Corruption Prevention and Governance in Hong Kong

This book analyses central questions in the continuing debate about success factors in corruption prevention and the efficacy and value of anti-corruption agencies (ACAs). How do ACAs become valued within a polity? What challenges must they overcome? What conditions account for their success and failure? What contributions can corruption prevention make to good governance? And in what areas might they have little or no effect on the quality of governance? With these questions in mind, the authors examine the experience of Hong Kong's Independent Commission Against Corruption (ICAC), widely regarded as one of the few successful examples of an ACA. The book is grounded in an analysis of ICAC documents and surveys, the authors' survey of social attitudes toward corruption in Hong Kong and interviews with former officials.

Ian Scott is Emeritus Professor and a Fellow of the Asia Research Centre at Murdoch University in Perth, Australia and Adjunct Professor in the Department of Public Policy, City University of Hong Kong.

Ting Gong is Professor in the Department of Public Policy, City University of Hong Kong and Distinguished Chair Professor in the School of International Relations and Public Affairs at Fudan University, China.

T0383072

Routledge Research in Public Administration and Public Policy

For more information about this series, please visit: www.routledge.com/
Routledge-Research-in-Public-Administration-and-Public-Policy/book-series/
RRPAPP

Corruption Prevention and Governance in Hong Kong

Ian Scott and Ting Gong

Routledge
Taylor & Francis Group

LONDON AND NEW YORK

First published 2019
by Routledge
2 Park Square, Milton Park, Abingdon, Oxon OX14 4RN

and by Routledge
605 Third Avenue, New York, NY 10017

First issued in paperback 2020

Routledge is an imprint of the Taylor & Francis Group, an informa business

British Library Cataloguing-in-Publication Data
A catalogue record for this book is available from the British Library

Library of Congress Cataloging-in-Publication Data
Names: Scott, Ian, 1943– author. | Gong, Ting, 1955– author.
Title: Corruption prevention and governance in Hong Kong /
    by Ian Scott and Ting Gong.
Description: Abingdon, Oxon ; New York, NY : Routledge, 2019. |
    Series: Routledge research in public administration and public
    policy | Includes bibliographical references and index.
Identifiers: LCCN 2018042209 | ISBN 9780815395133 (hardback) |
    ISBN 9781351184496 (ebook)
Subjects: LCSH: Corruption—China—Hong Kong—Prevention. |
    Political corruption—China—Hong Kong—Prevention.
Classification: LCC JQ1539.5.A56 C6497 2019 | DDC
    364.4095125—dc23
LC record available at https://lccn.loc.gov/2018042209

ISBN 13: 978-0-367-50415-1 (pbk)
ISBN 13: 978-0-8153-9513-3 (hbk)

Typeset in Galliard
by Apex CoVantage, LLC

Contents

PART III
Corruption prevention and governance   151

Figures

Tables

Acronyms

ACA	Anti-Corruption Agency
API	Announcement of Public Interest
CPD	ICAC Corruption Prevention Department
CPIB	Corrupt Practices Investigation Bureau
CRD	ICAC Community Relations Department
DAB	Democratic Alliance for Betterment and Progress of Hong Kong
EACO	Electoral Affairs Commission Ordinance
ECICO	Elections (Corrupt and Illegal Conduct) Ordinance
FC	Functional Constituencies
GC	Geographical Constituencies
GPPP	Guangdong Provincial People's Procuratorate
HKFTU	Hong Kong Federation of Trade Unions
HKSAR	Hong Kong Special Administrative Region
HKUPOP	University of Hong Kong Public Opinion Poll
ICAC	Independent Commission Against Corruption
ICACO	Independent Commission Against Corruption Ordinance
IMF	International Monetary Fund
KPK	Komisi Pemberantasan Korupsi (Indonesia)
OD	ICAC Operations Department
OECD	Organisation for Economic Cooperation and Development
POBO	The Prevention of Bribery Ordinance
PRC	People's Republic of China
SMEs	Small and Medium Enterprises
UNCAC	United Nations Convention Against Corruption
UNDP	United Nations Development Programme

Preface

Corruption has long been a major concern of international organisations and governments around the world. Yet progress in devising effective measures of prevention has, at best, been slow and, at worst, has seen a proliferation of different forms of corruption, increases in the systemic abuse of public resources for private purposes and few signs of change in the entrenched tolerance of corruption in many societies. In Asian countries, for example, a Transparency International report (2017: 4) found that only one in five people thought that the level of corruption was decreasing; that 900 million people had paid a bribe in the previous year although only 7 per cent reported it; and that in most countries, more than 50 per cent of those surveyed thought that their governments were doing badly in fighting against corruption.

Although successful corruption prevention has been a commodity in short supply, there has been continuing interest in whether the experiences of places where corruption has been controlled are transferable to other jurisdictions. Hong Kong's Independent Commission Against Corruption (ICAC) is widely regarded as a model of a successful anti-corruption agency (ACA). It has been the principal means by which a once highly corrupt government and society was transformed into one in which corruption was not tolerated either by the government or by most members of society. The ICAC's success, however, has been hard-won and serves as a reminder that there is no magic formula to transform rampantly corrupt governments and societies into clean ones. Even when specific anti-corruption policies and procedures seem to work in one jurisdiction, there is no guarantee that they will be equally successful in different political and cultural contexts. Nonetheless, there is value in identifying significant factors in successful corruption prevention and in studying the processes by which the ICAC brought about a dramatic change in probity in government and in societal attitudes and behaviour. If we can increase our understanding of the pre-conditions and processes for achieving effective prevention, then we are on the path to finding solutions for the increasingly complex and pervasive corruption issues which the world appears to be facing.

In this book, we address three broad questions: What factors need to be in place for an ACA to reduce levels of corruption? What does effective corruption prevention contribute to governance? Is the successful experience in corruption control, or some part of it, transferable to other jurisdictions?

For the first question, we acknowledge that there are other approaches to preventing corruption than setting up an ACA. Although we are principally concerned with the work of ACAs, good governance approaches endorsed by international organisations, such as the World Bank and the International Monetary Fund, also have something to say about corruption prevention. These approaches depend, however, on changes in values conducive to clean government and more transparent societies which may sometimes take generations to realise, if indeed they can be realised at all. Many governments and their citizens perceive the need for more immediate action and, as an antidote to corruption, have created ACAs with specific powers.

In Part I, we discuss the effects of introducing a new ACA into a political and bureaucratic environment which may be hostile to its very existence. We contend that ACAs are very likely to experience initial challenges to their powers and that the ability to overcome these challenges will be critical for their future success. As an example, we examine the challenges which faced the ICAC shortly after it was created in 1974.

In Part II, we consider the key factors which enabled the ICAC to operate successfully, paying particular attention to its ability to organise for effective action, enforce the law, win public support, and institutionalise its structures and processes. We argue that the institutionalisation of an ACA, so that its work becomes valued in the community, is an important means of generating trust in government and of increasing social capital.

In Part III, we consider the contributions that successful corruption prevention has made to good governance in Hong Kong and other areas in which corruption still potentially remains a problem and where governance has not been improved. We examine the means by which the ICAC has changed bureaucratic practices to ensure strict controls over financial management, policy implementation and civil service behaviour, and its programmes to engage the community in active corruption prevention. Good governance, however, depends on much more than what even the most successful ACA can offer. Within the constitutional and political order, its remit is necessarily restricted to matters relating to corruption, even if some formally sanctioned practices are inimical to the values underlying good governance. There are also usually threats to the work of the ACA from those who would prefer to reduce its powers and maintain opacity in their dealings. In the case of Hong Kong, we look at examples of these problems insofar as they affect such matters as investigating electoral conduct, cross-border corruption and perceptions of government–business collusion.

In the final chapter, we analyse the lessons which the ICAC experience might have for other ACAs and anti-corruption systems, and the extent to which the elements of its success might be transferable.

We have been conducting research on corruption in Hong Kong and the role of the ICAC over the past decade. This book is based on material in the public domain with the exception of our own survey research and some interviews with former ICAC officials and academics which were conducted in September and November 2017. In the course of the research, we have incurred numerous debts of gratitude. We are particularly appreciative of the support which we have received from both past and present Executive Directors of the Centre of Anti-Corruption Studies and International Training of the ICAC. They have been an invaluable sounding board on which we have tested our ideas over the years.

We have also benefited greatly from the help of serving senior ICAC officials. In 2013, we requested the then Director of Community Relations to release ICAC survey material from 1977 to 1990 into the public domain. She agreed to the request, and the material is now housed in the Special Collection of the University of Hong Kong. It tells a fascinating story of the ICAC's attempts to change public attitudes toward corruption and records their successes and difficulties in doing so. We are also grateful for permission to use the raw data from the ICAC annual surveys, which has enabled us to disaggregate information and to obtain a more precise sense of public perceptions of corruption, and for permission to publish the organisation chart in Chapter 5. Former ICAC officials whom we interviewed or who helped in other ways with the research made invaluable contributions. Tony Kwok, Alan N. Lai, Francis Lee, Yvonne Mui, Gerry Osborn, Vanessa and Spencer So, Ryan Wong and Helen C.P. Yu Lai were all generous with their time, ideas and recollections of the ICAC in times past. At an earlier stage of the research, Ian McWalters, then Director of Public Prosecutions, provided valuable assistance in understanding and compiling misconduct in public office cases.

We have been fortunate to enjoy funding support from the Hong Kong Research Grant Council. Two General Research Fund (GRF) awards (#9042104 and #9042596) funded some research activities and a large-scale survey, which was conducted for us in 2015 by the Social Science Research Centre at the University of Hong Kong under the direction of Professor John Bacon-Shone. Professor Simon Young of the University of Hong Kong provided valuable information on legal aspects of the ICAC's role. The Department of Public Policy at the City University of Hong Kong has been very supportive of our research, and we are grateful to the former Head, Professor Ray Forrest; to the Acting Head, Professor Xiaohu Wang; and to Professor Ray Yep for their support and interest in the project. Brian Brewer and Joan Y. H. Leung, both former members of the Department, worked with us in research on misconduct in public office and integrity management and provided important academic input. We are very grateful for their contributions. We would also like to acknowledge the wonderful support staff in the Department of Public Policy who has made our task much easier.

Finally, we have had excellent research assistance over the past years. We want to express our thanks to Hang Chow, Queenie Lijun Deng, Xinlei Sha, Wenyan

Tu and especially to Hanyu Xiao, who worked with us on our survey, and to Sunny Litianqing Yang, who has helped us in many different ways in putting this book together.

Any mistakes of fact or interpretation are, of course, our own responsibility.

Ian Scott
Ting Gong
August 2018

Reference

Transparency International (2017) *People and corruption: Asia Pacific.* Berlin: Transparency International.

1 Concepts, approaches and institutions

There are estimated to be more than 150 anti-corruption agencies (ACAs) around the world, and the number seems to be growing (Transparency International 2014). Yet the evidence suggests that many agencies are failures, at least if assessed in terms of their formal purpose. In the worst cases, governments have used ACAs to oppress opponents and facilitate even greater corruption (Heilbrunn 2004; Meagher 2005). What might improve the track record of these agencies? We believe that the experiences of the few successful agencies are instructive but not that they should lead to attempts to transfer entire laws, organisations and procedures which would be politically and culturally difficult, if not impossible. Rather, we argue that studying the process of institutionalising a successful ACA is likely to provide a more useful template for new or struggling agencies than a wholesale transfer of best practices. By institutionalisation, we mean organisations in which "practices are regularly and continuously repeated, are sanctioned and maintained by social norms, and have major significance in the social structure" (Abercrombie *et al* 1988: 124).

How does an ACA acquire such value? What challenges must it overcome? What qualities are necessary for success? Once institutionalised, what contributions can successful corruption prevention make to good governance?

With these questions in mind, we examine the experiences of Hong Kong's Independent Commission Against Corruption (ICAC), widely regarded as a leading example of a successful ACA. In this chapter, we provide a framework for discussion, considering, first, definitions of corruption and their impact on how corruption prevention is perceived and enforced. We then analyse the two major ideal-type corruption prevention strategies: value-based and compliance-based approaches. Neither approach by itself is practically feasible but attempts to prevent corruption are often based on their implicit assumptions. Value-based approaches assume that if such values as trust, honesty, transparency, accountability and integrity are widely held, corruption will be minimised. Compliance-based approaches focus on the deterrent effect of anti-corruption laws and regulations and are predicated on the underlying assumption that effective enforcement will reduce corruption. ACAs tend toward compliance-based approaches because they are often set up with the principal aim of enforcing the law. However, some ACAs, including the ICAC, do place considerable emphasis on the importance of supportive public values in effective corruption prevention. We analyse the mix of value-based and compliance-based factors that are necessary for the successful institutionalisation of ACAs. In later chapters, we explore the ICAC's experience and the impact of effective corruption prevention on governance.

Definitions

Corruption and corruption prevention are problematic terms whose meanings vary in different countries and with changing public perceptions of social experiences over time. We use definitions which are common in Hong Kong but which are not necessarily shared elsewhere (Gong *et al* 2015).

Corruption may be defined in ways that could include or exclude such offences as simple bribery, theft, extortion, embezzlement, fraud, some aspects of money laundering, serious conflicts of interest and even violations of social norms. It may also be seen as a failure to meet expected standards of behaviour either those which are expressly laid down in rules and regulations or those which may represent the strongly held values of an organisation or a society (Kurer 2015: 31). A common definition of corruption is the "abuse of entrusted power for private gain" (Transparency International 2016). This definition is appropriate in a legal sense in Hong Kong because it covers both the public and private sectors, but it does beg the question of what is meant by "abuse". In Mainland China, for example, abuse of entrusted power is defined, among a wide range of criminal offences, to include the notion of moral decay and violations of social norms such as committing adultery (Gong *et al* 2015). In Hong Kong, the public takes a much narrower view: corruption is often defined as synonymous with bribery even though simple bribery is now a relatively rare offence (Gong *et al* 2015).

Many scholars and international organisations also focus on political corruption, which is usually defined as the abuse of public office or public power for private gain (Heywood 1997; World Bank 1997; Philp 2015). This more specific definition has relevance in Hong Kong where much of the ICAC's early efforts were concentrated on dealing with police corruption and other bureaucratic misdemeanors and where, more recently, the Commission has been concerned with serious conflicts of interest at the highest levels of government (Lethbridge 1985; Scott 2014, 2017). Political corruption casts doubt on the integrity of the system, raises questions of legitimacy and may also have an impact on trust within the society (Rose-Ackerman 2017). In Hong Kong, it has also created a disjunction between a clean society and perceptions of a corrupt polity, resulting in concerns over whether the anti-corruption successes achieved by the ICAC can be sustained.

Definitions of corruption are not simply a matter of semantics. They can also cause problems in the formulation of corruption offences in law, in establishing priorities on the anti-corruption agenda and in detecting new forms of corruption. Until the *Prevention of Bribery Ordinance* (*POBO*) came into force in Hong Kong in 1970, it had proved difficult to devise an appropriate wording to satisfy the courts of the precise legal meaning of corruption. The previous legislation,

The Prevention of Corruption Ordinance, had included the words "corruptly accepts", which laid responsibility on the prosecution to prove that it had been in the mind of the accused to engage in a corrupt act (McWalters 2015: 9–13). The result was a lower number of convictions than the government or the public thought reflected the level of corruption. With the *POBO*, however, the government was able to circumvent the problem by re-defining the offence. Bribery is not specifically mentioned in the text of the ordinance, and the offence is defined instead in terms of accepting an advantage. Anyone holding a paid government position who solicits or accepts an advantage without the permission of the Chief Executive (*POBO* Section 3) or, in the private sector, without the permission of the principal is guilty of an offence (*POBO* Section 9(1)(4)(5)). An advantage is widely defined to include gifts, loans, fees, rewards or commissions, employment and contracts, any payment or liquidation of a debt, services and favours, the exercise or forbearance of any power or duty, and any offer of these advantages (*POBO* Section 2(1)).

Definitional problems may also arise in devising corruption prevention strategies. Since the ICAC has adopted a zero-tolerance policy in fighting corruption throughout government, business and society, we use the term *corruption prevention* broadly to cover the "universal" approach, which the Commission has adopted. Corruption prevention is defined, accordingly, as measures involving sanctions, rules and regulations, and education which are designed to prohibit, inhibit or influence behaviour in ways that enable the prosecution of the corrupt and avoid the perpetration of acts of corruption.

The ICAC's approach to corruption prevention is often called "three-pronged", involving investigation, prevention and education. This reflects the functions of the three major departments within its organisational structure: the Operations Department (OD), the Corruption Prevention Department (CPD) and the Community Relations Department (CRD). The work of the OD is focused on investigating complaints and enforcing the anti-corruption laws with the aim of prosecuting the corrupt and deterring potential future offenders. The CPD has specific statutory functions which include the examination of the procedures of government departments and public bodies in order to make recommendations for better corruption control. In the private sector, on invitation, it may also make recommendations on improved anti-corruption practices (*Independent Commission Against Corruption Ordinance* Section 12 (d–f); ICAC 2018: 59). The CRD is charged with responsibility to "educate the public against the evils of corruption" and to "enlist and foster public support in combatting corruption" (*Independent Commission Against Corruption Ordinance* Section 12 (g–h); ICAC 2018: 71). The functions of the Commission's departments constitute our understanding of what is meant by corruption prevention. What is understood by *corrupt practices*, however, presents more complex definitional challenges.

Corruption prevention strategies may be viewed in different ways by the ACA and the public. As Michael Johnston (2017: 175) remarks, "analysts and reformers, on the one hand, and citizens, on the other, may be talking about quite different things when they mention 'corruption' and can have very different reactions to it". What the public regards as corrupt practice may be conditioned by history, personal experiences or perceptions of wrongdoing within government or business. What an ACA believes is corruption may be limited by political considerations or restrictions contained within the terms of its jurisdiction. If a disjunction develops between an ACA's anti-corruption agenda and what the public is experiencing on the ground, support for the agency may well decline (Gong and Scott 2017: 6–8). From either perspective, what is believed to be corruption is critically important to efforts to prevent it.

Finally, definitions of corruption and perceived effective corruption prevention strategies may change over time. Dealing with the prevalent form of corruption is not the end of the story. Other, probably more sophisticated, forms of corruption may soon emerge; new weapons may be needed to deal with new threats. Thus, although bribery was virtually eliminated in the public sector in Hong Kong after the creation of the ICAC, serious conflicts of interest, which were more difficult to detect, soon took their place. The simple bribe was replaced with complex dealings relating, for example, to contracts for companies owned by relatives or friends and promises or suggestions of future benefits for compliant action. If an ACA is not alert to changes in the form of corruption and does not receive adequate support from the government to introduce new measures, perceptions of its ability to control corruption will be affected and it is likely to lose popular support.

Value-based and compliance-based approaches

Corruption prevention systems come in many different forms but we may categorise them initially into approaches which are predominantly value-based and those which are predominantly compliance-based. Value-based integrity systems, also referred to as the "high road" (Rohr 1978), place reliance on individual morality, congruent with society-wide beliefs, to determine the correct course of action when people are confronted with ethical dilemmas (Paine 1994; Maesschalck 2004; Brewer *et al* 2015). Compliance-based systems, or the "low road", rely primarily on sanctions to ensure that rules are obeyed and that their deterrent effects prevent transgressions (Hejka-Ekins 2001: 82–84; Roberts 2009). If we conceive of these approaches as a continuum with value-based approaches at one end and compliance-based approaches at the other, an ideal-type value-based approach would rest on the assumption that violation of social norms, such as honesty and integrity, was a moral impossibility and that, consequently, no corruption offences could be committed. At the other end of the continuum, an ideal-type compliance-based approach would depend on legal provisions that were so well constructed and so effectively implemented that anyone who committed an offence would be caught and that no one would therefore violate the law.

In reality, of course, although corruption prevention systems may lean toward one approach or the other, neither pure type is practicable. Value-based approaches require some form of sanction for those who contravene ethical expectations and engage in corrupt behaviour. An ideal compliance-based approach, aside from the difficulty of formulating absolutely effective laws, might create the perception that what is not prohibited is permitted. Patterns of corruption would probably shift accordingly to avoid compliance with the rules. As a consequence of these difficulties, all effective corruption prevention systems involve some combination of support for public values, and the moral actions stemming from them, and well-drafted laws which list precisely the offence and consequential punishments. The question is where the emphasis should rest and how an appropriate mix of value-based and compliance-based measures can be achieved as forms of corruption change.

Value-based approaches

Even though ideal-type value-based or compliance-based approaches are not feasible, corruption prevention practices usually tend to favour one approach or the other. In some systems, for example, particularly in Scandinavia, the United Kingdom, the Netherlands, Australia and New Zealand, corruption prevention rests primarily on a value-based approach (Roberts 2009). In these countries, the congruence between public values and the desired political end of a corruption-free society means that watchdog institutions play largely monitoring roles (Salminen 2013: 66–67, 73). They ensure that violations of widely held anti-corruption values and norms do not occur; if they happen, they are viewed as the exception rather than the rule (Salminen and Ikola-Norrbacka 2010; Salminen 2013; Johnston 2013). The critical element in these successful corruption prevention systems is generally agreed to be social trust. Rothstein and Eek (2009) argue, for example, that trust in authorities influences public perceptions and helps create a more trusting society. More trusting societies share common values and are less likely to be corrupt (Rose-Ackerman 2017). How such social trust has developed and whether such systems are transferrable remain matters of debate.

The focus on values and how to change them is an intrinsic component of the good governance model which has been adopted by the World Bank and International Monetary Fund (IMF) and promoted in many developing countries. A fundamental premise of the model is that corruption undermines public trust in government, which in turn hinders poverty reduction and efforts to increase economic growth (World Bank 2017; IMF 2017). It follows that World Bank and IMF assistance to developing countries should be aimed at improving institutional capacity and effectiveness with the aim of promoting good governance. To do this requires enhancing such values as transparency, integrity, accountability, participation and the rule of law and improving government procedures in such areas as financial regulation, procurement and money laundering. After 1996, the World Bank included effective corruption prevention as one of the indicators of good governance. There is still, however, the expectation that improvements in overall governance will lead to reduced corruption.

The World Bank's approach to corruption control has been subject to various criticisms (Ganahl 2012: 83–129). First, it has been argued that the Bank has allowed concerns about corruption to deflect attention from its principal goals of poverty reduction and economic growth (Khan 2006; Marquette 2007). A second strand of criticism contends that the concept of good governance is too imprecise to provide practical prescriptions (Andrews 2008; Grindle 2012). If it is to succeed, good governance probably requires a very slow, complex and comprehensive chain of developments and gradual improvements in institutional capacity. It is also assumed that the process will be linear. However, a change of regime, or even of policy, might well jeopardise any gains made in achieving cleaner government or better governance. Against this, a former Director of Governance and Anti-Corruption at the World Bank has claimed that quite rapid changes toward good governance can be realised. But he also concedes that standards of corruption control may be deteriorating even faster (Kaufman 2005). Transparency International's perceptions indices support the view that corruption has increased substantially over the past decade (Transparency International 2017). The implication is that more immediate solutions, such as the creation of effective ACAs, must be found.

If the World Bank believes that changing social attitudes and the institutionalisation of structures and processes are critical elements in successful corruption control, it might have been expected that the Bank would have shown strong support for the proliferating number of ACAs. But this has not been the case. Amid allegations that the Bank is pursuing a neoliberal agenda or violating sovereignty, sensitivity over offering support for such a highly political institution as an ACA is an issue. Equally important is the fact that many ACAs are not established for the purpose of controlling and preventing corruption and few are independent (Heilbrunn 2004: 2–3; UNDP 2005: 5; Rotberg 2017: 110). They may be established to assuage public opinion and legitimise the regime, to monitor management practices in the bureaucracy or, in the worst cases, to persecute political opponents. The Bank has generally taken the view that increasing the capacity of such institutions would not necessarily lead to better corruption prevention and could possibly impede progress toward good governance.

The United Nations has also lent its support to more effective corruption prevention by promoting good governance values. The Convention Against Corruption (UNCAC), which has been signed by 140 members and 45 other parties since its promulgation in 2003, has made improvements in international cooperation and mutual legal assistance on corruption cases, in the universal criminalisation of offences, and in asset recovery. The convention also describes what amounts to an ideal model of corruption prevention which specifies many of the values supported by the World Bank. Thus, for example, all parties to UNCAC are required, in accordance with their legal systems, to develop, implement or maintain effective, coordinated anti-corruption policies that promote the participation of society. Anti-corruption policies should also reflect the principles of the rule of law, proper management of public affairs and public property, integrity, transparency and accountability (UNCAC 2003: Article 5.1).

The convention stipulates that in each of the signatory states, there should be a body whose responsibility is to prevent corruption by implementing appropriate policies and by disseminating information (UNCAC 2003: Article 6). There is a formidable wish-list of values and practices designed to ensure that the public sector is clean. Public officials are to be recruited on merit, equity and aptitude and should display the qualities of integrity, honesty and responsibility (UNCAC 2003: Articles 7.1(a), 8.1). Procurement should be based on transparency, competition and objective criteria. The management of public finances should be accountable and electoral funding should be transparent (UNCAC 2003: Article 9). In the private sector, signatory states are expected to prevent corruption by, *inter alia*, enhancing accounting standards, promoting transparency and integrity and by preventing conflicts of interest (UNCAC 2003: Article 12).

The UNCAC is a comprehensive document. If it were fully implemented it would go some way toward reducing corruption. Yet, while the convention has helped improved international cooperation, the state of corruption in many developing countries is probably worse than ever before. The negotiations on the convention produced a clear division between states which were open to the review of their procedures and those which were not (Joutsen 2011: 313–314). The escape clause for the latter group is Article 4, which affirms the principles of state sovereignty and "non-intervention in the domestic affairs of other States". However valuable the ideas of the World Bank and UNCAC might be in preventing corruption, the harmonious value-based prevention systems of the Scandinavian countries and Japan remain a very distant goal in the face of a continuing implicit commitment in many countries to a corrupt status quo.

That is not to say that elements of value-based approaches cannot be incorporated within existing anti-corruption systems. Many governments, including that of Hong Kong, have sought to enhance awareness of the individual ethical dimension in decision-making – particularly conflicts of interest – and to increase personal responsibility for outcomes. In some cases, this represents an attempt to supplement a predominantly compliance-based system with practices which recognise that rules cannot cover all eventualities in ethically problematic situations. Whether a successful fusion of value-based and compliance-based systems can be achieved remains uncertain.

Compliance-based approaches

Compliance-based systems place emphasis on the external control of the behaviour of civil servants through strict rules, ethical codes and procedures and use legal constraints, control and discipline to manage organisational integrity (Paine 1994). People are expected to "do the thing right" according to the procedures rather than "do the right thing" by virtue of their values and personal integrity (Gregory and Hicks 1999: 5). In the Netherlands, for example, the development of a compliance-based approach, prior to its replacement by a more balanced ethics system, included a bureaucracy strongly rooted in rules, checks and compliance. The system was supplemented by the predominantly legal background of officials and the government's traditional experience with legislative and regulative instruments (Hoekstra *et al* 2008). Many Asian governments also use predominantly compliance-based approaches which stress the importance of following procedures and the disciplinary consequences for civil servants who step out of line.

If officials follow the rules, the advantage of a compliance-based approach is that it provides organisational protection from corrupt acts and reduces the discretion which civil servants need to use to arrive at ethical decisions (Roberts 2009). There is a danger, however, that informal rules will emerge which circumvent the formal regulations, or that some departmental rules are incompatible with the intent to reduce corruption and consequently permit personal behaviour that is ethically dubious. Rules cannot cover all ethical dilemmas, particularly conflicts of interest where different interpretations of a potential conflict may be possible and where there may be no rules covering expected behaviour. Compliance-based systems often attempt to overcome these problems by creating even more rules, but ambiguities in the wording of the regulations and the uniqueness of individual cases mean that it is a never-ending task. Once a compliance-based system is in place, it also seems to become more difficult to integrate value-based elements into the ethical framework. There is a tendency to try to turn values into rules, mistrusting individuals to arrive at appropriate answers (Roberts 2009; Brewer *et al* 2015).

Although ACAs may have many different anti-corruption functions, initially they often lean toward compliance-based approaches because they are usually set up to enforce the anti-corruption laws (Disch *et al* 2009: 15). It is assumed that corruption will be reduced by pursuing the corrupt, by the deterrent effect of sanctioning unlawful activities, and by imposing rigorous rules and monitoring mechanisms. Even if this simplistic vision were achieved – and many difficulties stand in the way of success – the assumption that the problem will remain unchanged and that the legislation and investigatory procedure will continue to be appropriate is likely to be challenged. New ways of evading the law develop quickly, and rules frequently lag behind prevailing corrupt practices. The anti-corruption agenda may become increasingly irrelevant or the credibility of the ACA will be stretched because it is unable to deal with the issues which led to its creation. ACAs ignore the resulting public perceptions of their performance at their peril. If, at the outset, there are signs that the ACA has little ability or inclination to combat corruption, it is unlikely to be able to win back public support in the future.

Anti-corruption agencies

Despite the influence of the compliance-based approach at the time of its creation, ACAs may have many different anti-corruption functions and may vary considerably in design. Meagher (2005) defines ACAs as

> separate, permanent agencies whose primary function is to provide centralized leadership in core areas of anti-corruption activity [which] include policy analysis and technical assistance in prevention, public outreach and information, monitoring, investigation and prosecution.

With regard to single-purpose ACAs, Heilbrunn (2004) has suggested that there are three main successful models: the universal model typified by the ICAC in Hong Kong, encompassing a zero-tolerance approach to corruption and involving "investigative, preventative and communicative" functions (Heilbrunn 2004: 3); the investigatory model exemplified by Singapore's Corrupt Practices Investigation Bureau (CPIB), which focuses on obtaining and preparing evidence for prosecutions (Heilbrunn 2004: 6; Quah 2013: 106–128); and the parliamentary model of the Australian state of New South Wales, which reports to Parliament and has a strong emphasis on preventing corruption (Heilbrunn 2004: 8).

These models have different strengths and weaknesses. The ICAC's universal model is expensive, and although there are advisory committees for each of its departments which help ensure accountability, there have been questions about its human rights record and whether it should be accountable to the Chief Executive. The investigatory model is narrowly focused and has been criticised for its lack of accountability (Heilbrunn 2004). In addition, although the CPIB does have an outreach programme (Quah 2013: 224), the Singaporean government itself has largely taken on the function of public engagement and the promotion of anti-corruption values. The parliamentary model maximises accountability, concern over human rights and the importance of prevention, but lacks the investigative powers and strong anti-corruption laws of the other models. Whichever model is adopted, there is always potential conflict between values which are sometimes difficult to reconcile such as accountability and enforcement.

If a *modus vivendi* can be achieved and the ACA becomes institutionalised, the historical and social context in which it has acquired value for citizens will be important. This makes it difficult to transfer anti-corruption models successfully. The issue is complicated further in situations where value-based elements have been introduced in what were originally compliance-based organisations. These elements often focus on individual morality and best behaviour in specific circumstances and relate to local practices which may have less relevance or acceptability in other jurisdictions.

Heilbrunn's three models describe successful practice, but as he notes, most ACAs are at best limited successes and at worst are not worth the trouble taken to establish them. Some seem to be set up with failure in mind, as a means of relieving political pressure to do something about corruption rather than as a lasting solution to the problem. Others find difficulty in making any progress against entrenched corrupt elites who are usually intent on clipping the wings of a new ACA before it can fly. Many ACAs also suffer from organisational shortcomings such as insufficient powers, inadequate funding, poorly trained personnel and a lack of support from other government departments and private sector bodies. In Asia, Quah (2017: 241) has calculated that twenty-nine ACAs were created in twenty-three countries over the period between 1952 and 2014. Of these, only the CPIB and the ICAC are regarded as successes although the jury is still out on Indonesia's Komisi Pemberantasan Korupsi (KPK) (Rotberg 2017: 123–129; Schütte 2017; Widoyoko 2017).

ACAs themselves came together in Jakarta in 2012 to try and promulgate principles which they thought might lead to greater success. Their joint statement stipulates that ACAs should have a "clear mandate to tackle corruption through prevention, education, awareness raising, investigation and prosecution" (Jakarta Statement 2012). It contains sensible provisions on the need for accountability, respect for the law, ethical conduct, security of tenure for the official in charge, remuneration of employees, and collaboration with the public and other public sector agencies. But there is little by way of specifics on the methods that might be employed to reduce corruption. In common with the UNCAC, the guidelines which the statement provides remain at a very general level and reflect the lowest common denominator that the parties were willing to accept.

Assuming that an ACA is set up by a government which is intent on combating corruption by combining compliance-based and value-based approaches, more specific guidelines are required. What kinds of pitfalls might be experienced in striking a balance between value-based and compliance-based approaches and in institutionalising an ACA's practices? What factors promote effective performance?

Success factors

There is a substantial academic literature on the necessary conditions for success (see, for example, Heilbrunn 2004; Meagher 2005; de Sousa 2009; Quah 2013, 2017; Choi 2009, 2017; Rotberg 2017). When all the requirements are considered together, it is perhaps not surprising that there are so many cases of failure. For a new ACA, the task is not only to catch the corrupt but also to maintain a syndrome of success factors. If any one of those factors is compromised, the performance of the ACA will be affected, often critically. We consider below the essential elements of the syndrome with a view to exploring later in the book how the ICAC has managed to avoid or to mitigate the difficulties which they entail.

Political will

Political commitment to combating corruption is usually seen as the most important criterion for the successful performance of ACAs (Kpundeh 1998; Brinkerhoff 2000; Persson and Sjöstedt 2012; Quah 2013: 453–456; Quah 2015a, 2017a: 242–244; Choi 2017; Rotberg 2017: 45–49). However, it may be defined in different ways. In its broadest context, political will might refer to the common resolve of the government, legislature and the courts to combat corruption. In our discussion of the ICAC, we use a narrower definition focusing on the extent of support provided by the political executive, particularly in relation to government intervention on behalf of the Commission and to funding issues (see Ch. 4). We consider the roles played by the legislature and the courts on the occasions when the ICAC has been the subject of their attention. Political will may also be taken to subsume some issues which may account for loss of confidence in an ACA: ineffective anti-corruption laws, lack of trained personnel, and lack of independence and organisational deficiencies, especially the creation of multiple anti-corruption agencies with competing jurisdictions (Quah 2017a: 246). We treat these separately in the following discussion of the other features of the syndrome.

Independence

Independence is critical for the credibility of an ACA. Its ability to pursue the corrupt without fear or favour is an essential requirement for success. In many countries, the influence of politicians or business people is such that investigations are not properly conducted. Similarly, where ACAs come under the control of the police force, they fail to perform well. The police are often the most corrupt of government departments and the public, understandably, usually has suspicions about outcomes when policemen investigate policemen. Independence is better preserved when anti-corruption functions are centralised in a single agency. If jurisdiction is shared between agencies as it has been, for example, in South Korea and Taiwan, there is a tendency for turf wars to develop, to the detriment of the anti-corruption effort as a whole (Choi 2009; Ko *et al* 2015). Even when a single, independent agency is established, there still remains the issue of its accountability. Giving strong powers to an independent law-enforcement agency without proper accountability raises human rights issues and the integrity of the authority to whom the agency is accountable (see Ch. 4).

Well-trained staff with high integrity

The ACA's organisation has to be fit for purpose, whether its strategy is to follow a universal model with multiple anti-corruption functions, a model focusing mainly on investigations, or a parliamentary model with an emphasis on prevention. There is no single ideal structure, but it is important that the structure relates to the ACA's functions and that there is adequate coordination with government departments and private sector organisations, such as chambers of commerce and business associations. The ACA must also ensure that its personnel are qualified for the task. Increasingly, successful corruption investigations involve tracing flows of money in "paper trails" or electronic surveillance to obtain useful leads. Both types of investigation require well-trained personnel who may not be readily available in many countries. Another recruitment problem is ensuring that those who are selected are people of integrity. There is often public suspicion that ACA personnel are themselves corrupt and, if a case surfaces which seems to confirm that suspicion, the effect on the reputation of the ACA can be very damaging (see Chs. 5, 6).

Effective anti-corruption laws

To be effective, anti-corruption laws must be sufficiently strong to ensure that the corrupt are caught and prosecuted. They must also relate to the prevalent forms of corruption and not to some previous conception of the nature of the threat. There is always the possibility that the law will lag the form of corruption, that there will be insufficient political will to bring in new legislation, and that the ACA will be enforcing laws which the corrupt have already circumvented. Another important aspect of anti-corruption law is that it should be implemented with the certainty that, on conviction, appropriate penalties will be applied to the offender. Since the public often regards prosecutions and convictions as the most significant indicator of an ACA's success, the relationship between investigations and the prosecutorial function must be clear and founded on mutual trust. Even if the ACA itself is able to conduct investigations impartially, its efforts will be seriously compromised if some prosecutorial decisions are not based on the evidence but on political direction (see Ch. 5).

Corruption-proof procedures

Although ACAs sometimes view themselves as principally reactive organisations, pursuing and prosecuting corruption where it appears, prevention is clearly better than cure. One dimension of prevention is ensuring that bureaucratic and private sector procedures are as corruption-proof as possible. Particularly when new policies are introduced and where procurement or large-scale expenditure is involved, there are likely to be opportunities for corruption unless effective preventive measures are in place. An ACA is probably the most suitable institution to undertake this function, although it may also be performed within government departments or specialised commissions, or within private companies (see Chs. 4, 8).

Public engagement

There are three critically important reasons why an ACA needs to engage with the public to be successful. First, many investigations arise from public complaints. If there is no proactive effort to encourage the public to report corruption, then the information that the ACA needs to deal with the problem may well dry up. Second, public attitudes toward corruption may be inimical to its prevention. If corruption is viewed as a "way of life" and something that cannot be changed, then the ACA may find that its efforts are not supported or are treated with suspicion. Changing public perceptions and attitudes toward corruption is no easy task and is likely to require research into social attitudes. Third, institutionalising an ACA depends ultimately on evidence that the ACA is valued by the community. That support legitimises its power to act and provides sustenance in potential conflicts with politicians, the bureaucracy (particularly the police) and the private sector. For all these reasons, an ACA that neglects its relationship with the public is unlikely to be able to perform entirely effectively (see Ch. 7).

Our overarching argument is that for an ACA to be successful it must become institutionalised and valued within government, the private sector and society for the contributions which it makes to a clean public service, economic prosperity and a good quality of life. The process of institutionalisation is fraught with difficulties. We examine the failed attempts at corruption control in Hong Kong before the creation of the ICAC, the reasons for its creation and the serious challenges which it had to overcome from the police, the business sector and the Hong Kong civil service in its early years. We argue that any ACA, especially a new one, is likely to face significant challenges to its authority from many different quarters and that resolving these challenges is a necessary requirement if the agency is to become effective and institutionalised.

Overcoming such challenges is a necessary but not a sufficient condition if an ACA is to perform effectively. Political determination to support anti-corruption policies, adequate funding, and essential legal and organisational mechanisms are all required for successful anti-corruption efforts. The ICAC's policies on public engagement, its efforts to influence public perceptions of corruption and its relationship with civil society organisations provide insights into the way ACAs can interact with citizens and create partnerships to prevent corruption. We argue that ACAs should attempt to create a "virtuous circle", strengthening relationships between capacity, effectiveness, trust and institutionalisation.

An institutionalised ACA can make contributions to good governance, but we do not hold that successful corruption prevention necessarily has positive effects across the entire political, economic and social spectrum. Rather, we seek to identify areas in which the ICAC has made a marked contribution to good governance in Hong Kong and areas which continue to pose challenges. We note that successful corruption prevention has had a significant impact in promoting legitimacy, on the monitoring and improvement of government procedures and practices, and in building a more trusting society. We also analyse the other side of the problem – namely, those areas in which there is concern about governance in Hong Kong and potential consequences for corruption, such as contentious elections and electoral conduct, public perceptions of government–business collusion, serious conflicts of interest and cross-border corruption. Finally, we analyse the problems with institutionalising ACAs and the extent to which the ICAC model is applicable elsewhere in the world.

References

Abercrombie, Nicholas, Stephen Hill and Bryan S. Turner (1988) *Dictionary of sociology*. Harmondsworth: Penguin.

Andrews, Matt (2008) "The good governance agenda: Beyond indicators without theory", *Oxford Development Studies*, 36(4): 379–407.

Brewer, Brian, Joan Y.H. Leung and Ian Scott (2015) "Value-based integrity management and bureaucratic organizations: Changing the mix", *International Public Management Journal*, 18(3): 390–410.

Brinkerhoff, Derick W. (2000) "Assessing political will for anti-corruption efforts: An analytical framework", *Public Administration and Development*, 18(2): 239–252.

Choi, Jin-wook (2009) "Institutional structures and the effectiveness of anti-corruption agencies: A comparative analysis of South Korea and Hong Kong", *Asian Journal of Political Science*, 17(2): 195–214.

Choi, Jin-wook (2017) "Corruption prevention: Successful cases" in Ting Gong and Ian Scott (eds.) *Routledge handbook of corruption in Asia*. London: Routledge: 262–276.

de Sousa, Luis (2009) "Anti-corruption agencies: Between empowerment and irrelevance", *Crime, Law and Social Change*, 53(1): 5–22.

Disch, Arne, Endre Vigeland, Geir Sundet and Sam Gibson (2009) *Anti-corruption approaches: A literature review*, www.sida.se/contentassets/3f5c8afd51a6414d9f6 c8f8425fb935b/15047.pdf.

Ganahl, Joseph Patrick (2012) *Corruption, good governance and the African state: A critical analysis of the political-economic foundations of corruption in sub-Saharan Africa*. Potsdam: Potsdam University Press.

Gong, Ting and Ian Scott (2017) "Introduction" in Ting Gong and Ian Scott (eds.) *Routledge handbook of corruption in Asia*. London: Routledge: 1–10.

Gong, Ting, Shiru Wang and Jianming Ren (2015) "Corruption in the eye of the beholder: Survey evidence from Mainland China and Hong Kong", *International Public Management Journal*, 18(1): 458–482.

Gregory, Robert and Colin Hicks (1999) "Promoting public service integrity: A case for responsible accountability", *Australian Journal of Public Administration*, 58(4): 1–15.

Grindle, Merilee (2012) "Good governance: The inflation of an idea" in Bishwapira Sanyai, Lawrence J. Vale and Christina D. Rosen (eds.) *Planning ideas that matter*. Cambridge, MA: Massachusetts Institute of Technology Press: 259–282.

Heilbrunn, John R. (2004) *Anti-corruption commissions: Panacea or real medicine to fight corruption?* Washington: World Bank.

Hejka-Ekins, April (2001) "Ethics in in-service training" in Terry L. Cooper (ed.) *Handbook of administrative ethics*. 2nd edition. New York: Marcel Dekker: 79–103.

Heywood, Paul (1997) "Political corruption: Problems and perspectives", *Political Studies*, 45(3): 417–435.

Hoekstra, Alain, Alex Belling and Eli Van der Heide (2008) "A paradigmatic shift in ethics and integrity management within the Dutch public sector? Beyond compliance: A practitioner's view" in Leo W.J.C. Huberts, Jeroen Maesschalck and Carole L. Jurkiewicz (eds.) *Ethics and integrity of governance: Perspectives across frontiers*. Edward Elgar: Cheltenham: 143–158.

ICAC (2018) *Annual report 2017*, www.icac.org.hk/filemanager/en/content_27/ 2017.pdf.

IMF (International Monetary Fund) (2017) "The IMF and good governance", 2 August, www.imf.org/About/Factsheets/The-IMF-and-Good-Governance?pdf=1.

Independent Commission Against Corruption Ordinance (ICACO) (Cap 204).

Jakarta Statement on Principles for Anti-Corruption Agencies (2012), www.unodc. org/documents/corruption/WG-Prevention/Art_6_Preventive_anti-corruption_ bodies/JAKARTA_STATEMENT_en.pdf.

Johnston, Michael (2013) "The great Danes: Successes and subtleties of corruption control in Denmark" in Jon S.T. Quah (ed.) *Different paths to curbing corruption: leSunny, ssons from Denmark, Finland, Hong Kong, New Zealand and Singapore*. Bingley: Emerald: 23–56.

Johnston, Michael (2017) "Thinking about corruption as though people mattered" in Ting Gong and Ian Scott (eds.) *Routledge handbook of corruption in Asia*. London: Routledge: 165–178.

Joutsen, Matti (2011) "The United Nations Convention Against Corruption" in Adam Graycar and Russell G. Smith (eds.) *Handbook of global research and practice in corruption*. Cheltenham: Edward Elgar: 303–318.

Kaufman, Daniel (2005) "Myths and realities of governance and corruption", http:// siteresources.worldbank.org/INTWBIGOVANTCOR/Resources/2-1_Govern ance_and_Corruption_Kaufmann.pdf.

Khan, Mustaq (2006) "Governance and anti-corruption reform in developing countries: Policies, evidence and ways forward", *G-24 Discussion Paper Series*, http:// unctad.org/en/docs/gdsmdpbg2420064_en.pdf.

Ko, Ernie, Yu-chang Su and Chilik Yu (2015) "Sibling rivalry among anti-corruption agencies in Taiwan: Is redundancy doomed to failure?" *Asian Education and Development Studies*, 4(1): 101–124.

Kpundeh, Sahr J. (1998) "Political will in fighting corruption" in Sahr J. Kpundeh and Irene Hors (eds.) *Corruption and integrity development initiatives*. New York: UNDP: 91–110.Kurer, Oskar (2015) "Definitions of corruption" in Paul M. Heywood (ed.) *Routledge handbook of political corruption*. London: Routledge: 30–41.

Lethbridge, Henry James. (1985) *Hard graft in Hong Kong: Scandal, corruption and the ICAC*. Hong Kong: Oxford University Press.

Maesschalck, Jeroen (2004) "Approaches to ethics management in the public sector: A proposed expansion of the compliance-integrity continuum", *Public Integrity*, 7(1): 21–41.

Marquette, Heather (2007) "The World Bank's fight against corruption", *The Brown Journal of World Affairs*, XIII(2): 27–39.

McWalters, Ian, David Fitzpatrick and Andrew Bruce (2015) *Bribery and corruption law in Hong Kong*. 3rd edition. Singapore: LexisNexis.

Meagher, Patrick (2005) "Anti-corruption agencies: Rhetoric versus reality", *Journal of Economic Policy Reform*, 8(1): 69–103.

Paine, Lynn S. (1994) "Managing for organizational integrity", *Harvard Business Review*, (March-April): 106–115.

Persson, Anna and Martin Sjöstedt (2012) "Responsive and responsible leaders: A matter of political will", *Perspectives on Politics*, 10(3): 617–632.

Philp, Mark (2015) "The definition of political corruption" in Paul M. Heywood (ed.) *Routledge handbook of political corruption*. London: Routledge: 17–29.

Prevention of Bribery Ordinance (POBO) (Cap 201).

Quah, Jon S.T. (2013) *Curbing corruption in Asian countries: An impossible dream?* Singapore: ISEAS Publishing.

Quah, Jon S.T. (2015) "The critical importance of political will in combating corruption in Asian countries", *Public Administration and Policy*, 18(2): 12–23.

Quah, Jon S.T. (2017) "Controlling corruption in Asian countries: The elusive search for success" in Ting Gong and Ian Scott (eds.) *Routledge handbook of corruption in Asia*. London: Routledge: 241–261.

Roberts, Robert (2009) "The rise of compliance-based ethics: Implications for organizational ethics", *Public Integrity*, 11(3): 261–278.

Rohr, John A. (1978) *Ethics for bureaucrats: An essay on law and values*. New York: Marcel Dekker.

Rose-Ackerman, Susan (2017) "Corruption in Asia: Trust and economic development" in Ting Gong and Ian Scott (eds.) *Routledge handbook of corruption in Asia*. London: Routledge: 85–96.

Rotberg, Robert I. (2017) *The corruption cure: How leaders and citizens can combat graft.* Princeton: Princeton University Press.

Rothstein, Bo and Daniel Eek (2009) "Political corruption and social trust: An experimental approach", *Rationality and Society*, 21(1): 81–112.

Salminen, Ari (2013) "Control of corruption: The case of Finland" in Jon S.T. Quah (ed.) *Different paths to curbing corruption: Lessons from Denmark, Finland, Hong Kong, New Zealand and Singapore.* Bingley: Emerald: 57–77.

Salminen, Ari and Rinna Ikola-Norrbacka (2010) "Trust, good governance and unethical actions in Finnish public administration", *International Journal of Public Sector Management*, 23(7): 647–668.

Schütte, Sofie Arjon (2017) "Two steps forward, one step backwards: Indonesia's winding (anti-) corruption journey" in Ting Gong and Ian Scott (eds.) *Routledge handbook of corruption in Asia.* London: Routledge: 42–55.

Scott, Ian (2014) "Political scandals and the accountability of the Chief Executive in Hong Kong", *Asian Survey*, 54(5): 966–986.

Scott, Ian (2017) "The challenge of preserving a successful anti-corruption agency", *Asian Education and Development Studies*, 6(3): 227–237.

Transparency International (2014) *Fighting corruption: The role of the anti-corruption commission*, www.transparency.org/news/feature/fighting_corruption_the_role_of_the_anti_corruption_commission.

Transparency International (2016) "What is corruption?" www.transparency.org/what is corruption/define.

Transparency International (2017) *Corruption perceptions index.* Berlin: Transparency International, www.transparency.org/news/feature/corruption_perceptions_index_2016.

UNCAC (United Nations Convention Against Corruption) (2003), www.unodc.org/documents/treaties/UNCAC/Publications/Convention/08-50026_E.pdf.

UNDP (United Nations Development Programme) (2005) *Institutional arrangements to combat corruption: A comparative study*, www.un.org/ruleoflaw/files/10%20Institutional%20arrangements%20to%20combat%20corruption_2005.pdf.

Widoyoko, Johannes Danang (2017) "Indonesia's anti-corruption campaigns: Civil society versus the political cartel" in Marie dela Rama and Chris Rowley (eds.) *The changing face of corruption in the Asia Pacific: Current perspectives and future challenges.* Amsterdam: Elsevier: 253–266.

World Bank (1997) *Helping countries combat corruption: The role of the World Bank.* Washington: The World Bank.

World Bank (2017) "Combating corruption", 11 May, www.worldbank.org/en/topic/governance/brief/anti-corruption.

Part I

Corruption prevention in colonial Hong Kong

2 Corruption in Hong Kong, 1842–1973

The colony of Hong Kong was a corrupt place for a very long time. For 130 years after the onset of British rule in 1842, corruption was a feature of many bureaucratic, social and commercial practices. Some periods were more venal than others and some organisations, depending on the opportunities for extracting illegal payment for goods and services, were more corrupt than others. But, until 1974, there was always widespread acceptance that bribes and commissions were the way to do business, to obtain advantages and favourable treatment and to facilitate the provision of public services. The colonial government, sometimes prodded by London, did make sporadic attempts to bring corruption under control, but those foundered, partly for the reasons that ACAs elsewhere fail today. There was no sustained commitment to corruption prevention and the laws were inadequate and poorly implemented, not least because anti-corruption efforts were placed under the control of a corrupt police force.

Attempts to control corruption also failed because senior government officials subscribed to two important articles of faith. The first was that British colonial policy should not disturb Chinese customary practices unless they affected law and order or contributed to the spread of epidemics. Payment of "tea money" was regarded as customary practice. *Guanxi*, based on social connections and cemented by gift-giving, was regarded as a necessary condition for commercial and bureaucratic transactions (Smart 1993). But maintaining an appropriate balance between the contextual importance of the relationship and the value of the gift was not always easy. Gift-giving at festivals, described in one government report on corruption as an "age old custom", often seemed to stretch beyond customary requirements to include what amounted to a bribe (Advisory Committee 1961: 64–65).

Second, there was a widely held belief that the higher levels of the civil service, and especially the administrative grade, were clean and that corruption in the public service was essentially lower-level petty corruption. None of the administrative grade officers was ever convicted of corruption although some were asked to resign (Tsang 2007: 110). Other civil servants were dismissed under the civil service regulations. There were relatively few court cases because it was difficult to secure convictions and penalties were light. Corruption was believed to be an endemic and immutable part of the nature and lives of Hong Kong citizens;

action to prevent corruption was expected to have only a transitory effect and was ultimately futile.

In this chapter, we explore the forms that corruption took in colonial Hong Kong and the efforts that were made to control it, the sea-change in the level of corruption in the 1960s, the Godber affair in 1973 and its role in changing the official and public mind-set, and the creation of the ICAC in 1974 as an antidote to what by then was regarded as a serious problem rather than a minor irritation.

Attempts to control corruption in colonial Hong Kong

Public administration in early colonial Hong Kong was chaotic. The police were corrupt from the time of the creation of the force in 1844. The judicial system was little better. The Governor did attempt to improve the court system in the 1850s, but there were still suspicions of corruption, which were not helped by friction between the government and the judges (Eitel 1983: 268). In 1856, the Attorney-General, Thomas Anstey, brought a charge of "malversation of office" against the Assistant Magistrate for allegedly accepting bribes from prisoners in exchange for pardons (Munn 2001: 423). He was acquitted, but Anstey clearly thought that corruption also permeated the police force because he claimed that, when off duty, they "roamed about plundering people", producing their badge of office to assist in extortion (Endacott 1962: 91). Court interpreters, who were first used in the 1850s, were also believed to be corrupt. Many cases were interpreted by the Assistant Police Superintendent, Daniel Caldwell, the only senior member of the government who could speak Cantonese and who was himself soon to be the subject of a major corruption investigation (Munn 1997).

Caldwell rose to the position of Registrar-General and Protector of the Chinese and by all accounts was a prominent figure in the government of the time. However, when a pirate, Ma Chow Wong, with whom Caldwell had a long association, was convicted in 1857, Anstey brought charges of complicity against him, claimed that he should never have been appointed as a Justice of the Peace, and alleged that he had long associations with criminal elements and a financial interest in a brothel (Endacott 1962: 98, 1964: 103–104). After potentially incriminating material was allegedly burned by another senior official, Anstey's allegations were based only on circumstantial evidence and Caldwell was censured but not dismissed. The matter did not end there. The British government, tired of the squabbles within the colonial government, replaced the Governor, appointed Sir Hercules Robinson to the position in 1859 and ordered a new investigation, the Civil Service Abuses Enquiry, into the Caldwell affair (British Parliamentary Papers 1971: 10–28). The committee found considerable evidence of a corrupt relationship between Ma Chow Wong and Caldwell, and concluded that he should be dismissed from the public service (British Parliamentary Papers 1971: 28).

At a different time in Hong Kong history, Caldwell would probably have been sent down for many years. It is illustrative of the sanguine attitude toward corruption in nineteenth century Hong Kong that, despite his dismissal, Caldwell continued to assist the Hong Kong government in various ways (Endacott 1962: 99). Nonetheless, the affair did focus attention on the parlous state of the Hong Kong civil service. In 1861, Robinson introduced the cadet scheme, the fore-runner of the future administrative grade, which enabled recruits from British universities to undergo Chinese language training and eventually take on high-ranking positions in the government. The idea was probably also that they would be of impeccable moral character and that the ethics of the civil service would improve accordingly (Lethbridge 1978: 222). It is possible that the idea that government was clean at the higher levels dates from this time although as Tsang (1995: 6) points out, the "negative side . . . was that petty corruption was rampant among functionaries as senior officials were somewhat out of touch and did not do much about it".

The police force remained largely unreformed. McDonnell, who succeeded Robinson in 1866, reportedly said that he had never seen a body of men so corrupt and inefficient as the Hong Kong Police Force (Sinclair 1982: 28). He wrote to the Colonial Secretary that "more than half of the Inspectors [had] monthly allowances, higher than their salaries, from the Keepers of Brothels and gaming establishments" (Tsang 1995: 166). An attempt to charge an Inspector of Brothels with corruption failed because, although McDonnell was certain of the man's guilt, not a single witness would testify against him. He then dismissed the inspector. (Tsang 1995: 177). McDonnell also tried to reduce corruption by licencing gambling activities and applying the costs of the licence to funding the force and increasing the salaries of policemen. It seemed to work, but moralists in Britain objected and the scheme was discontinued.

McDonnell's experiences illustrate two important features of corruption control that were to last for the next century. First, the licencing of vice – gambling establishments, brothels, and opium divans – was a more effective way of controlling corruption than declaring those activities to be illegal. It was also more profitable for a government that was often financially stretched. However, the British government, under pressure from religious and other advocacy groups, wanted the Hong Kong government to close down all vice establishments. The results were sometimes disastrous not only for the control of corruption but for the public health of the community, especially when licenced brothels were closed down in 1935 (Miners 1987: 205–206). Second, McDonnell's problem with charging corrupt officers was not uncommon. Witnesses were usually unwilling to testify, and with good reason; the principal witness in the Witchell case, the biggest corruption case in nineteenth century Hong Kong, was found murdered, bound hand and foot, in a Canton canal (Norton-Kysshe 1971: 497). The problem was subsequently compounded by the anti-corruption laws, which made it difficult to prove corruption and to secure convictions. As a consequence, many senior officials, faced with corruption in their departments, followed in McDonnell's footsteps and resorted to dismissal rather than to the uncertainties and complications of a court case.

In 1897, records seized from an illegal gambling establishment showed police corruption stretching back 42 years (Sinclair 1982: 25). A European police inspector, Job Witchell, was subsequently charged and sentenced to six months in prison. Five other inspectors, six sergeants, nineteen Indian police and forty-four Chinese police were dismissed, compulsorily retired or resigned, reducing the size of the police force by almost half (Norton-Kysshe 1971: 498–499). There was widespread public interest in Witchell's trial. According to the *Hong Kong Telegraph* (1897), it was

> watched with the keenest interest by every section of the community, by people of high and low estate, by rich and by poor. Even schoolboys were to be seen eagerly devouring newspaper reports of the trial while in the tea-shops, opium divans and coolie lodging houses hundreds of the lowest class of residents were to be seen nightly gathered round educated men who read to them the Chinese version of the reports of proceedings.

The police force was corrupt – "honey-combed with corruption", as Norton-Kysshe (1971: 496–497) describes it – and the government accepted the view that stronger measures were needed to deal with it. These three features of the Witchell scandal – intense public interest, a belief that the police were corrupt and the need to take unequivocal action to change the situation – were significant factors in the outcome of the notorious Godber scandal, some 76 years later.

Until 1898, the principal rules dealing with corruption were the common law provisions of bribery and extortion and misconduct in public office and the civil service regulations. As a response to the Witchell case, the government introduced the *Misdemeanors Punishment Ordinance*, which remained in force until 1948 and was the first legislation to seek to control corruption explicitly (McWalters *et al* 2015: 6). Its most significant features were that it defined corruption exclusively in terms of bribery and focused on the offer and acceptance of a bribe by a public servant (*Misdemeanors Punishment Ordinance*, Sections 3 and 4). Kuan (1981: 18) notes that it was not the acceptance of a bribe which was an offence but rather its inducing influence on the public servant's conduct, honesty and integrity. The penalty on conviction was imprisonment not exceeding two years and a fine not exceeding 500 dollars but could include hard labour which had not been part of previous sentences for corrupt offences. Corruption in the private sector was not included in the ordinance. The prevailing view in both government and society was that corruption in the public service was a much more heinous crime than in business.

The *Misdemeanors Punishment Ordinance* did not have much deterrent effect, but there were no more spectacular cases of the Witchell type. The government preferred simple dismissals of corrupt officials to avoid the adverse publicity of court cases, the problem with witnesses and legal interpretations of the meaning of corruption, and because as Lethbridge (1978) argues, corruption was not seen to be a major social problem. Instances of corruption were still common in the public service. In 1902, the Governor established a Commission to investigate inefficiencies in the Public Works Department, which were thought to have contributed to the irregular water supply, the collapse of some buildings with loss of lives and the deteriorating quality of the roads. The Commissioners clearly suspected that corruption was one of the causes of the problems (Hong Kong Government 1902: 150–155), although they eventually accepted the view of the Director of Public Works that the inefficiencies resulted from a lack of manpower.

Four years later, another commission was able to identify corrupt practices more conclusively. It was set up to investigate the implementation of the health and building laws and the existence of corruption within the Sanitary Department (Hong Kong Government 1907a). The Department was run by a board comprised of three official and two *ex officio* members appointed by the Governor. Although it was more autonomous than other government departments, it was funded by the Hong Kong government and its employees were regarded as public servants. It was supposed to implement the health and sanitation regulations whose deficiencies were the cause of outbreaks of bubonic plague in the 1890s.

The Commission produced a scathing report on the Sanitary Department's failure to implement the regulations, but it was what it said about corruption that caused the greatest concern. It concluded that corruption was "rampant" and extended throughout the organisation (Hong Kong Government 1907a: 5). Transactions with contractors were not properly recorded and, in some cases, not recorded at all, leading to the suspicion that a bribe had been paid. The principal clerk in the department, who opened all correspondence in Chinese, was a partner in one of the firms with which the Department did business and was able to subvert the sealed tender system by alerting the firm to the expected price of a contract. It was common practice for the Department's inspectors to tell a contractor that work was not up to standard and could not be passed and to follow that with a request for a loan which, it was clearly understood, did not have to be repaid (Hong Kong Government 1907a: 43). The Commission found that

> No man is apparently too poor to be exploited and there is no form of exaction, however mean and contemptible, to which the Inspectors and servants of the Sanitary Department will not stoop . . . If a contractor attempts to resist these exactions, he is ruined, and in order to retain his business, he is forced to submit.
>
> (Hong Kong Government 1907a: 44)

The Principal Civil Medical Officer, who was a doctor and also the administrative head of the Sanitary Department, objected strongly to this passage, noting that the Department had thirty-five Sanitary Inspectors of whom, up to the date of his minute, five had been dismissed for corrupt practices and two were under suspension (Hong Kong Government 1907b). He felt that it was unfair that the entire department should be categorised as corrupt. The government also disagreed with some of the Commission's findings, treating its report as evidence of the need for reform but objecting to the factual basis on which other recommendations had been made. The Colonial Secretary minuted that it was not surprising that there was corruption among subordinates in the Sanitary Department when the senior officers did not speak Cantonese and he questioned whether a doctor with other responsibilities should serve as head of a large department (Hong Kong Government 1907c). The government later brought in an experienced public servant to run the Department on a full-time basis. Since the inspectors were European officers, the government may also have wanted to avoid the negative publicity that would have resulted from a court case. According to the government's annual report for 1907, the offenders were "tried by the Executive Council" (Hong Kong Government 1908: 296) and then dismissed from the service.

The Witchell case and the subsequent revelations about the Sanitary Department both display characteristics of corruption which were still present when the ICAC was created. In both cases, there were elements of syndicated corruption in which public servants jointly conspired to subvert bureaucratic rules to their own advantage. Corruption syndicates were one of the main reasons for the creation of the ICAC. Because of their organisational form, they proved much more difficult to break than cases of individual corruption. There is also some fragmentary evidence that social attitudes toward corruption did not change significantly between the early part of the century and the 1970s. The evidence to the Commission on the Sanitary Department suggests that corruption was seen as a nuisance but was very difficult for the contractors to avoid because there were threats both to their businesses and of physical violence if they did not comply (Hong Kong Government 1907a: 107–131). Commenting on the Commission's report, the Acting Governor, Frederick May, who as head of police force had investigated the Witchell case, made the interesting point that there seemed to be insufficient public knowledge that it was "as wicked to give as to receive a bribe" (Hong Kong Hansard 1907: 4). The ICAC faced the same problem when it tried to change public attitudes toward corruption seventy years later.

From the Sanitary Department investigation in 1906 until just before the Japanese invasion in 1941, there is a curious silence about corruption. That corruption continued to exist in much the same way as previously is difficult to doubt, but the government seemed either to have ignored it or to have swept it under the carpet. There were good reasons why it might have done so. Although the Hong Kong government operated with a good deal of autonomy from London, Miners (1987) notes that there were areas which generated concern in Britain: the government's opium monopoly; the *mui tsai* system which was regarded as a form of slavery and the Hong Kong government's regulation of prostitution. All of these areas were potentially vulnerable to corruption. If corruption had come to be seen a major social issue in the colony, the prospect of more direct intervention by the British government would have considerably increased. As it was, the Hong Kong government tried to appease British opinion in order to maintain its autonomy and because it did not want to undermine its fundamental principle of non-interference with Chinese customary practices.

Of the three contentious areas, the opium monopoly probably offered the greatest opportunities for corruption. The Hong Kong government had an opium monopoly for nearly one hundred years from 1845 to 1941. The monopoly contributed to the colony's often-stretched finances and Governors and senior civil servants were reluctant to lose such an important source of revenue. Initially, the opium contract was let out to a single opium farmer but in 1914 the Hong Kong government itself took over the preparation and sale of opium (Miners 1987: 227–228). Aside from growing British and international pressure to close down the opium trade, the government was also confronted with the problem of how to maintain the monopoly. The importation of illicit opium and the proliferation of illegal opium divans provided fertile ground for corruption. In 1923, the Superintendent of Imports and Exports reported that 716 keepers of illegal opium divans had been convicted and more than 3300 smokers of illegal opium had been charged (Hong Kong Government 1924: 24). He said that if he had the resources, he could have charged many more. Corruption is quickly passed over at the end of his report. "Considerable corruption and dishonesty were prevalent . . .". Seven officers were dismissed, nine resigned and two absconded but none were taken to court. In a dispatch to the Colonial Office in 1934, the Governor also refers to the problems of corruption in the Police and Revenue Departments in relation to the opium monopoly (Miners 1987: 267). But these are isolated references and corruption does not seem to have been regarded as a problem which needed more careful attention.

The British government also wanted to stop the *mui tsai* system, under which young daughters of poor Chinese families were sold into the domestic service of rich families, and to put an end to the state regulation of prostitution. Although there is no evidence that the *mui tsai* system led to increased corruption, there were fears that more *mui tsai* would be sold into prostitution if the practice was banned. The British government also pressed the Hong Kong government to close the tolerated brothels which were quite strictly controlled by the Secretary for Chinese Affairs. Prostitutes were registered, the fees they could charge were specified and they could be required to have a hospital examination if venereal disease was suspected (Miners 1987: 197). In 1935, the Hong Kong government closed down the tolerated brothels which, as it had predicted, led to unregulated illegal prostitution, with more opportunities for police corruption, and the rapid spread of venereal disease.

The government's lack of action on corruption may have been partly because the *Misdemeanors Punishment Ordinance* was regarded as unlikely to secure convictions. The burden of proof lay with the prosecution to show that the bribe had caused the recipient to act corruptly which was difficult to prove. Hong Kong juries were also inclined to acquit when the evidence was based solely on the testimony of an accomplice (Hong Kong Hansard 1948: 217–218). In 1936, Lo Man-kam, an unofficial member of the Legislative Council, said that he thought that "it is quite futile . . . to expect that evidence of bribery and corruption will be forthcoming as will secure a verdict of guilt in a Court of Law" (Hong Kong Hansard 1936: 57).

By the end of the 1930s, corruption was beginning to be seen as a major problem. In the Legislative Council, Lo said that "the public views with some concern the numerous recent cases of police constables demanding or accepting bribes"

(Hong Kong Hansard 1938: 160). In 1939, seven police officers were convicted of corruption offences (Hong Kong Government 1940: 9). In 1941, there were suspicions of corruption in the Immigration Department and some fears that it may have affected air raid precautions (Lethbridge 1985: 38–48). At the end of October 1941, the Governor, Sir Mark Young, announced that the Chief Justice, Sir Atholl McGregor, would conduct a widespread investigation into corruption in the public service and make recommendations on how it might be stamped out (Hong Kong Government 1941). Six weeks later, the Japanese invaded Hong Kong and the enquiry never took place.

After the war, Young returned to Hong Kong. He wanted to introduce a limited form of democracy which would have led to a municipal government but opposition to the proposal led to its abandonment (Scott 2015: 187–189). One of the objections was that it would increase corruption. In a dispatch to the Colonial Office, Young reported that there was far too much corruption in the Hong Kong government for his "peace of mind" but did not think it would be any different if a municipal government was introduced (Tsang 1995: 128). The government did take some action, however, introducing a new ordinance, *The Prevention of Corruption Ordinance*, in 1948.

The ordinance was based on English legislation on corruption which had previously been considered for inclusion in a Hong Kong ordinance to supercede the *Misdemeanors Punishment Ordinance*. In 1919, the government had tabled a bill in the Legislative Council to introduce a new ordinance which would have incorporated English laws passed in 1906 and 1916. But it was withdrawn without debate or explanation (Hong Kong Hansard 1919: 45). The new *Prevention of Corruption Ordinance* extended the provisions of the law to the private sector and increased the penalty on indictment to a maximum of five years imprisonment and a fine of $10,000 (*Prevention of Corruption Ordinance*, Section 5(2)b). Although the ordinance was an improvement on the previous legislation, there was still difficulty in obtaining convictions. There was considerable legal debate over the meaning of the phrases "corruptly solicits" and "corruptly accepts". The ordinance did not resolve the problem that it was not enough to show that an advantage had been received: it was still necessary to prove that a bribe was an inducement to some form of conduct or action (McWalters *et al* 2015: 9–13). Investigation of corruption remained with the police which set up a specialised Anti-Corruption Branch (later the Anti-Corruption Office) in 1952 (Palmier 1985: 125ff).

Judicial uncertainty over the meaning of the ordinance and continuing evidence of widespread corruption may have led the Governor, Sir Alexander Grantham, to supplement the ordinance by creating a Standing Committee on Corruption in 1956. The Committee was to advise the government on the means to reduce corruption and to review its incidence in the civil service. It was initially chaired by a Principal Crown Counsel but was strengthened in 1960 when the Attorney-General became the Chair and three Executive Councillors, the Establishment Officer (in charge of civil service personnel) and the Deputy Commissioner of Police were appointed as members (McWalters *et al* 2015: 14).

Corruption in the 1950s still often seemed to be viewed as an occasional nuisance, sometimes worse if an individual had frequent dealings with the public service or the police. The Korean War provided a fillip for corruption, but Grantham took a soft approach to some of the corrupt practices that developed (Manion 2004: 29; Goodstadt 2005: 149–150). Government policies were increasing the interaction between civil servants and the public, providing more opportunities for corruption. In 1955, for example, the government embarked on a large-scale public housing programme which involved re-settling the hundreds of thousands of squatters who had flooded into Hong Kong after the communist takeover in China in 1949. The process of clearing the squatters off Crown land was undertaken by the Resettlement Department which had to rotate its workers to try to ensure that they would not be bribed by squatter landlords (Smart 2006: 42). When the squatters lived on the hill-sides, they may have had corrupt dealings with their landlords and among themselves, but they had little reason to interact with the Hong Kong government. Once they were re-located in public housing blocks, they were turned into citizens and had to deal with the government as their landlord and the police as their protectors in a climate where bribery was the expected means of completing a transaction.

The 1960s and the *Prevention of Bribery Ordinance* (*POBO*)

Corruption in the 1960s and the early 1970s has come to play such a part in Hong Kong's understanding of its own history that many of the details have now become embedded in folk-lore and in film. The ICAC has used it as the dark-side counterpoint of its own efforts to sustain a clean government, economy and society. In 2018, for example, the ICAC website described corruption in the 1960s and early 1970s as

> rampant in the public sector. Ambulance crews would demand tea money before picking up a sick person. Even hospital amahs asked for "tips" before giving patients a bedpan or a glass of water. Offering bribes to the right officials was also necessary when applying for public housing, schooling and other public services. Corruption was particularly serious in the Police Force. Corrupt police officers offered protection to vice, gambling and drug activities.
>
> (ICAC 2018)

ICAC senior officials have added further details in their speeches on corruption prevention: firemen who refused to turn on their hoses unless offered a bribe, buying a driving licence from the examiner, illegal kickbacks in business (ICAC 2008). This is a description of corruption of a different order from that of the previous one hundred years. It is pervasive and pernicious, affecting life at every turn, from cradle to grave. How did this come about? Why was there a change in the level of corruption in the 1960s?

The principal explanation focuses on two related factors: the changed circumstances resulting from massive immigration from China in the late 1940s, which more than doubled the population to about three million by the beginning of the 1960s, and the consequences of rapid economic growth. As the ICAC (2018) sees it, the government "while maintaining social order and delivering the bare essentials in housing and other services, was unable to meet the needs of the swelling population". Scarce goods and services could be obtained more quickly by paying a bribe (Manion 2004: 29; Scott 2015: 191).

This explanation places the emphasis on public demand for goods and services, but there was also pressure from a corrupt bureaucracy which was coming into increasing contact with citizens in fields which had not previously been part of the government's responsibilities. Between 1949 and 1962, the establishment of the public service more than tripled from 17,500 to 56,910 (Hong Kong Government 1963: 354). The establishment of the police force grew from 3852 to 8593 (Hong Kong Government 1963: 203), with uniformed police on the beat composing about two-thirds of the total. In the Resettlement Department, a memorandum in 1963 noted that the Department's personnel were "in daily contact with 1,200,000 people: 550,000 settlers in Resettlement Estates and Cottage Areas, 100,000 in the process of being resettled and 550,000 squatters waiting to be re-settled" (quoted in Smart 2006: 169). New policies, increased contact between the government and the public and a largely unregulated economy created many fresh corruption opportunities for entrepreneurial civil servants.

In 1960, the Standing Committee on Corruption decided to change its name to the Advisory Committee on Corruption in which capacity it made recommendations to the Governor on establishing working parties on public consultation, departmental procedures and legal matters (Advisory Committee 1960: 1–2). In its sixth report, produced in April 1961, the Committee provided a critical assessment of the state of corruption (Advisory Committee 1961: 41–75). It believed that the most susceptible departments were those in continuous contact with the public, such as the police and the Urban Services Department, but that – and here it accepted the long-standing government view – corruption was "largely confined to the Inspectorate and lower grades, although it does on occasions reach higher levels" (Advisory Committee 1961: 46). It recognised, however, that many "responsible members" of the public believed that corruption was rife throughout the government. Although it made some sensible recommendations for reducing corruption in government departments, in dealing with the public and in amending the law, the Committee's report ended on a note of despair:

> Corruption is too deep-rooted in Hong Kong society for the remedies that we have put forward to have any obvious and immediate success. It will be necessary to maintain a sustained campaign against all aspects of corruption, perhaps indefinitely, and alter tactics in the light of experience.
>
> (Advisory Committee 1961: 66)

Despite these observations, the Committee downgraded its own role and status by recommending that its membership should in future consist only of a non-official Chairman, three Unofficial Members of Council and the Establishment Officer (Advisory Committee 1961: 74).

The police were the major problem. By the 1960s, corruption within the force had become systemic and widespread. Bribes were extorted by constables on the beat and syphoned up through the organisation to the highest levels (Cheung and Lau 1981). They covered a wide range of activities from protection rackets for illicit activities, to what amounted to taxes on legitimate small businesses and people on the streets, to the collection of bribes to avoid fines for traffic violations and other offences. The organisational structure of the force was subverted to the extent that a parallel hierarchy was in place which used public resources for the purpose of extracting bribes for the benefit of its members. The span of control was such that even if senior officers had been clean, which many were not, their numbers were insufficient to control the activities of junior officers. Staff sergeants virtually became a law unto themselves and were able to acquire hundreds of millions of dollars. After the creation of the ICAC, the most notorious sergeants fled to Taiwan and Thailand to avoid prosecution (Mok 2011).

A fervent campaigner against corruption and an elected member of the Urban Council, Elsie Elliot (later Elsie Tu), attempted to bring many examples of police extortion and other bureaucratic corruption to the attention of the media, the Commission of Inquiry investigating the 1966 riots, and to the British government (Elliot 1971; Tu 2003). But she was ignored by both the British and Hong Kong governments and charged by the Commission of Inquiry with contempt although she was not imprisoned or fined (Hong Kong Government 1967: Appendix 11). There was increasing public resentment of petty corruption on the streets, especially among the young, and growing awareness of the problem at the highest levels in government. The 1966 Star Ferry riots showed that there was widespread mistrust and even hatred of the police and provided many further examples of extortion (Hong Kong Government 1967). But the Commission of Inquiry into the riots made no recommendations for better control of police corruption (Scott 2017).

Although the Anti-Corruption Branch did make some progress in prosecuting corrupt officials in the 1960s, the fact that the police were both poachers and gamekeepers did nothing to increase public confidence in the system. The Branch nonetheless was responsible for initiating changes in the legislation in the late 1960s, drawing attention to deficiencies in the *Prevention of Corruption Ordinance* (McWalters *et al* 2015: 18). The government set up a working party to examine possible amendments to the legislation. After considering anti-corruption legislation in Ceylon and Singapore, it decided instead to recommend an entirely new ordinance. The explanatory memorandum on the new legislation, which came into effect in 1971, said that the reason for its introduction was that success against corruption had only been "moderate" (Hong Kong Hansard 1970: 143).

The *Prevention of Bribery Ordinance* (*POBO*), as subsequently amended, remains the cornerstone of Hong Kong's efforts to control corruption. It represents a significant break from the past and contains within its clauses the implication of zero tolerance of corruption, a willingness to shift the burden of proof to the defendant, and the provision of powers of investigation which, critics were to claim, infringed civil liberties. Rather than trying to define corruption, the new ordinance simply provided that it was an offence, both in the public and in the private sector, to solicit or accept an advantage (*POBO*: Section 4). As McWalters *et al* (2015: 21) note, "[t]he only defence was that the accused had permission from the Governor to accept the advantage". In prosecuting civil servants, the legislation removed the requirement in the previous ordinance to prove a connection between the acceptance of a bribe and the performance of official functions. It was sufficient to show that a civil servant had obtained an advantage. Resting the burden of proof on the defendant was also central to another novel provision. Any civil servant who had a standard of living or assets disproportionate to emoluments without satisfactory explanation was guilty of an offence (*POBO*: Section 10). Penalties for all offences were raised with a maximum sentence of ten years and a fine of $100,000 reserved for offences relating to procurement, contracts and tenders (*POBO*: Section 12).

When the Attorney-General introduced the bill in Legislative Council, he noted that the powers of investigation had been widened and that these might cause inconvenience to the public, but he said that "[i]f some infringement of traditional liberty and privacy is involved, then I believe it is a price which the community ought to be prepared to pay, if it really wishes to see corruption ousted from our daily life" (Hong Kong Hansard 1970: 133, 137). The powers of investigation now included access to information such as bank accounts, tax returns, living expenses of the accused and property owned singly or with a spouse. It required anyone with knowledge of an alleged offence to provide a full disclosure of information, and it increased the ease with which search warrants could be obtained. The question of whether the investigation of corruption should remain with the Anti-Corruption Branch or whether it should be transferred to an independent body was also considered. The Attorney-General thought that it should remain with the police and ruled out the creation of a "small independent organization", which he believed would not have sufficient authority or expertise to do the job properly and would reduce confidence in the police (Hong Kong Hansard 1970: 133).

A new Governor, Sir Murray MacLehose, was appointed in 1972 and delivered a landmark speech on social policy reforms in October of that year. There was no mention of corruption in his speech although reportedly he had been asked by his most senior civil servant, Jack Cater, to include some indication of what the government was doing about it (*Daily Telegraph* 2006; Yep 2013). Goodstadt (2005: 145) suggests that MacLehose may have been concerned that references to corruption might detract from the positive image of his administration which he was attempting to cultivate. He also reports that in the early days of his governorship, MacLehose attempted to persuade journalists to drop campaigns against corruption because he thought the Chinese community was not interested in controlling it (Goodstadt 2005: 145). If that was MacLehose's view, then the public reactions to the Godber scandal must have quickly changed his mind.

The Godber scandal

The Godber scandal and its direct outcome, the creation of the ICAC, mark in the public mind a seismic divide between old and new ways of relating to corruption prevention. Yet there were also some improvements in the two years between the enactment of the *POBO* and the revelation of Godber's transgressions. Charles Sutcliffe was appointed Commissioner of Police in 1969 and instituted an organisational reform programme which was designed, *inter alia*, to reduce the power of the staff sergeants who were all offered promotion to inspectors (Cheung and Lau 1981: 211). The Anti-Corruption Office in the police force also began to take a stronger line on corruption within the force and in the wider public service (Manion 2004: 32–32; Yep 2013). Despite acknowledging these tighter controls and accepting Sutcliffe's view that the Anti-Corruption Office needed time to show its mettle, the judge who investigated the Godber scandal still concluded that there had not been "any spectacular breakthrough in the battle against corruption" (Blair-Kerr 1973b: 19). In any event, the affair itself, and particularly Godber's flight from Hong Kong, cast doubt on the value of some of the provisions of the *POBO* and the efficacy of the Anti-Corruption Office's methods.

In April 1973, Sutcliffe received information that Godber, who had held the very senior position of Deputy District Police Commander, Kowloon (Blair-Kerr 1973a: 3), was remitting money abroad. Sutcliffe passed the information on to the Anti-Corruption Office, which then investigated the case. In early June, Godber, who had tried to take early retirement, was charged with possessing "pecuniary resources or property disproportionate to his present or past official emoluments" under Section 10 of the *POBO*. He was also served with a notice asking for an explanation of the disparity between his assets and his salary. Under the *POBO*, as it then stood, he was not immediately arrested but was given a week to explain the discrepancy. He was estimated to have accumulated HK$4.377 million, nearly six times his net salary over the period of his service from 1952 to 1973 (Blair-Kerr 1973a: 5). On 8 June, Godber boarded a plane for Singapore and fled to England (Blair-Kerr 1973a: 3–11). The Hong Kong government's initial reaction was that it could not extradite him because of the provisions of the *Fugitive Offenders Act* and because of a lack of evidence (Lam 2004: 162). However, a public campaign and some demonstrations persuaded the government to be more proactive. Godber was eventually extradited from London in January 1975, where he had spent ten months in jail. He was tried and sentenced to four years in prison and was ordered to pay HK$25,000 in restitution. He was convicted on the testimony of two tainted witness and in an earlier period under different corruption laws might have expected a jury to acquit him.

The public took an intense interest in the case. Godber became an anti-hero, a villain who epitomised the problem with the police and its corruption syndicates

(Lethbridge 1985: 94). The demonstrators, mostly young people, had called for Godber's extradition, removing corruption cases from police control and the creation of an independent commission. There was some suspicion that Godber had been able to escape from Hong Kong with help from within the police force. MacLehose then asked a senior judge, Sir Alastair Blair-Kerr, to report on how Godber had been able to leave for England unimpeded, how the *POBO* could be improved and what other changes might be necessary to increase effective corruption prevention (Blair-Kerr 1973a, 1973b).

Blair-Kerr produced two reports. In the first report, he explained how Godber could have used his police security pass to evade immigration controls even though he had been on the watch-list at the airport (Blair-Kerr 1973a: 18–19). In his second report, he provided an analysis of corruption in Hong Kong and made detailed recommendations to tighten the *POBO*. He described corruption in the police force as "syndicated" (Blair-Kerr 1973b: 23–26). Groups of officers (the syndicate) would act together to require small businesses, vice establishments, taxi and mini-bus drivers, prostitutes and many others to pay bribes on a regular basis (Cheung and Lau 1981; Lo 2003). Other police officers were involved in drug trafficking or in the systematic circumvention of government regulations. As virtual head of a syndicate, Godber had little more to do than to sit back and collect his share of the proceeds.

Although Blair-Kerr focused on police corruption, he saw the entire public sector and illegal commissions in the private sector as replete with opportunities for corrupt behaviour. He recommended *inter alia* strengthening the *POBO* to prevent the loopholes that had allowed Godber to flee, giving investigators the power to inspect bank accounts, increased financial penalties for offences, and an end to the right of suspects to remain silent to avoid incrimination (Blair-Kerr 1973b: 27–34). He did not arrive at a conclusion on whether corruption control should remain under the Anti-Corruption Office or whether a new independent commission should be created but he did lay out the arguments both for maintaining control within the force and the case for an independent agency. As he saw it, the argument for control to remain with the Anti-Corruption Office related principally to the organisational abilities of the police to investigate crimes and the difficulties of recruiting equivalent personnel to play that role. The opposing argument was that there were widely held public perceptions that the police force was corrupt and that corrupt officers could not be expected to investigate offences impartially (Blair-Kerr 1973b: 49–50).

The creation of the ICAC

The decision was left to MacLehose, who told the Legislative Council on 17 October 1973 that he had decided to set up a "separate Anti-Corruption Commission under a civilian Commissioner" (Hong Kong Hansard 1973: 17). The "conclusive argument", he said, was that "public confidence is very much involved [and that] the public would have more confidence in a unit that was entirely independent and separate from the Government, including the police" (Hong Kong

Hansard 1973: 17; Hong Kong Hansard 1974: 447). MacLehose had already asked Jack Cater to serve as the first Commissioner and he had travelled to Malta to persuade John Prendergast, a former policeman, to come out of retirement and serve as Director of Operations (OD). P. T. Warr, a former Director of Audit, was appointed as Director of the Corruption Prevention Department (CPD), and Helen C.P. Yu Lai, then a young Administrative Officer in the Hong Kong government, became the first head of the Community Relations Department (CRD).

The speed with which the ICAC was created is an indication of the importance which was attached to the corruption issue and the concern that it might affect the legitimacy of colonial rule. The 1966 riots, which had stemmed in part from police corruption and brutality, resulted in some reforms (Hong Kong Government 1967; Scott 2017). More serious disturbances in the following year and MacLehose's promises of further social reforms further emphasised that the old colonial system was coming to an end. Although the government probably felt under less pressure in 1973 than it had done in 1966, the widespread perception of police corruption, exacerbated by the Godber affair, was still a highly sensitive political issue. Dealing effectively with corruption was one means of building legitimacy (Lethbridge 1985: 205–207; Scott 1989: 146–152; Cheung 2008).

The Hong Kong colonial civil service did not normally act precipitately, even in times of crisis. Yet, in this instance, it took less than five months after MacLehose's announcement to create the ICAC. The amendments which Blair-Kerr had proposed were quickly passed into law together with some other changes to strengthen the ordinance and the powers granted to the Commission (McWalters 2015: 30). On 13 February 1974, the *Independent Commission Against Corruption Ordinance* was read for a second and third time and two days later the ICAC opened its doors. Its initial concern was to convince the public that the Commission was a very different kind of organisation from its predecessor. The staff of the Anti-Corruption Office, 181 police officers and 44 police-employed civilians, were transferred to the Commission but the Director of Operations made it clear that this was a temporary move, pending recruitment of the ICAC's own staff (ICAC 1975: 7–8). Some of the staff later returned to the police force or were released. The OD began work immediately, focusing on corruption in the police force and the public service. The CPD was not able to start its assignment work in government departments until September 1974 but it began by taking on issues which had prompted public concern about corruption: for example, the process of issuing driving licences; soliciting by minor staff in hospital wards; and procedures governing illegal immigrants from China (ICAC 1975: 15). The CRD began by explaining its role to government departments and community organisations. Its efforts were met with an enthusiastic response from younger people, former participants in the anti-Godber demonstrations, some of whom joined the department (Yu 2017).

The history of anti-corruption efforts in Hong Kong until 1974 is a tale of false starts, of political failure to confront the problem and of laws which were not fit for purpose. Colonial beliefs that corruption and Chinese culture were intertwined and should not be disturbed and that the public service was clean aside from the petty transgressions of its most junior employees were obstacles to reform. The Godber scandal challenged those assumptions, changed the official mind-set, and led to the creation of an agency which developed more effective ways of dealing with corruption. It is a matter of speculation whether an increasingly economically advanced and educated Hong Kong could have continued to live with the kind of corruption which it experienced in the 1960s and 1970s; if it had not been for Godber, perhaps some other incident would have created a scandal and provided the stimulus for change. Even so, in 1974, the new order had still to become established. There were forces opposed to change in the police and the public service, in business and in society where many were inclined to wait and see whether another false start was in the making. In the next chapter, we examine how the ICAC addressed these issues and how it sought to extend its zero-tolerance policy on corruption throughout polity, business and society.

References

Advisory Committee on Corruption (1960) *First report*. Hong Kong: mimeo.

Advisory Committee on Corruption (1961) *Sixth report*. Hong Kong: mimeo.

Blair-Kerr, Sir Alastair (1973a) *First report of the Commission of Inquiry under Sir Alastair Blair-Kerr*. Hong Kong: Government Printer.

Blair-Kerr, Sir Alastair (1973b) *Second report of the Commission of Inquiry under Sir Alastair Blair-Kerr*. Hong Kong: Government Printer.

British Parliamentary Papers (1971) *China 25 Hong Kong 1862–1881*. Shannon: Irish University Press.

Cheung, Anthony B.L. (2008) "Combating corruption as a political strategy to rebuild trust and legitimacy" in Bidya Bowornwathana and Clay Westcott (eds.) *Corruption governance reform in Asia: Democracy, corruption and government trust*. Bingley: Emerald: 55–84.

Cheung, Tak-sing and Chong-chor Lau (1981) "A profile of syndicate corruption in the police force" in Rance P.L. Lee (ed.) *Corruption and its control in Hong Kong*. Hong Kong: The Chinese University Press: 199–221.

Daily Telegraph (2006) "Sir Jack Cater", 26 April, www.telegraph.co.uk/news/obit uaries/1516154/Sir-Jack-Cater.html.

Eitel, Ernst Johann (1895, reprinted 1983) *Europe in China*. Hong Kong: Hong Kong University Press.

Elliot, Elsie (1971) *The avarice, bureaucracy and corruption of Hong Kong*. Hong Kong: Friends Commercial Printing Factory.

Endacott, George B. (1962) *A biographical sketch-book of early Hong Kong*. Singapore: Eastern Universities Press.

Endacott, George B. (1964) *A history of Hong Kong*. 2nd edition. Hong Kong: Oxford University Press.

Goodstadt, Leo F. (2005) "The business of corruption" in Leo F. Goodstadt (ed.) *Uneasy partners: The conflict between public interest and private profit in Hong Kong*. Hong Kong: Hong Kong University Press: 139–157.

Hong Kong Government (1902) "Report of the Commission to enquire into the Public Works Department", http://sunzi.lib.hku.hk/hkgro/view/s1907/1993. pdf.

Hong Kong Government (1907a) "Report of the Public Health and Buildings Ordinance Commission", http://sunzi.lib.hku.hk/hkgro/view/s1907/1993.pdf.

Hong Kong Government (1907b) "Minute of the Principal Civil Medical Officer on the report of the Public Health and Buildings Ordinance Commission", 13 May, http://sunzi.lib.hku.hk/hkgro/view/s1907/1993.pdf.

Hong Kong Government (1907c) "Minute by the Colonial Secretary on the report of the Commission to enquire into the working of the Public Health and Building Ordinance in the Sanitary Department", http://sunzi.lib.hku.hk/hkgro/view/s1907/1993.pdf.

Hong Kong Government (1908) "Report on the blue book for 1907", http://sunzi.lib.hku.hk/hkgro/view/s1907/1993.pdf.

Hong Kong Government (1924) "Report of the Superintendent of Imports and Exports for the year 1923", http://sunzi.lib.hku.hk/hkgro/view/s1907/1993.pdf.

Hong Kong Government (1940) "Report of the Commissioner of Police, 1939", http://sunzi.lib.hku.hk/hkgro/view/s1907/1993.pdf.

Hong Kong Government (1941) *The Hong Kong Government Gazette*, 31 October, http://sunzi.lib.hku.hk/hkgro/view/s1907/1993.pdf.

Hong Kong Government (1963) *Hong Kong 1962*. Hong Kong: Government Press.

Hong Kong Government (1967) *Kowloon Disturbances 1966: Report of the Commission of Inquiry*. Hong Kong: Government Printer.

Hong Kong Hansard 16 May 1907; 21 June 1919; 19 March 1936; 16 November 1938; 11 July 1948; 21 October 1970; 17 October 1973; 13 February 1974.

Hong Kong Telegraph (1897) 4 August.

ICAC (1975) "Annual report 1974", www.icac.org.hk/filemanager/en/Content_27/1974.pdf.

ICAC (2008) "Speech of the Director of the Community Relations, ICAC at the opening ceremony of the 6th Postgraduate Certificate course in corruption studies", 4 November.

ICAC (2018) "About ICAC: Brief history", www.icac.org.hk/en/about/history/index.html.

Kuan, Hsin-chi (1981) "Anti-corruption legislation in Hong Kong – a history" in Rance P.L. Lee (ed.) *Corruption and its control in Hong Kong*. Hong Kong: The Chinese University Press: 15–43.

Lam, Wai-man (2004) *Understanding the political culture of Hong Kong: The paradox of activism and depoliticization*. Armonk, NY: M.E. Sharpe.

Lethbridge, Henry James (1978) "The emergence of bureaucratic corruption as a social problem in Hong Kong" in H.J. Lethbridge (ed.) *Hong Kong: prosperity and stability: A collection of essays*. Hong Kong: Oxford University Press: 214–237.

Lethbridge, Henry James (1985) *Hard graft in Hong Kong: Scandal, corruption and the ICAC*. Hong Kong: Oxford University Press.

Lo, T. Wing (2003) "Minimizing crime and corruption in Hong Kong" in Roy Godson (ed.) *Menace to society: Political-criminal collaboration around the world*. New Brunswick: Transaction: 231–256.

Manion, Melanie (2004) *Corruption by design: Building clean government in Mainland China and Hong Kong*. Cambridge, MA: Harvard University Press.

McWalters, Ian, David Fitzpatrick and Andrew Bruce (2015) *Bribery and corruption law in Hong Kong*. 3rd edition. Singapore: LexisNexis.

Miners, Norman (1987) *Hong Kong under imperial rule*. Hong Kong: Oxford University Press.

Mok, Danny (2011) "Tsang Kai-wing dies aged 94 after 35 years as corruption fugitive", *South China Morning Post*, www.scmp.com/article/736079/tsang-kai-wing-dies-aged-94-after-35-years-corruption-fugitive.

Munn, Christopher (1997) " 'Giving justice a second chance': The criminal trial in early British Hong Kong, 1841–1866", *China Information*, 12(1–2): 36–65.

Munn, Christopher (2001) *Anglo-China: Chinese people and British rule in Hong Kong, 1841–1880*. Richmond: Curzon Press.

Norton-Kysshe, James (1971) *The history of the laws and courts of Hong Kong from the earliest period until 1898*. Vol. 2. Hong Kong: Vetch and Lee.

Palmier, Leslie (1985) *The control of bureaucratic corruption in Asia*. New Delhi: Allied Publishers.

Scott, Ian (1989) *Political change and the crisis of legitimacy in Hong Kong*. London: Hurst.

Scott, Ian (2015) "Governance and corruption prevention in Hong Kong" in Leon van den Dool, Frank Hendriks, Alberto Gianoli and Linze Schaap (eds.) *The quest for good governance: Theoretical reflections and international practices*. Wiesbaden: Springer: 185–204.

Scott, Ian (2017) "Bridging the gap: Hong Kong senior civil servants and the 1966 riots", *Journal of Imperial and Commonwealth History*, 45(1): 131–148.

Sinclair, Kevin (1982) *Asia's finest*. Hong Kong: Unicorn.

Smart, Alan (1993) "Gifts, bribes and guanxi: A re-consideration of Bourdieu's social capital", *Current Anthropology*, 8(3): 308–408.

Smart, Alan (2006) *The Shek Kip Mei myth: Squatters, fires and colonial rule in Hong Kong, 1950–1963*. Hong Kong: Hong Kong University Press.

Tsang, Steve (ed.) (1995) *A documentary history of Hong Kong: Government and politics*. Hong Kong: Hong Kong University Press.

Tsang, Steve (2007) *Governing Hong Kong: Administrative officers from the nineteenth century to the handover to China, 1862–1997*. London: I.B. Taurus.

Tu, Elsie (2003) *Colonial Hong Kong through the eyes of Elsie Tu*. Hong Kong: Hong Kong University Press.

Yep, Ray (2013) "The crusade against corruption in the 1970s: Governor MacLehose as a zealous reformer or a reluctant hero?" *China Information*, 27(2): 197–221.

Yu Lai, Helen C.P. (2017) "Interview with Helen C.P. Yu Lai, former Head of the Community Relations Department", 17 November.

3 Crisis and challenge
The early years of the ICAC

A new ACA often finds itself working in an atmosphere where there is some ambivalence about what it is trying to do and some scepticism about its ability to achieve it. While there may be initial enthusiasm for its creation, as there was among youth in Hong Kong, memories of past failures and the need to make an immediate positive impression means that the agency needs quick results. If the ACA takes a quiet approach to corruption prevention or is unable to fight its own corner, it is unlikely to win public support, its efforts may be treated with indifference and the process of institutionalisation becomes much more difficult. Incremental improvements, however valuable, do not signal the kind of radical changes that are often promised by the authorities who set up the agency. If, on the other hand, the ACA vigorously pursues the corrupt and welcomes the publicity that goes with their prosecution, there is likely to be a backlash from those who are affected by its actions. Organised opposition to the ACA aimed at limiting its powers is likely to follow and may even win support from those who are not corrupt but doubt whether the ACA will bring about significant change. In consequence, the first few years of an ACA's life are critical for its credibility. It must win the battle to establish its vision of how corruption will be stamped out and show by its endeavours that it has the determination and the means to do so.

Based on the ICAC's experience, we postulate that, soon after their creation, effective ACAs will usually have to confront corrupt and unacceptable practices in the bureaucracy, especially in the police; deal with embedded supportive public attitudes toward corruption in the private sector; and meet challenges to their status and funding from within the government, the bureaucracy or the legislature. This is by no means an exhaustive list of the possible challenges faced by an ACA. Critically, confrontation often revolves around attempts to restrict its operations. These may take the form of assertions or even action by the police force to show that they alone are capable of investigating corruption, attempts by the legislature to weaken the powers of the ACA, public or private sector practices that fly in the face of the law, and efforts to cut the budget of the ACA and render it ineffective. Crises and confrontations between the ACA and its opponents will consequently depend on the political, economic and social configurations in each jurisdiction. In Indonesia, for example, there has been a long and bitter confrontation between the KPK, the police and the legislature over the KPK's powers

(Dick and Mulholland 2016; Schütte 2017). In Papua New Guinea, after the agency had helped serve an arrest warrant on the Prime Minister, the government cut the ACA's budget to the point where it could no longer function effectively (Walton and Hushang 2017).

The ICAC's experience does not cover the multiplicity of conflictual situations in which ACAs may find themselves. However, it does provide some indication of how these situations may be overcome and the political dynamics that must work in the ACA's favour if the outcome is to be successful. In the following sections, we consider four areas of tension or concern: between the ICAC and the police in a period when many corrupt policemen were arrested and the government proclaimed a partial police amnesty; between the ICAC and the public after the amnesty when public support for the Commission was in question and the campaign to change social attitudes toward corruption had only recently begun; between the ICAC and the private sector over illegal business commissions; and between the ICAC and the government and the legislature over a funding issue.

The partial police amnesty and its aftermath

Corruption control in many British colonies, including Hong Kong before 1973, was under police control. When MacLehose created the ICAC as an independent agency in the face of strong police arguments for its retention, and the Commission subsequently initially focused mainly on its investigations into corruption in the police, the stage was set for tense relationships. Although Blair-Kerr (1973: 23–24) had warned about the extent of police corruption, its sheer scale and pervasiveness had probably not been anticipated. In the first two years of its life, the ICAC felt that it did not have sufficient capacity to deal with syndicated corruption and officers were prosecuted on an individual basis rather than as part of what was later called a "conspiracy". By 1976, however, the ICAC investigators were able to make very considerable inroads into the syndicates, resulting in large numbers of prosecutions and convictions. The dramatic nature of many cases strengthened the position of the ICAC in the community but also resulted in fear and resentment within the police force which eventually took the form of demonstrations and violent action.

Table 3.1 lists the number of public reports of corruption, investigations and prosecutions of police officers. Between 1974 and 1980, 150 police officers were convicted on charges of corruption (ICAC 1975–1981) and a further 108 were convicted between 1981 and 1985 (ICAC 1982–1986). In addition, between 1974 and 1985, the ICAC referred 1011 police officers to the force for possible disciplinary or administrative action, some of whom were subsequently dismissed (ICAC 1974–1986). Table 3.1 shows the increase in confidence in the ICAC as anonymous complaints dropped and more complainants proved willing to identify themselves and help with further investigations. The sharp drop in complaints after the partial police amnesty in 1977 was taken as evidence that public confidence in the Commission had been badly shaken rather than as evidence of a decline in police corruption.

Table 3.1 Corruption reports, investigations, prosecutions and convictions of police officers, 1973–1978

	Reports of police corruption[1]	*Investigations*	*Prosecutions*	*Convictions*[2]
1973[3]	–	–	7	5
1974	1443 (1026)	419	30	17
1975	1492 (978)	602	58	27
1976	1119 (468)	345	55	19
1977	729 (377)	386	126	39
1978	487 (230)	344	62	19

Sources: Blair-Kerr 1973: 18; ICAC 1975: Appendices VIII, IX, X; ICAC 1976: Appendices X, XI, XII, XIII; ICAC 1977: Appendices X, XI, XII, XIII; ICAC 1978: Appendices X, XI XIII, XIV; ICAC 1979a: Appendices XIII, XIV, XVI, XVII

Notes:
[1] The figures in brackets are of reports which were made anonymously.
[2] Figures for convictions are best seen over a period longer than a year, as in the text, because many cases were pending from one year to the next.
[3] The figures for 1973 are cases brought by the Anti-Corruption Office of the Hong Kong Police Force. Figures from 1974 onward are ICAC cases.

By 1975, the ICAC was well aware of the "vast amounts of money made by comparatively low-ranking officers involved in syndicated corruption" (ICAC 1976: 20). One retired station sergeant (previously called staff sergeants), for example, had assets of more than HK$6 million on a salary which probably did not exceed a few thousand dollars per month. Station sergeants (the "caterers" as they were called) were the focal point of syndicated corruption, organising more junior staff to collect bribes from small businesses, taxi and mini-bus drivers, hawkers and prostitutes and passing on a portion of the proceeds to more senior officers as a form of protection (Lethbridge 1985: 123). Police officers who did not want to become part of the syndicate found themselves posted to "dry" areas where there was little opportunity for corruption.

The effects of the prosecutions and convictions did much to increase the credibility of the ICAC but the public were still uncertain about the outcome. The first survey carried out by the ICAC's Community Research Unit in September 1977 showed that about 40 per cent of respondents believed that the ICAC had a positive effect on the efficiency of government employees, including the police, but 57 per cent thought that there had been a negative effect on police morale with possible consequences for the maintenance of law and order (ICAC 1979b: 34–35). Nearly 30 per cent of respondents believed that the Commission should concentrate on catching the "big tigers" rather than the "small flies" (ICAC 1979b: 37).

The "big tigers" were housed in the syndicates which proved difficult to break. The problem, not only in the police force but also in syndicates in the Prisons and Public Works Departments, lay in the complexity of the investigations. The collection and collation of material took time; potential witnesses were intimidated; some of those implicated absconded; and there were long trial and appeal processes before convictions could be secured (ICAC 1975: 19). The ICAC was concerned that the syndicates would learn about its investigative procedures through the court cases and that their defences would improve as a result. Nonetheless, by 1976, when its numbers had been strengthened by the recruitment of officers from overseas and the creation of an intelligence unit specifically concerned with syndicates, the ICAC was in a much better position to deal with organised corruption.

The syndicates were composed of police officers organised to commit such crimes as extortion, drug trafficking, illegal gambling, permitting breaches of government regulations and various kinds of protection rackets. In the first major syndicate case, the Kowloon Traffic conspiracy in May 1976, sixteen officers were charged with conspiracy for accepting bribes from transport operators and lorry drivers, and for altering statements after accidents; thirteen were found guilty and three were acquitted (ICAC 1976: 17). The ICAC estimated that the syndicate had collected HK$400,000 per month between 1972 and 1974 (ICAC 2014: 17). In the Wanchai conspiracy case, twelve officers and three civilians were charged with accepting money from hawkers in exchange for protection from harassment and prosecution. The activities of the syndicates were widespread, involving, for example, false accusations of possessing drugs, allowing illegal book-making in exchange for bribes at the race course and accepting bribes for permitting breaches of many different government regulations (ICAC 1977: 18–19). But some progress was made, and by mid-1977, the ICAC commissioner was able to report to the Governor that no major syndicates remained and those that did "had been shattered into smaller and, therefore, financially less rewarding groups" (ICAC 1978: 9).

The problem was not entirely resolved, however. At the end of 1976, ICAC officers began investigations into the Yau Ma Tei fruit market conspiracy, the largest and most troublesome of the syndicates. The syndicate was involved in trafficking heroin and had developed into a wider network, which not only included policemen but also customs officials. Between January and October 1977, the ICAC arrested 119 officers, all but one of whom were policemen. A further eighty-four were interviewed without arrest. The ICAC suspected that 262 serving or former government officers had dealings with the syndicate between May 1975 and August 1976 (ICAC 1978: 29). In the event, only twenty-six officers (twenty-four police officers and two customs officers) were prosecuted because the partial police amnesty enabled fifty-five suspects to escape charges.

By October 1977, it appeared to the police that the ICAC was mounting a campaign against the entire force. The arrest of more police officers on 25 October sparked a response. On the following day, 300 police officers met in the Kowloon headquarters canteen to discuss points which they wished to raise with the Commissioner of Police. They alleged unfair treatment at the hands of the ICAC, that prosecution witnesses were tainted, that the process of investigation caused stress and hardship to their families and that police morale had been badly affected by the ICAC's activities (*Off-beat* 1977). Two days later, 2000 off-duty police officers gathered in central Hong Kong to request the Commissioner of

Police to permit the creation of a Junior Police Officers' Association (*Ming Pao* 1977). He agreed to their demand but, as the crowd dispersed, a breakaway group, variously estimated at between 40 and 200, tried to storm the ICAC headquarters in Hutchison House, injuring five ICAC officers (*Off-beat* 1977; Lethbridge 1985: 139).

Before MacLehose decided on how to deal with the crisis, he consulted with the Commissioner of Police, the ICAC Commissioner and the Director of Operations. He was concerned about the number of cases under investigation that would have to be dropped if an amnesty were granted and whether public support for anti-corruption work could be retained (Yu 2017). The Director of Operations was sent back to his office to determine the number of affected cases and reported that investigations on eighty-three cases would have to be terminated (ICAC 1978: 9). The Head of the CRD was confident that her department could still convince the public that the ICAC would pursue corruption seriously in the event of an adverse reaction to the amnesty (Yu 2017).

Armed with this information, MacLehose went on television on 5 November and announced that henceforth the ICAC would not normally act on corruption complaints relating "to offences committed before 1 January 1977 except for persons who had already been interviewed, persons against whom warrants had been issued and persons now outside Hong Kong" (Hong Kong Hansard 1977: 157). According to a newspaper report, police officers were jubilant, believing that they had scored an important victory over the ICAC (Sinclair 1977). Two days later, however, when MacLehose repeated the message in the Legislative Council, he also noted that the *Police Force Ordinance* would be amended to allow for summary dismissal and that policemen would be required to pledge their loyalty to the Commissioner of Police (Hong Kong Hansard 1977: 159).

MacLehose clearly had to act quickly in the light of the turmoil within the police and the possibility that it would undermine much of what the ICAC had achieved in the previous three years. But it has always been something of a puzzle why he chose to take the partial amnesty route. Coincidentally, the ICAC's Community Research Unit had conducted a survey of 1974 respondents in September 1977, the month before the police demonstration, about their views on an amnesty. Only 10 per cent supported such a measure (ICAC 1979b: 21). Better educated and younger respondents were more likely to favour an amnesty on the grounds that, before the creation of the ICAC, corruption might be based on ignorance or that the police should be given the chance to reform. Some respondents believed that an amnesty would be unfair to those who had already been convicted of corruption. The vast majority, however, believed that corruption was a crime and ought to be punished (ICAC 1979b: 27). Based on these survey results, there was no reason for MacLehose to suppose that there was any public pressure on the government to grant an amnesty.

Commentators have looked elsewhere for reasons for the amnesty. The principal explanation appears to be that MacLehose feared a wider police mutiny which would have seriously compromised law and order. But there are other factors which might have been part of the decision-making process. Lethbridge

(1985: 147–148) even explores the possibility that some in high circles might have been concerned that evidence of homosexuality, on which the police apparently kept confidential files, might be leaked. This seems unlikely if only because the threat, if there were such a threat, would surely have been used earlier. Perhaps MacLehose was simply buying time with the amnesty so that he could reorganise the police force and speed up the transformation to clean government (David 2010). Perhaps he was concerned about Hong Kong's image of political stability at a time when a case was being made to the PRC government to allow British administration to continue in Hong Kong after 1997. That case was roundly rejected by the PRC government in September 1979, but it would have undermined the British position if law and order in Hong Kong had become an issue in the interim.

Whatever the reasons for MacLehose's decision, it was widely expected that it would have a detrimental impact on the way in which the ICAC worked. It did have an immediate effect on corruption reports which declined from 2433 in 1976 to 1700 in 1977 and to 1234 in 1978, gradually increasing to 2349 in 1982 (see Figure 3.1). Thereafter, the ICAC's "normal" expectation of corruption reports was that they would range between 2000 and 3000 reports per year; a total of more than 3000 was taken to mean that corruption was rising, and a total of less than 2000 was taken to mean that public confidence in the ICAC had dropped. As Figure 3.1 shows, the number of anonymous corruption reports, a sign of confidence in ICAC procedures, continued to fall over the period 1974–1982 and appears to have been little affected by the amnesty.

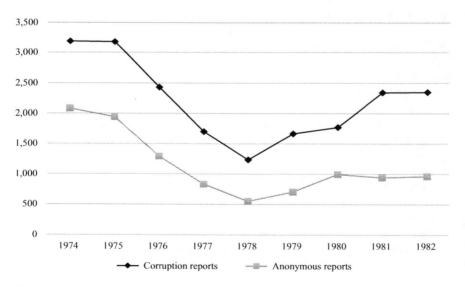

Figure 3.1 Corruption reports, 1974–1982

Source: ICAC Annual Reports (1975–1983)

Remarkably, the number of non-corruption reports received by the ICAC between 1977 and 1987 out-numbered the number of corruption reports in each of those years and amounted in total to almost 50,000 complaints by the end of 1987 (Ma Man 1988: 44). Non-corruption reports, as an ICAC survey discovered, were not usually made because of lack of knowledge of the Commission's jurisdiction but rather because the complainants were aggrieved by the way in which government departments had treated their complaints and/or believed that their complaints would receive more careful attention if they were referred to other government departments by the ICAC (Ma Man 1988: 96). The number of non-corruption reports was taken to be evidence of growing public trust in the ICAC and as an indication of its independence and impartiality. After the creation of an ombudsman and as other complaint-handling government bodies became more effective, the number of non-corruption complaints gradually dropped.

In January and February 1978, the Community Research Unit conducted a specific sub-survey of 858 respondents on public confidence in the ICAC to discover whether there had been "changes in public reactions and responses to its activities in the wake of the Governor's announcement of the partial amnesty . . ." (ICAC 1979c: I). The results provide an interesting comparison with September 1977 survey, which showed high levels of confidence in the ICAC and the government's sincerity in fighting corruption. The Unit found that there had been a drop in public confidence of those who thought the ICAC's performance was good or very good from 73 per cent in 1977 to 63 per cent in 1978 (ICAC 1979c: paras 52–53). When asked whether they thought the government was sincere in fighting corruption, only 67 per cent thought so, compared with the 84 per cent who had responded positively in 1977. When asked the same question about the ICAC, there was a drop from 91 per cent in 1977 to 80 per cent in 1978, not as substantial a fall as that of the government but still sufficient to concern the Unit (ICAC 1979c: para 55). It concluded:

> The immediate problem which the Commission has to face is not merely to sustain but more importantly how to restore confidence in the Commission. The Commission should highlight and emphasize the Community Relations and Corruption Prevention aspects of its work . . . so that the Commission's effectiveness will not be judged solely by the success of the Operations Department.
>
> (ICAC 1979c: para 10)

The Unit also noted that the government itself needed to do more to show that it was sincere in fighting corruption.

Although the Unit was unequivocal in its finding that there had been a loss of public confidence after the amnesty, another reading of the survey might suggest that matters were not quite so bad. Almost one-third of the respondents had not heard of the amnesty and presumably had insufficient information on which to base a change of their attitudes to the ICAC (ICAC 1979c). Of those who had heard of the amnesty, over half approved of it, a surprising number, given that only 10 per cent had approved of an amnesty in the 1977 survey. The reasons given for their approval were largely similar to previous supporters of an amnesty, namely that "bygones should be bygones", that the gravity of the situation warranted an amnesty, and that the police should be given an opportunity to turn over a new leaf (ICAC 1979c: para 99). Two-thirds of respondents thought that the ICAC would continue to fight corruption in the same way as it had before the amnesty (ICAC 1979c: 52–53). However, there were also negative sentiments. Half of the respondents, especially those with no formal education, thought that the ICAC had overplayed the problem of corruption in Hong Kong. Many respondents thought that the amnesty would affect the ICAC's morale, make its work more difficult and waste its past efforts. And about one-third of respondents, especially the young and better educated, believed that there was corruption within the ICAC itself (ICAC 1979c: para 62).

Despite this somewhat gloomy picture of loss of confidence in the ICAC and concerns about the impact of the amnesty, the Commission was able to recover lost ground relatively quickly. Hui and Lo (2016: 185) attribute the restoration of confidence to three factors: the conclusion of the Yau Ma Tei fruit market case, which had triggered the unrest within the police force; the dismissal of 119 police officers who had been involved in the case and probably in the attack on ICAC headquarters; and the Hong Kong government's continuing commitment to the ICAC. Each of these factors was important in restoring confidence in the short-term. The dismissal of police officers sent a strong message to the force that the amnesty did not mean that corruption would be tolerated or, as MacLehose subsequently put it, that "things would slip back into the bad old days" (Hong Kong Hansard 1978: 12). It was also important that the government should give indications to counter the perception that the ICAC was about to be wound up. The Governor and other senior officials continued to proclaim that anticorruption policy was based on zero tolerance and that its support for the ICAC was unequivocal. There was an immediate increase of establishment from 1068 officers in 1977 to 1121 officers in 1978 and the number of officers in post rose from 903 to 957. New sub-offices, which had previously been on hold, were opened and added to the Commission's capacity to engage with the community.

Each of these short-term factors was important in restoring confidence. Yet, in the longer-term, it was the CRD's publicity and face-to-face campaign on the ground, to which we now turn, which helped win back support for the ICAC and changed social attitudes toward corruption.

Winning hearts and minds

Every new ACA must decide on its community relations policy. Even if that policy is simply to carry out investigations without seeking to change attitudes, the consequences must be weighed against the impact which it will have on its effectiveness. From the outset, those who set up the ICAC were convinced of the need to change social attitudes to corruption. Implementation of the policy required allocating limited resources for best use in community relations efforts.

In its early years, the ICAC had to make a choice between territory-wide publicity and setting up more sub-offices which would have direct contact with the public through liaison activities. It chose to put its resources into publicity, especially on television, with the specific aim of persuading people to report corruption. Liaison work with community groups on the ground was still an important objective but it was not comprehensive. In 1976, the first full year of CRD liaison activities, more than two-thirds of its efforts were focused on government and schools (ICAC 1977: Appendix XVIII). In September 1977, a Community Research Unit survey found that 68 per cent of respondents thought that public education in the media about corruption was sufficient while 25 per cent had never heard of the ICAC's liaison activities. As the report concluded,

> Publicity efforts through the mass media, such as posters, pamphlets, television APIs and ICAC Spot [a five-minute television promotion] are meant to and generally are able to reach a large sector of the public whereas liaison activities of the Commission which are conducted on a face-to-face basis are meant and able to reach a smaller sector of the public in a more intensive way.
>
> (ICAC 1979c: para 76)

The survey on the effects of the amnesty showed that the Commission was not reaching a wide enough audience and that there was a need to increase awareness of its activities. The more pressing concern, however, was that the ICAC should win back lost public support and confidence quickly.

One of the most important consequences of the amnesty was a massive ICAC campaign designed to achieve the multiple objectives of bringing about a clean Hong Kong, persuading the public that the Commission was still very much in business, and changing social attitudes toward corruption. The CRD orchestrated the campaign focusing on groups which the ICAC thought were "at risk" or could help in disseminating its message. The department was unique in Hong Kong's colonial government at that time in that it was almost entirely composed of young, ethnically Chinese, officers (Scott and Gong 2015; Yu 2017). At the beginning of 1980, the average age of the department was 26, with an establishment of 274 and a strength of 212 (ICAC 1981a: 49). The task before them, as many former officers, including its then head, Helen C.P. Yu Lai, have attested in their recollections to us, seems to have been conceived of as a moral crusade. They were convinced that Hong Kong had to rid itself of corruption and they were willing to spend long hours moving from housing block to housing block and to meeting with the "hard to reach" and "at risk" groups to convey the message that corruption was not acceptable and that its consequences were detrimental to the quality of life.

The campaign was based on a sequential strategy to increase awareness of the ICAC's work, to penetrate local community groups, and then to invite them to become partners in anti-corruption work (Leung 1981: 18–19; Scott 2013b: 87; Scott and Gong 2015). With that in mind, the ICAC had set up sub-offices (later called regional offices) which were subsequently to provide almost all its face-to-face liaison activities. The initial targets were schools and other educational institutions, religious organisations, voluntary associations, trade unions, area and district committees and other community organisations, but contact with the private sector also gradually increased (see Table 3.2). Although the ICAC message was tailored to the needs and interests of specific groups and organisations, there was a common approach and a central core of ideas. Katie Leung (1981: 20–23) describes a liaison package as talks, film shows, group discussions, simulations and door-knocking where the message was that corruption was a social evil which could involve extortion, reduced standards of living and inflation, a poor quality of life, and social instability and injustice. Housewives, for example, were asked if they wanted their daughters to grow up in in a corruption-ridden environment and taxi and mini-bus drivers were told that their profits would increase if they reported corruption and did not pay "tea-money" to police officers. In line with the "awareness" criterion of the strategy, liaison officers also tried to increase public confidence in the ICAC and to improve knowledge of the *POBO*.

Table 3.2 shows the range and rapid increase in the number of liaison activities undertaken by the CRD. The government increased funding for the Commission after the amnesty, which enabled it to open more sub-offices and to extend the scope of its liaison work. The Community Research Unit conceived of exposure to corruption as one big circle that was composed of three rings. The innermost

Table 3.2 Number of liaison activities, 1977–1980

	1977	1978	1979	1980
Primary schools		1311	1395	893
Secondary schools	1729	1171	1214	947
Adult education centres	73	67	451	160
Post-secondary colleges/universities	102	111	98	117
Clansmen/district/kaifong associations	136	117	147	107
Mutual aid committees/owners' corporations	512	619	696	868
Area/district/village committees	106	121	218	301
Religious organisations	222	273	212	161
Charitable/welfare/voluntary organisations	373	401	475	662
Factories/offices/shops	646	1023	1734	3046
Youth groups	365	411	498	521
Professional trade associations	167	123	80	189
Government departments (including staff associations)	588	795	1304	1531
Public bodies	54	72	231	263
Hospitals/clinics	28	74	61	90
Others	293	459	209	45
Total	5394	7148	9023	9901

Sources: Adapted from ICAC 1979a: Appendix XXIII; ICAC 1982: Appendix XXIV

Note: Liaison activities included visits, talks, meetings, group discussions and film shows.

ring consisted of a hard core of corrupt members of the community who could not be persuaded to change their ways and could only be investigated and then prosecuted. The next ring was made up of those who were not corrupt but had a high likelihood of exposure to corrupt activities and opportunities. People and groups within this ring, it was argued, should be the principal focus of liaison work. In the outermost ring, the exposure to corruption was very low and a "general moral education" was considered to be sufficient to meet their needs (ICAC 1981b: 77).

This conceptualisation of exposure to corruption had implications for resource allocation. In 1977, 35 per cent of liaison activities were conducted in schools and tertiary institutions; by 1986, this had fallen to less than 20 per cent (ICAC 1978: Appendix XXI; ICAC 1987: Appendix 23). Youth, secondary schools and universities were still significant targets but primary schools were no longer seen as important as they had been in 1977. By contrast, liaison activities with commercial and industrial establishments rose to 50 per cent of all activities, from 813 functions in 1977 to 8804 in 1986 (ICAC 1977: Appendix XXI; ICAC 1987: Appendix 23). By 1986, despite the spread of liaison functions to cover a broader proportion of society, television remained the primary source of information about the ICAC. The struggle to win public support and to convince citizens that Hong Kong was better off with the ICAC had largely been won. About 63 per cent of respondents to the 1986 mass survey thought that without the ICAC, there would be a return to the rampant corruption of the past, and 79 per cent thought that it was performing well. There were still doubts, however, about whether the Commission was paying sufficient attention to catching the "big tigers" (ICAC 1987: 4–7).

Illegal commissions and private sector corruption

Illegal commissions, most of which were bribes paid by firms to obtain business, became the touchstone of the ICAC's sometimes fractious relationships with the private sector in its earliest years. Commissions in themselves were not illegal but became so if they were solicited or accepted without the principal's consent (*POBO*: Section 9). Blair-Kerr said that these "kickbacks" were either explicitly or tacitly condoned by most Hong Kong companies. One of his informants told him that "the whole of Hong Kong operates on a commission basis" and the judge concluded that there was "good reason to believe that the vast majority of businessmen . . . would not have it otherwise" (Blair-Kerr 1973: 23). The ICAC, consistent with its emphasis on corruption as a social evil, argued that the effects of illegal commissions could be very damaging, bringing businesses to the brink of ruin or representing a tax on employment which many could ill-afford to pay. Illegal commissions, so the ICAC contended, increased the price of products for everyone (ICAC 1976: 23).

Illegal commissions also raised the wider issue of whether the ICAC should restrict its pursuit of corruption to the public sector. The *POBO* gave the ICAC the power to investigate corruption in both the public and private sectors, provisions that were strongly supported by the public. The first ICAC survey found that almost 75 per cent of respondents thought that, "contrary to what some (in particular people in the business sector) would like to believe", the Commission should pay attention to both sectors (ICAC 1979b: 31). The ICAC Commissioner was not convinced that there was any difference in principle between corruption in the public sector and corruption in the private sector (ICAC 1976: 2–3). The public thought otherwise: 32 per cent of survey respondents believed that the ICAC was bad for trade and business and more respondents were intolerant of corruption in the public sector than in the private sector (ICAC 1979b: 36). The business associations argued that the ICAC should focus exclusively on the public sector rather than pursue private sector cases, arguing that if illegal commissions were crimes, they were commercial crimes and should not be prosecuted under the *POBO*.

The issue came to a head in May 1976 with the prosecution and conviction for offering advantages of Gilman, a leading company which had been in Hong Kong since the founding of the colony in 1841. The trial judge concluded that its prosecution was meant to be a warning to all businesses that illegal commissions would no longer be tolerated (Lethbridge 1985: 184–185, 191). Meanwhile, the Chinese Manufacturers Association had formally lobbied the government to amend the *POBO* to exclude the payment of commissions from the legislation. The government stood firm, however. In April 1976, the Chief Secretary used his speech on the Appropriation Bill to tell the Legislative Council that there was no question in the government's mind that accepting a commission, rebate, discount or kickback for personal benefit was corruption because it deprived the employer of a benefit. For similar reasons, inducing anyone to offer an illegal commission also constituted corruption (Hong Kong Hansard 1976a: 786). The Attorney-General returned to the point in a speech to the Council in November 1976 when he claimed that Section 9 of the *POBO*, which concerns private sector corruption, was now well understood (Hong Kong Hansard 1976b: 201–203). For its part, the ICAC noted that "underhand dealings with an employee of a private sector business are not, as sometimes seems to be implied, less reprehensible than underhand dealings with a civil servant" (ICAC 1977: 21).

Although accepting or inducing illegal commissions was the major private sector offence which the ICAC prosecuted in its early years, the number of cases remained small, only comprising about 1 per cent of the ICAC's work in 1976 (ICAC 1976: 21). The Commission had its hands full with police cases. Private sector corruption cases were seen to be a distraction from the main task of dealing with corruption in the public sector. The official position was that the ICAC would not actively seek out cases of illegal commissions but that it would investigate all complaints that were made (Hong Kong Hansard 1976a: 786). There was a gradual rise in prosecutions of illegal commissions in the 1980s but there were still problems in persuading the public to report such cases. In the Community Research Unit's 1990 survey, the last which it conducted, nearly half of the respondents considered reporting corruption in the private sector to be useless because not enough evidence could be obtained for prosecution

(ICAC 1990: 11). Although 10 per cent fewer respondents in 1990 considered illegal commissions to be necessary in business than in 1980, 17 per cent were still prepared to tolerate them (ICAC 1990: 12). Older, less educated respondents were more inclined to believe that illegal commissions were prevalent and, if they regarded them as prevalent, were more likely to see them as an acceptable way of doing business. Respondents thought that illegal commissions were most common in the construction, manufacturing, and wholesale and retail sectors (ICAC 1990: 15).

In 1985, the Overseas Trust Bank, which at the time was the third largest bank in Hong Kong, and the Ka Wah Bank collapsed (Li n.d.). The ICAC's involvement in these cases raised its profile in private sector investigations. The government suspected that corruption was a factor in the collapse of the banks and requested the ICAC to investigate. Both cases were complicated by absconding suspects (ICAC n.d.). The former chairman of the Overseas Trust Bank was arrested at the airport and eventually sentenced to a prison term, but other members of the senior management team were able to escape. In the Ka Wah bank investigations, the Low brothers, who ran the bank, absconded to Taiwan and had to be brought back to Hong Kong to face trial (Lo 1991: 126). The cases attracted considerable media attention and, by inference, made the point that the ICAC would now pursue major private sector corruption cases.

The Carrian case was even more complicated than the bank cases and lasted much longer. Carrian had been founded in 1977 by a Singaporean civil engineer, George Tan, and made some spectacular property purchases in its first few years of operation. In 1980, it purchased Gammon House for HK$1 billion and six months later sold it for HK$1.6 billion. Within a few years, it was the fifth largest company by capitalisation in Hong Kong. In 1982, however, it experienced cash flow problems and was eventually suspended from the Hong Kong Stock Exchange and liquidated in October 1983. The police suspected fraud and the Bank Bumiputra Malaysia Berhad believed that its local office had illegally approved loans to Carrian. The bank estimated that it had lost US$1 billion in the Carrian collapse. Its internal auditor, who was sent to Hong Kong to investigate the case, was murdered (ICAC 2014: 28–29). The Malaysian Auditor-General then sent a committee to Hong Kong which discovered that there had been corruption involved in the loans. A member of the committee lodged a complaint with the ICAC in April 1985. The case dragged on and was not finally concluded until April 2000.

The ICAC's investigation was hampered by difficulties in extraditing suspects and incorrect legal decisions. Although there was sufficient evidence to secure a conviction of George Tan in 1987, the judge found, after a trial that lasted for well over a year, that Tan had no case to answer (Lo 1991: 127); relatively minor players in the saga, by contrast, were given long sentences. In 1996, Tan was eventually convicted and sentenced to three years in prison. Lorraine Osman, a former Bank Bumiputra executive, was extradited from Britain, where he had served seven years in prison, and sentenced to one years' imprisonment on conspiracy to defraud. In 2000, the case was finally completed when a former employee of

Wardley's Bank, Ewan Launder, was sentenced to five years' imprisonment for accepting HK$4.5 million from Tan to facilitate a loan to Carrian.

In each of these cases, the significant outcome, from a public relations perspective, was that the ICAC was taking on major private sector cases and investigations. The government's supportive stance in 1976 had settled the question of whether the ICAC would investigate both public and private sector corruption but its impact on private sector corruption cases was relatively limited until the Overseas Trust Bank, Ka Wah Bank and Carrian cases required highly complex investigations. The decline in public sector corruption also meant that there were more resources available for investigating private sector cases including illegal commissions. This was matched by a corresponding shift in the nature of corruption reports. By 1988, private sector corruption reports to the ICAC for the first time exceeded those concerning the public sector.

Every new ACA, if it is to be successful, must develop a strategy for dealing with the private sector. It is difficult to imagine a system in which the public sector is clean and the private sector is corrupt or vice-versa. Inevitably, interaction between them determines the level of corruption that pervades the entire society. Bringing the private sector within the anti-corruption net, as the ICAC discovered, is a complex task that is likely to meet with resistance. It requires effective legislation and government support to plug loopholes and prevent successful lobbying for escape clauses. The ICAC was fortunate that it enjoyed the government's support in its conflict with the business associations and that it could produce enough evidence to secure convictions in both private and the public sector cases.

Funding and the bureaucratic milieu

Any new agency must find and consolidate its place within the bureaucratic and economic environment. This may involve jurisdictional issues, such as those with the police and private sector in Hong Kong, but the level of funding is also critically important. One of the easiest ways for a political executive to clip the wings of an ACA is to reduce its funding. New ACAs are particularly vulnerable to funding cuts because they do not yet have sufficient bureaucratic legitimacy and public support to use as a counterweight against adverse political pressures. Carpenter (2001: 34) has shown, for example, that the more autonomous an agency, defined in terms of its supportive public constituency, the more likely it is to be able to attract funding for new projects and to resist detrimental jurisdictional changes or budgetary cuts.

In the ICAC's case, there was an important and evident level of political support for its activities. While its initial budget was generous by the Hong Kong standards of the day, the Commission was still subject to normal government budgetary procedures for recurrent and capital expenditure. In March 1975, largely because of the oil crisis, the Financial Secretary budgeted for a deficit, a rare occurrence in Hong Kong. He described expenditure control for the following financial year as "tight, very tight" and cut back on all departmental submissions for new expenditure (Hong Kong Hansard 1975: 515). The ICAC was no exception and, arguably, suffered more than most because, only a year after its creation, some planned expenditure had not yet been budgeted for, yet alone made. At risk were the introduction of sub-offices (later called regional offices) and the positions for the senior staff needed to head them, the establishment of a Community Research Unit, and a public education unit (ICAC 1976: 32–33).

The sub-offices were an essential element in the ICAC's "universalist" strategy. The initial plan was to establish eight sub-offices in high density areas (four in Kowloon, two on Hong Kong Island and two in the New Territories), which would serve the dual functions of accepting corruption reports and providing a base for liaison work in the community. The first sub-office was set up in Kowloon City in July 1975 and was followed by two more in Tsuen Wan in the New Territories and in Sham Shui Po in Kowloon. The sub-offices were expensive because premises had to be rented and senior officers had to be recruited to run them. After the financial constraints were imposed, the Commission decided that community relations funding should be spent largely on publicity and that the remaining five sub-offices could not immediately be opened. As the ICAC's 1975 annual report (1976: 33) noted, "the 'freeze' has unquestionably made for unevenness and improper balance in the development of the ICAC's programme for publicity and public re-education".

It had been hoped that better financial circumstances in 1976, when the freeze was lifted, would enable the Commission to open the remaining sub-offices. However, by the end of the year, only one more sub-office had been launched. Although financial constraints had eased, there were still difficulties with the Finance Committee over the appointment of suitable people to head the sub-offices. The Commission was looking to appoint officers with the "usual leadership qualities" but also wanted candidates "who had already made some impact preferably in the field of community work" (ICAC 1977: 34). The Finance Committee of the Legislative Council, however, would not support the appointment of the head of a sub-office at Grade I (Senior Commission Against Corruption Officer) level. Although the ICAC tried three times to recruit at the lower Grade II level, and received seventy-nine applicants in one case, it was unable to find satisfactory candidates to fill the positions (ICAC 1977: 25). In May 1977, the Finance Committee finally agreed to appointments at Grade I level, and three new sub-offices were opened (ICAC 1978: 30). Following the police amnesty, as more funding became available, the CRD was able to increase the number of sub-offices to a total of eleven by 1982. In 1981, it was estimated that the liaison functions conducted from these sub-offices had enabled the Commission to contact some 132,500 people (ICAC 1982: 61). The Commission's establishment also increased significantly but there were still difficulties in recruiting suitable staff. Between 1977 and 1980, the strength of the ICAC was on average about 10 per cent below its establishment (ICAC 1978–1981).

The willingness of the Finance Committee to increase the Commission's establishment by providing additional posts and supporting the creation of new sub-offices was an indication that the difficulties in funding had passed. By the early 1980s, the ICAC was already seen, both within government and by the public, as a feature of the institutional landscape. In Carpenter's terms, it had developed sufficient autonomy to argue forcefully for funding that it thought was required. Although it was still dependent on government for its expenditure, there was a gradual realisation that the Commission's work was beneficial to the economy and the society and to the efficiency of government itself.

***

We have examined the crises and challenges faced by the ICAC in its early years in depth because we believe that such immediate potential conflicts must be overcome if an ACA is to be successful. It is unlikely to be successful if it is unable to assert its role impartially and to the full extent of its jurisdiction. It might be argued that there was an element of *fortuna* in the ICAC's eventual success. The partial police amnesty could well have gone wrong if it had spelt the emasculation of the Commission. If more people had been aware of the amnesty, it might have caused difficulties in winning back support. If the police crisis had occurred any earlier, there would have been less opportunity for the ICAC to build its own reputation. As it was, the vast majority of survey respondents still thought that the ICAC was "sincere" in fighting corruption. Similarly, it was important that the government should stand firm against the efforts of the business associations to dilute the powers of the ICAC and that it should continue to back the ICAC's plans with financial support. The outcome of these conflicts was a self-confident organisation that knew that it had both government and public support and had, in the process of resolving its various struggles, become a valued part of the institutional framework.

References

Blair-Kerr, Sir Alastair (1973) *Second report of the Commission of Inquiry under Sir Alastair Blair-Kerr.* Hong Kong: Government Printer.
Carpenter, Daniel (2001) *The forging of bureaucratic autonomy.* Princeton: Princeton University Press.
David, Roman (2010) "Transitions to clean government: Amnesty as an anticorruption measure", *Australian Journal of Political Science*, 43(3): 391–406.
Dick, Howard and Jeremy Mulholland (2016) "The politics of corruption in Indonesia", *Georgetown Journal of International Affairs*, 17(1): 43–49.
Hong Kong Hansard 26 February 1975; 7 April 1976a; 11 November 1976b; 7 November 1977; 11 October 1978.
Hui, Cora Y.T. and T. Wing Lo (2016) "Anti-corruption" in Wing Chong Chui and T. Wing Lo (eds.) *Understanding criminal justice in Hong Kong.* 2nd edition. London: Routledge: 175–193
ICAC. (1974–1986) "Annual reports", www.icac.org.hk/en/about/report/annual/index.html.
ICAC (1975) "Annual report 1974", www.icac.org.hk/filemanager/en/Content_27/1974.pdf.

ICAC (1975–1983) "Annual reports", www.icac.org.hk/en/about/report/annual/index.html.

ICAC (1976) "Annual report 1975", www.icac.org.hk/filemanager/en/Content_27/1975.pdf.

ICAC (1977) "Annual report 1976", www.icac.org.hk/filemanager/en/Content_27/1976.pdf.

ICAC (1978) "Annual report 1977", www.icac.org.hk/filemanager/en/Content_27/1977.pdf.

ICAC (1979a) "Annual report 1978", www.icac.org.hk/filemanager/en/Content_27/1978.pdf.

ICAC (1979b) *Mass survey 1977 final report*. Hong Kong: mimeo.

ICAC (1979c) *Mass survey 1978 final report*. Hong Kong: mimeo.

ICAC (1981a) "Annual report 1980", www.icac.org.hk/filemanager/en/Content_27/1980.pdf.

ICAC (1981b) *Final report of the 1980 mass survey*. Hong Kong: mimeo.

ICAC (1982) "Annual report 1981", www.icac.org.hk/filemanager/en/Content_27/1981.pdf.

ICAC (1987) *ICAC mass survey 1986*. Hong Kong: mimeo.

ICAC (1990) *ICAC mass survey 1990*. Hong Kong: mimeo.

ICAC (2014) "40 years in the Operations Department", www.icac.org.hk/filemanager/en/content_28/ops2014.pdf.

ICAC (n.d.) "The collapse of the OTB -the inside story", www.icac.org.hk/new_icac/eng/cases/otb/invest.htm.

Lethbridge, Henry James (1985) *Hard graft in Hong Kong: Scandal, corruption and the ICAC*. Hong Kong: Oxford University Press.

Leung, Sui-ying Katie (1981) *Public education as a means of combating corruption*. Unpublished M. Soc. Sc. dissertation, Department of Political Science, University of Hong Kong.

Li, Raymond (n.d.) "Banking problems: Hong Kong's experience in the 1980s", www.bis.org/publ/plcy06d.pdf.

Lo, Tit-wing (1991) "Law and order" in Sung Yung-wing and Lee Ming-kwan (eds.) *The other Hong Kong report 1991*. Hong Kong: The Chinese University Press.

Ma Man, Paula Su-lan (1988) *A study of the ICAC's role in handling non-corruption complaints*. Unpublished M. Soc. Sc. dissertation, Department of Political Science, University of Hong Kong.

Ming Pao (1977) "Police seek interview with Commissioner", 26 October.

Off-beat (1977) "Diary of events", 3 November.

Schütte, Sofie Arjon (2017) "Two steps forward, one step backwards: Indonesia's winding (anti-) corruption journey" in Ting Gong and Ian Scott (eds.) *Routledge handbook of corruption in Asia*. London: Routledge: 42–55.

Scott, Ian (2013) "Engaging the public: Hong Kong's Independent Commission Against Corruption's Community Relations Strategy" in Jon S.T. Quah (ed.) *Different paths to curbing corruption: Lessons from Denmark, Finland, Hong Kong, New Zealand and Singapore*. Bingley: Emerald: 79–108.

Scott, Ian and Ting Gong (2015) "Evidence-based policy-making for corruption prevention in Hong Kong: A bottom-up approach", *Asia Pacific Journal of Public Administration*, 37(2): 87–101.

Sinclair, Kevin (1977) "Corruption amnesty: Police camp jubilant", *South China Morning Post*, 6 November.

Walton, Grant and Husnia Hushang (2017) "Promises, promises: A decade of allocations for and spending on anti-corruption in Papua New Guinea", *Development Policy Discussion Paper, No.60*, Australian National University, https://papers.ssrn.com/sol3/papers.cfm?abstract_id=3009987.

Yu Lai, Helen C.P. (2017) "Interview with Helen C.P. Yu Lai, former Head of the Community Relations Department", 17 November.

Part II

Success factors in corruption prevention

4 Political will

There is almost unanimous agreement among academics that political will is an important, perhaps critical, determinant of successful corruption prevention (Kpundeh 1998; Quah 2013: 453–456; Quah 2015a, 2017: 242–244; Choi 2017; Rotberg 2017: 45–49; Ankamah and Khoda 2018). But what *political will* means, who exercises it, what kinds of actions are required, and the relevance of varying degrees of political commitment to corruption reform over time are viewed in different ways.

In its broadest application, the concept of political will is understood to be "the will of leaders to initiate and sustain reform" (Persson and Sjöstedt 2012). In relation to corruption, Kpundeh (1998: 92) suggests that the political actors might consist not only of the government but also of the legislature, civil society watchdog groups and stakeholders in society provided they show "demonstrable credible intent . . . to attack perceived causes or effects of corruption at a systemic level". The difficulty lies in linking those outside government with specific actions to bring about reform. Pressure on government or political leaders to initiate change may, of course, come from civil society but introducing, funding and sustaining new anti-corruption measures usually requires action from those in positions of authority. Perhaps for that reason, many authors focus their attention on the anti-corruption efforts of the government and its leadership, which include relationships with the ACA (Brinkerhoff 2000; U4 Anti-Corruption Resource Centre 2010). Brinkerhoff (2000: 242), for example, defines political will as

> the commitment of actors to undertake actions to achieve a set of objectives – in this case, anti-corruption policies and programmes – and to sustain the costs of those actions over time. This commitment is manifested by elected or appointed officials and public agency senior officials.

This definition has the value of emphasising the importance of implementation and continuing support and that the initiation of reform measures normally comes from governments.

The actions of political leaders within government are also important. Rotberg (2017: 46) defines political will as "the exercise of political leadership to influence, direct or alter public choice outcomes within particular contextual situations". For him, leaders mobilise governments and, if successful, "dramatically alter the direction and thrust of government accomplishments" (Rotberg 2017: 46). While this observation may not be applicable to all public policy decisions, it is directly relevant to anti-corruption reform and fits the Hong Kong experience for three reasons. First, the leadership of MacLehose as Governor and Cater as the first ICAC Commissioner was critical for the creation of the Commission and for its subsequent successes. For more than thirty years, until about 2007, the commitment of political leaders to strong anti-corruption policies was scarcely in doubt. Second, power was strongly vested in the Governor and, after 1997, was constitutionally entrenched in the position of the Chief Executive (Gittings 2013: 96–98). The ICAC is directly accountable to the Chief Executive (*The Basic Law* 1990: Article 57), and anti-corruption reform is consequently a designated responsibility of the political leader. Third, problems with the exercise of political will, which we consider in this chapter, centred on the ICAC's investigation of two Chief Executives, Donald Tsang Yam-kuen and Leung Chun-ying, for allegedly corrupt practices. While the Chief Executives were themselves the subject of investigations, it was not possible for them to argue convincingly that they would exercise their authority to improve corruption prevention.

If political will is a critical determinant of successful corruption prevention, what consequences result when leaders themselves are constrained in their ability to provide positive political support for the ACA? With the decline in political will after 2007, it might have been expected that the functions of the ICAC would have diminished or perhaps even collapsed and that public support for the Commission would have evaporated. Instead, the ICAC has emerged from the most troublesome decade in its history with its processes and structures intact and with a continuing high level of public support. It could only have done so, we argue, if it were able to rely on the sound practices and social trust which had been accumulated over three decades of successful corruption prevention. In short, the ICAC was already institutionalised before the ethical behaviour of the most senior members of the government became an issue. It was institutionalised in the sense that it had over time conducted its enforcement procedures regularly, impartially and effectively, that its aims were consistent with the norms of the society, and that the outcomes which it had achieved in terms of corruption prevention were valued by the community.

In this chapter, we explore the relationship between political will and institutionalisation and the ways in which it has helped insulate the ICAC from the political turmoil surrounding the investigations of the Chief Executives. How did institutionalisation reduce the need for political leaders to exercise political will? What kind of political commitment did the ICAC still need to adapt sufficiently rapidly to changing patterns of corruption? To what extent does public support, central to the notion of an institutionalised ACA, allow the agency to function effectively without overt political commitment? What happens when issues affecting the relationship between the political leaders and the ACA become matters of contentious political debate?

Other political actors may be involved, or want to be involved, in the exercise of political will. In Hong Kong; however, their ability to determine or to implement significant action is limited. The Legislative Council, for example, has often been involved in the debate over the powers and needs of the ICAC. The Council, however, has restricted powers and is not fully democratically representative of the Hong Kong people. Those who wanted corruption reform over the period 2007 to 2017 were principally democrats who did not have a majority in the Council and were voted down when they sought change. Unless there are serious issues at stake, the ICAC also usually functions at arm's length from the Council and its heated politics. Similarly, although the ICAC has enjoyed continuing widespread support, the effects of public opinion on the relationship between the executive and the Commission are indirect. Public opinion may, nonetheless, provide a constraint on the actions of the executive because the Commission is seen as a valued part of the institutional firmament. We argue, for example, that, even if it wanted to do so, it would be difficult for the executive to reduce the ICAC's budget substantially because this would be seen by the public, and their representatives, as going "soft" on corruption and undermining a trusted institution.

With these factors in mind, we explore the contributions that political will can make to successful corruption prevention policies, to effective anti-corruption laws and to public support for a well-established ACA.

The decline of political will

The perception that a government is prepared to deal with corruption is a valuable commodity but political rhetoric does not always translate into action. Fine words often turn into empty promises because, even if political leaders do intend to act against corruption, resource constraints and entrenched opposition to reform may result in failed policies. At worst, there may never be any intention to combat corruption and the ACA becomes simply a vehicle for the use of power in a biased and self-interested manner (Heilbrunn 2004). Corruption may be a useful charge with which to label political opponents or to claim additional powers which may be used to disguise the leadership's own corrupt practices. Regime change does not necessarily provide a solution. Often, one set of corrupt leaders is simply replaced by another. If ACAs are to be successful, they need more stable and committed support, especially when they are first established.

In Hong Kong, by the 1980s, the ICAC had already achieved a *modus vivendi* with the political executive and widespread public backing for its efforts. It was perceived to be effective and able to act independently in pursuit of the corrupt. It was increasingly embedded in the society and its recommended anti-corruption procedures in government departments were making a difference. In this state of equilibrium, which was reflected in a stable number of corruption reports and prosecutions, all that was required of the political executive was the periodic reiteration of its support for the Commission and the provision of adequate funding. The form that this usually took was a short, but strong, statement of support in the Governor's annual policy address, repetition of the same message in other speeches (see Table 4.1) and a budget which sustained the Commission at levels commensurate with its work. In the policy addresses, there were

Table 4.1 The political executive and the ICAC: selected policy addresses and other statements

Year	Occasion	Comment
1984	Policy address	The Governor, Sir Edward Youde, notes increases in corruption-related frauds and pledges the government's "fullest possible support".
1992	Policy address	The Governor, Chris Patten, says that the stability and prosperity of Hong Kong require "a relentless assault on corruption before and after 1997".
1995	Policy address	The Governor, Chris Patten, describes the corruption situation as "acute". Notes the creation of a new ICAC Ethics Development Centre and more liaison and information-sharing with China.
1997	Policy address	The Chief Executive, Tung Chee-hwa, promises more funding for the ICAC to strengthen investigative procedures.
1998	Policy address	The Chief Executive, Tung Chee-hwa, announces that the ICAC will set up two new sections to analyse electronic data and to investigate complex financial cases.
2005–2016	Policy addresses	Little or no mention of the ICAC.
2012–2016	Chief Executive's question and answer sessions in the Legislative Council	Legislative Council members raise the issue of the Chief Executive's payments from UGL. The Chief Executive, Leung Chun-ying, declines to answer.
July 2016	Press report	The Chief Executive, Leung Chun-ying, denies involvement in the decision to revert the ICAC Acting Director of Operations to her substantive position.
January 2017	Policy address	Outgoing Chief Executive, Leung Chun-ying, says that the government is committed to combating corruption and that the ICAC enforces the law impartially.
October 2017	Policy address	Incoming Chief Executive, Carrie Lam Yuet-ngor, strongly supports the ICAC and promises to amend Sections 3 and 8 of the *POBO* to bring the Chief Executive within its provisions.

Sources: Hong Kong Hansard 4 October 1984; 7 October 1992; 11 October 1995; 7 October 1998; 17 October 2012; 16 January 2013; 18 January 2017; 11 October 2017; Siu 2016

occasional references to particular corruption problems and some mention of the importance of clean government and a corruption-free system for economic development (see Table 4.1). But during this period of equilibrium there was no need to test the strength of the political executive's commitment to corruption prevention.

The importance of political support became evident, however, whenever the Commission faced a challenge or a significant crisis. In the 1990s, two issues were of particular importance: concerns about civil liberties and the ICAC's powers in the context of the resumption of Chinese sovereignty (see pp. 84–86) and the rising tide of corruption. In 1995, the last British Governor, Chris Patten, said that corruption had become an area of acute concern and asked how it could be otherwise when corruption complaints had risen by 45 per cent in the previous three years (Hong Kong Hansard 1995: para 114). The reasons for the apparent increase in corruption were thought to relate to the belief that China would be more lenient on corruption after 1997 and to the effects of closer economic relationships with the Mainland. As the Legislator Simon Ip Sik-on remarked, "burgeoning trade with and in China has produced the assumption that corruption will become an inevitable way of life after 1997 and that opportunities that present themselves now ought not to be missed" (Hong Kong Hansard 1994: 2131).

There were other factors that contributed to the creation of a climate in which it was widely believed that corruption was again beginning to flourish. Corruption complaints exceeded 3000 reports per year for the first time between 1994 and 1997 (ICAC 1997b: 12; ICAC 1998: 9) and there were concerns about the possible re-emergence of bureaucratic corruption. In 1996, the government gave the Director of Immigration, Leung Ming-yin, the option of retiring or of being dismissed. He had been investigated by the ICAC for possessing assets in excess of his income but the ICAC did not proceed with a prosecution because some of his wealth had been inherited and his wife had commercial interests. The Select Committee set up by the Legislative Council to investigate the issue chided the government for its failure to provide a "full and frank disclosure" of the real reasons for the decision to force Leung to retire (Legislative Council 1997). The government claimed that the reason for the forced retirement was Leung's failure to re-pay a government housing loan but there was much speculation that it was linked to a leak from the Immigration Department to the PRC government of the names of the 50000 Hong Kong residents who had been granted full British citizen rights (O'Clery 1997; Scott 2000: 165–167).

Surveys also produced supporting evidence of public perceptions of a likely increase in corruption after 1997. In his 1996 annual report, the ICAC Commissioner noted that "[f]or three consecutive years, public opinion surveys repeatedly indicated the worrying sign that the younger the respondents, the more tolerant they were of corruption" (ICAC 1997b: 12). Based on surveys between 1993 and 1996, Manion (2004: 63–64, 73) has calculated that about one-third of respondents believed that corruption would revert to pre-1974 levels after the resumption of Chinese sovereignty. In 1997, an ICAC survey found that 70 per cent of those surveyed expected corruption to increase (ICAC 1997a).

The increase in corruption complaints around the time of the handover remains something of a puzzle. Although there was an increase in reports of cross-border corruption, the numbers were very low amounting to only 2 to 3 per cent of all reports. Total corruption reports continued to increase after 1997 until they reached their highest-ever level of 4390 in 2000 (ICAC 2001: 29). The ICAC Commissioner, Alan N. Lai (2001), attributed the increase to the Asian financial crisis rather than to cross-border corruption. The figures seem to provide some evidence to support his view. There were, for example, almost equally large increases in reports across the board from both the public and the private sectors. Whatever the cause, the government clearly took the increase in the number of complaints as a proxy for a rising level of corruption and was prepared to do what it could to enable the Commission to bring the situation under control. Both Patten and his successor, the first Chief Executive of Hong Kong Special Administrative Region (HKSAR), Tung Chee-hwa, supported such ICAC initiatives as setting up a business ethics centre within the Commission, increasing liaison and information-sharing with China, and strengthening investigative powers, electronic data analysis, and mutual cooperation with other jurisdictions (Hong Kong Hansard 1995: para 115, 1997: para 144, 1998: para 155). After 2000, corruption complaints gradually declined and the state of equilibrium was restored.

Up to this point, the political executive had behaved toward the ICAC in much the same way as it had always done. It was generally supportive and willing to provide additional resources when the ICAC signalled that it needed assistance. However, attitudes began to change. Formally, there was still rhetorical support from the political executive for corruption prevention but less apparent willingness to act, especially after 2012, when the ICAC began an investigation of Chief Executive Donald Tsang Yam-kuen over conflicts of interest. Two years later, his successor, Leung Chun-ying, came under the scrutiny when it was revealed that he had received undisclosed payments from an Australian firm. Table 4.1 shows that, from about 2005 onward, both Chief Executives began to omit mention of the ICAC in their policy addresses. We date the beginning of the decline in political will to about mid-2007 when the Legislative Council began to consider ways in which the Chief Executive might be brought within the provisions of the *POBO*.

In July 2007, after procrastinating for a decade, the government introduced more stringent rules governing the position of the Chief Executive under the ordinance. It proposed to do so by amending Sections 4, 5 and 10 (Hong Kong Hansard 2007: 10356). Sections 4 and 5 of the *POBO* proscribed bribery for which the Chief Executive was already liable for prosecution under the common law. Section 10 covered unexplained assets. The government did not include the Chief Executive under the provisions of Sections 3 or 8, which deal with accepting an advantage, claiming that there was a constitutional issue. There were rumours that the stumbling block was the PRC government which did not wish to see its appointee, the Chief Executive, made subject to a strongly prohibitive section of the law which could be seen to be damaging to his or her authority.

After almost another year in committee, legislators had another opportunity to debate the amendment. The democrats could still see no good reason why the Chief Executive should not be included under Sections 3 and 8 and wanted other amendments to the legislation (Legislative Council 2008; Hong Kong Hansard 2008: 9142ff). The government argued that the Chief Executive could not decide both on whether a prescribed officer (a civil servant) could accept an advantage and still be personally subject to the same law. It rejected the democrats' suggestion that an independent body could be set up to decide on whether the Chief Executive could accept an advantage. The legislation amending Sections 4, 5 and 10 to include the Chief Executive was passed, but the democrats' proposed amendments were all defeated.

Hong Kong's Basic Law (Article 47) stipulates that the Chief Executive should be a person of high integrity and it was presumed that the amended provisions of the *POBO* would rarely, if ever, have to be applied. On 20 February 2012, however, the *Oriental Daily News* alleged that the Chief Executive, Donald Tsang Yam-kuen, had accepted travel, hospitality, accommodation and other advantages from friends (*Oriental Daily News* 2012; Hong Kong Hansard 2012: 6324–6325; Scott 2014). If the acceptance of these advantages were offences, they would seemingly have fallen under Section 3 of the *POBO*. Tsang was eventually charged in 2015 and convicted on a charge of misconduct in public office in 2017 (see Lau 2015 and p. 185).

Immediately following the revelations in the *Oriental Daily News*, Tsang set up an independent committee under a former Chief Justice to review the prevention and handling of conflicts of interest. The Committee considered the *POBO* provisions and recommended that Sections 3 and 8 should be amended to include the Chief Executive and that if the issue affected the Chief Executive, it should be referred to an independent panel (Independent Review Committee 2012: 44–55). The Committee was unequivocal in its view that

> as a matter of principle, in order to command public confidence, the Chief Executive should observe rules which are at least as stringent as those applicable to the PAOs (politically appointed officials) and the Civil Service, which he leads.
>
> (Independent Review Committee 2012: 44)

Tsang accepted some of the Committee's recommendations immediately and the incoming Chief Executive, Leung Chun-ying, said that he would seek "to implement [the remainder] as soon as possible after taking office" (Hong Kong Hansard 2015: 1395).

During the five years of Leung's tenure in office, nothing was done to bring the Chief Executive under the provisions of Section 3 and Section 8. The matter became something of a running sore. Democrats frequently asked the government what was happening to the amending legislation and criticised Leung for not living up to his promises. The issue was debated again in the Legislative Council in November 2015 but the Chief Secretary for Administration, Carrie Lam Yuet-ngor, simply reiterated the government's contention that the unique constitutional status of the Chief Executive would be affected if potential Section 3 offences were to be considered by a panel under the Chief Justice (Hong Kong Hansard 2015: 1396). The democrats once more stressed the importance of equality before the law and their inability to comprehend why the constitutional status of the Chief Executive had any relevance to Sections 3 and 8 (Hong Kong Hansard 2015: 1402, 1421). Their motion to amend the legislation was voted down.

Leung himself soon became so embroiled with issues concerning the ICAC that prospects of amending the ordinance disappeared. On 8 October 2014, Fairfax media revealed that before he became Chief Executive, Leung had entered into an agreement with the Australian firm UGL relating to the sale of DTZ property agency of which he had been the Chief Executive Officer for North Asia (Legislative Council Secretariat 2017: Appendix 1). The agreement provided that UGL, upon the sale of DTZ, would pay Leung £1.5 million (HK$18.5 million). Two further payment tranches of £2 million (HK$25 million) each were to be made in December 2012 and December 2013, by which time Leung was already Chief Executive. In 2014, the Chief Secretary for Administration told the Legislative Council that Leung had disclosed his assets, including presumably the payment of £1.5 million, on assuming office as Chief Executive; the payments after he became Chief Executive were "non-compete" arrangements which the Chief Secretary described as "standard business practice" (Hong Kong Hansard 2014a: 852). No declaration was made of the two tranches of £2 million that he was supposed to have received and no tax was paid on them (Legislative Council Secretariat 2017: Appendix 1). Leung's office later said that he had sought the advice of an accountant on whether the amounts were liable for tax (Legislative Council 2017: Appendix 1).

On 9 October 2014, the day after the details of the agreement were revealed, the Neo-Democrats lodged a complaint with the ICAC. The Legislative Council, which was deeply concerned by the Occupy Central movement and the civil disobedience campaign at that time, did consider setting up a select committee to investigate the matter (Legislative Council House Committee 2014). The democrats saw the payments as "illicit kickbacks" and were concerned about potential conflicts of interest, the system of declaration of interests and the taxation implications (Legislative Council Secretariat 2017: 7–8). The pro-establishment members voted down the call for a select committee on the grounds that Leung's behaviour was normal commercial practice and that it was merely a ploy by the democrats to remove him from office (Legislative Council House Committee: 10; Hong Kong Hansard 2014b: 1588ff).

Two years later, a select committee was eventually set up but soon ran into controversy when the Vice-Chairman, Holden Chow Ho-ding, proposed 47 amendments to the terms of reference. It was discovered that the amendments had actually come from Leung's office and that Chow had not formulated them himself. Leung admitted that he had been in contact with Chow and claimed that, as the subject of the investigation, he had the right to express his views on its terms of reference (Cheung and Kao 2017). The democrats thought otherwise. Two members of the Democratic Party lodged a complaint with the ICAC alleging misconduct in public office and another member and a former legislator also made complaints to the Commission. Chow resigned from the Committee.

In the fractious atmosphere in which Hong Kong politics was conducted, the prospect of the executive bringing changes supportive of the ICAC's campaigns against corruption soon died away. A former Chief Secretary of Administration under Tsang, Rafael Hui Si-yan, was convicted of corrupt offences.

The Secretary for Development in Leung's administration was forced to resign after only 12 days in office and the actions of two Executive Councillors were also investigated by the ICAC (Scott 2017). In the unlikely event that Leung had sought to initiate proposals for strengthening the ICAC, the effect would have been to draw even more attention to the UGL incident and to the ethical problems which bedevilled his administration. After 2005, even the ritual annual acknowledgement of political commitment to the role of the ICAC in the policy address became a thing of the past. Leung mentioned the ICAC only briefly in his final policy address (Hong Kong Hansard 2017: 3156; see also Table 4.1).

The ICAC had its own integrity issues to deal with during Leung's tenure in office. A former Commissioner, Timothy Tong Hin-ming, was found to have over-spent on duty visits, gifts and entertainment (see pp. 86–87). Although the Department of Justice decided not to lay charges against Tong, the loss of public confidence in the Commission was reflected in the declining number of corruption reports and in the questions raised in the legislature about the effectiveness of the ICAC (Hong Kong Hansard 2014c: 1687; Ewing 2016). The Tong affair and the charges and counter-charges stemming from the investigations of the Chief Executives and members of their administrations affected the ICAC's reputation for probity. (Ewing 2016; see also pp. 104–105). For a time, the Commission's strategy seemed to be to avoid adding more fuel to the fire by proposing major new initiatives. It concentrated instead on strengthening its financial control system and ensuring continuing public support. There was little political will on either the side of the political executive or of the ICAC to engage in major reform to improve the corruption prevention process.

The wheel turned full circle when Carrie Lam Yuet-ngor, the former Chief Secretary for Administration, succeeded Leung as Chief Executive in July 2017. Lam had vigorously defended the government's decision not to bring the Chief Executive under the provisions of Sections 3 and 8 of the *POBO*. But in her first policy address as Chief Executive in October 2017, it was evident that she had changed her mind. She said that she would "resolve as soon as possible those constitutional and legal issues pertinent to the amendment of the *Prevention of Bribery Ordinance* to extend the scope of sections 3 and 8 to cover the Chief Executive" (Hong Kong Government 2017a: para 29). There was also a strong, and probably necessary, statement of support, echoing the words of the Chief Executive and Governors before 2007, that the ICAC would continue to investigate all complaints impartially. Lam said that the ICAC "remains independent in its operation" and "is fearless, robust and effective in pursuing the corrupt" (Hong Kong Government 2017a: para 29). She also promised additional resources for anti-corruption training for civil servants and international exchanges (Hong Kong Government 2017b). However, the question of whether there was sufficient political will to pursue the kinds of corruption problems that were perceived to afflict Hong Kong – serious conflicts of interest, cross-border corruption, government–business collusion and continuing attempts to subvert the electoral system – remained unanswered.

The costs of declining political will

Quah (2015a) argues that there are five indicators of political will: comprehensive anti-corruption legislation; an adequate budget, trained personnel and up-to-date equipment coupled with operational autonomy; impartial enforcement of the anti-corruption laws, regardless of the offender's position, status, or political affiliation, and without political interference; avoiding the use of corruption measures as a weapon against political opponents; and the maintenance and monitoring of anti-corruption efforts. By 2007, the ICAC was well placed on all of these indicators and had also achieved significant success in changing public attitudes toward corruption (see Chs. 2, 7). Declining political will nevertheless posed questions in three respects. First, would financial resources continue to be provided as generously as they had been in the past? Second, did the failure to bring the Chief Executive under Sections 3 and 8 of the *POBO* create problems? Could the anti-corruption legislation be amended to enable the ICAC to deal more effectively with the increasing problem of serious conflicts of interest? Third, would the level of public support for the ICAC be affected by the complaints against, and convictions of, senior figures in the administration? We consider each of these issues in turn.

Providing resources

ACAs are dependent on the government for funding. A political leadership at odds with an ACA might simply decide to reduce its impact by cutting its budget or stopping funding altogether. The ICAC was never in any danger of this happening because it was sufficiently autonomous that significant cuts in expenditure would have aroused public opposition and objections in the Legislative Council. The Council has to approve to approve the budget and members have traditionally paid close attention to the details of the ICAC's proposed expenditure. In 2017, for example, there were thirty-four written questions from Councillors, the answers to which suggest that the ICAC was principally using the increased funding to strengthen existing functions rather than to introduce new initiatives (Hong Kong Government 2017c).

Historically, however, the ICAC has relied on the government to provide funding for new measures in times of crisis. During the rise in corruption complaints just before and after 1997, for example, the government provided substantially increased funding. The ICAC's expenditure increased by 44 per cent, from HK$552 million in 1996–1997 to HK$796 million in 1999–2000, at a time when every other Hong Kong government department was experiencing budget cuts because of the effects of the Asian financial crisis (ICAC 2000: 10). The ICAC seems always to have been able to persuade the government that corruption prevention should be high on the policy agenda if complaints began to rise or decline rapidly or if areas of concern have been identified. In the wake of the Tong incident when corruption reports were declining, for example, expenditure on publicity was increased in an attempt to persuade more people to complain about corruption and to re-assure the public that the ICAC was still functioning as it had in the past.

Aside from the problem of funding the regional offices in the mid-1970s, the only other significant budgetary cuts have been a 3.1 per cent reduction in the 1992–1993 estimates and a small reduction in the 2005–2006 budget (ICAC 2006: Appendix 3). In 1992, the Commissioner said that he could deal with the cuts through trimming the public education programme, although he was quick to emphasise "how much the Commission depends on the trust, confidence and good will of the community" (ICAC 1992: 9). The small reduction in 2005–2006 was somewhat counter-balanced by capital expenditure on a new purpose-built ICAC headquarters building which opened in 2007. Figure 4.1, which is based on the ICAC's actual expenditure up to 2016, shows that the Commission has continued to be well-funded. Even when it was mired in its own integrity crises between 2012 and 2017, the Hong Kong government did not reduce the ICAC's funding. There is a steady rise in its budget during the Leung administration, followed by a more substantial increase in 2017–2018 when estimated expenditure jumped from HK$1011 million in 2016–17 to HK$1074.2 million under a new Chief Executive (Hong Kong Government 2014–2017).

After the investigations into the Chief Executives and the ICAC Commissioner began, neither the state of the Commission nor the political climate were conducive to new anti-corruption initiatives, and only a few new areas of funding were considered. In 2014, as a result of the Tong incident, the ICAC's internal audit system was strengthened (Independent Review Committee 2013; Hong Kong Government 2014: 132). There were also projects to review internal codes of practice in government departments and to promote CRD youth initiatives. In 2017, the Commission created new posts to help in complex investigations

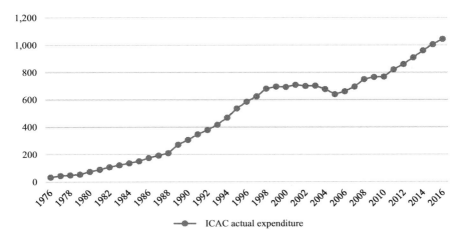

Figure 4.1 ICAC actual expenditure, 1976–2017 (in millions of Hong Kong dollars)

Source: Hong Kong Government (1976–2018)

Note: US$1 = HK$7.80.

of listed companies, to strengthen the capacity to handle complaints and to enhance information technology capabilities (Hong Kong Government 2017c). But major projects which had characterised the relationship between the ICAC and the government in the past, such as the introduction of ethics officers in all government departments initiated in 2006, were not introduced.

Although ICAC expenditure as a ratio of total government expenditure has declined from 0.37 per cent in 1999 to 0.28 per cent in 2017, the Commission remains three times better funded per capita than any other ACA in Asia and one of the best funded in the world (Quah 2017a: 244). At the end of 2017, its establishment was 1472 with a strength of 1386 (ICAC 2018: 26), which, measured in staff/population ratios, is 1:5366, by far the lowest in Asia. The institutionalisation of the Commission's role and procedures provides it with security against major detrimental funding changes, although the amount of funding still remains dependent on healthy government revenues.

Keeping anti-corruption legislation relevant

In the absence of political will, it is difficult to keep anti-corruption legislation relevant. Types of corruption can change quickly and require appropriate amendments to the powers and procedures of the ACA to ensure effective prevention. In the saga over the proposed inclusion of the Chief Executive under Sections 3 and 8 of the *POBO*, the issue was not initially seen as pressing but became rather more so once corruption charges were laid against Tsang in 2015. His subsequent conviction supported the government's claim that any Chief Executive who committed a corruption offence was liable to be charged under the *POBO* or the common law offence of misconduct in public office. But, by that stage, the amendments to Sections 3 and 8 of the *POBO* were being presented by their proponents not only as anti-corruption measures but as necessary for equality before the law. It was argued that in a murky ethical climate, the amendments would re-assure the public that the ICAC was still able to pursue anyone who behaved corruptly.

The question that also required attention was how the ICAC was going to deal with the issue of government–business collusion and serious conflicts of interest which seemingly became increasingly prevalent when political will to prevent corruption declined. The ICAC, the Department of Justice and the courts had developed the common law offence of misconduct in public office as a means of dealing with these problems (see pp. 97–100). However, unlike the *POBO*, misconduct in public office does not give the ICAC strong investigatory powers. The consequence was that evidence was more difficult to collect and cases took some time to come before the courts. Tsang was not charged until three and a half years after the investigation began and Hui's case took a full six years' investigation before he appeared in court (Lau 2017). There has been a suggestion from a high-ranking ICAC official that the misconduct in public offence should be brought under the *POBO*, but the political atmosphere has not so far been conducive for this reform to be put to the legislature (Lau 2017; *South China Morning Post* 2017).

Public support and the decline in political will

Did the decline in political will and the integrity problems encountered during the Leung administration result in reduced public support for the ICAC? The ICAC annual surveys between 2012 and 2017 and our own 2015 survey suggest that it did not (Gong and Xiao 2017). It might be presumed that two Chief Executives, a former Chief Secretary of Administration, a minister and two Executive Council members in the news about their alleged transgressions and a former ICAC Commissioner who was called before several committees to explain his behaviour might raise questions in the public mind about whether the Commission was still able to control corruption. But institutionalisation provides some insulation from short-term failings and some recognition that the ICAC is not necessarily equally effective in all areas. Support does not entirely depend on perceptions of present effectiveness.

It might be assumed that if the level of corruption were perceived to be low, then the ICAC might be thought to be effective. Yet, as Figure 4.2 shows, perceptions that corruption was common or quite common were around 20 and 30 per cent of respondents between 2004 and 2017. Where did this perception come from? Between 2014 and 2017, an average of over 98 per cent of respondents said they had no personal experience of corruption in the previous year (ICAC 2014–2017: XIV). It is unlikely therefore that the perception arose from experience of corruption on the streets. The more likely explanation seems to be that the figures relate to perceptions of rising cross-border corruption, government–business collusion and closer economic ties with Mainland. These factors coincide with the reasons given in the ICAC annual surveys by those who expected a rise in corruption in the following year (ICAC 2014–2017; see also Ch. 10) and may also reflect the corruption cases in the courts or under investigation during

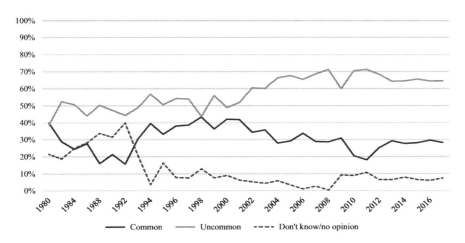

Figure 4.2 Perceived prevalence of corruption in Hong Kong, 1980–2017

Source: ICAC Annual Survey (1980–2017)

the Leung administration. The public, in short, strongly supports the ICAC but may have doubts about its effectiveness in controlling certain types of corruption. Paradoxically, successful prosecutions in these areas may not allay public fears but rather fuel the perception that there is more corruption under the surface.

Strong statements from political leaders on their support for anti-corruption measures can do no harm under such circumstances. The peculiar situation in which both a current and a former Chief Executive were being investigated at the same time obviously would have stretched the credibility of such a statement of support. But even for an institutionalised ACA in more normal times – in which autonomy serves to separate perceptions of the government's anti-corruption efforts from those of the ACA – there is value in the political leaders' strong endorsement of the work of the ACA and support for its future activities.

We have argued that institutionalisation provides protection for an ACA from a decline in political will. In subsequent chapters, we will also argue that the repetition of procedures – sanctioned by social norms that are valued by the community, a central feature of institutionalisation – is essential for the success of ACAs. In the following chapters, we explore the major characteristics of the ICAC which have contributed to its success:

- the development of an efficient organisation focused on sanctions, corruption prevention by improved procedures and public education, and staffed by people of integrity who are accountable for their actions (Ch. 5);
- the effective enforcement of the anti-corruption laws (Ch. 6); and
- the development of an effective community relations policy focusing on changing public perceptions of corruption in support of the Commission's zero-tolerance approach to corruption (Ch. 7).

In the final chapter of this section (Ch. 8), we examine how institutionalisation may help build capacity, effectiveness and trust in controlling corruption.

References

Ankamah, Samuel Siebie and S.M. Manzoor E. Khoda (2018) "Political will and government anti-corruption efforts: What does the evidence say?" *Public Administration and Development*, 38(1): 3–14.
The Basic Law of the Hong Kong Special Administrative Region of the People's Republic of China (1990), www.basiclaw.gov.hk/en/basiclawtext/images/basiclaw_full_text_en.pdf.
Brinkerhoff, Derick W. (2000) "Assessing political will for anti-corruption efforts: An analytical framework", *Public Administration and Development*, 20(3): 239–252.
Cheung, Tony and Ernest Kao (2017) "Hong Kong leader admits intervening in probe into HK\$50 million payment", *South China Morning Post*, 16 May, www.scmp.com/news/hong-kong/politics/article/2094482/hong-kong-leader-cy-leung-admits-role-proposal-change-scope.
Choi, Jin-wook (2017) "Corruption prevention: Successful cases" in Ting Gong and Ian Scott (eds.) *Routledge handbook of corruption in Asia*. London: Routledge: 262–276.

Ewing, Kent (2016) "Decadence and decline at Hong Kong's once proud anti-corruption agency", *Hong Kong Free Press*, 14 July, www.hongkongfp.com/2016/07/14/decadence-and-decline-at-hong-kong-once-proud-anti-corruption-agency/.

Gittings, Danny (2013) *Introduction to the Basic Law*. Hong Kong: Hong Kong University Press.

Gong, Ting and Hanyu Xiao (2017) "Socially embedded anti-corruption governance: Evidence from Hong Kong", *Public Administration and Development*, 17(3): 176–190.

Heilbrunn, John R. (2004) *Anti-corruption commissions: Panacea or real medicine to fight corruption?* Washington: World Bank.

Hong Kong Government (1976–2018) *Estimates of Expenditure*. Hong Kong: various publishers.

Hong Kong Government (2014) "The policy address: The policy agenda", www.policyaddress.gov.hk/2014/eng/pdf/Agenda.pdf.

Hong Kong Government (2014–2017) "Estimates of expenditure", Head 72, www.budget.gov.hk/2017/eng/pdf/head072.pdf.

Hong Kong Government (2017a) "Policy address", www.policyaddress.gov.hk/2017/eng/pdf/PA2017.pdf.

Hong Kong Government (2017b) "Policy agenda", www.policyaddress.gov.hk/2017/eng/agenda.html.

Hong Kong Government (2017c) "Replies to initial written questions raised by Finance Committee members in examining the estimates of expenditure 2017–18", www.legco.gov.hk/yr16-17/english/fc/fc/w_q/icac-e.pdf.

Hong Kong Hansard 4 October 1984; 7 October 1992; 26 November 1994; 11 October 1995; 8 October 1997; 7 October 1998; 11 July 2007; 25 June 2008; 29 February 2012; 17 October 2012; 16 January 2013; 29 October 2014a; 5 November 2014b; 6 November 2014c; 11 November 2015; 18 January 2017; 11 October 2017.

ICAC (1980–2017) *Annual surveys*. Hong Kong: mimeo.

ICAC (1992) "Annual report 1991", www.icac.org.hk/filemanager/en/Content_27/1991.pdf.

ICAC (1997a) *Key statistics for briefing media interviews*. Hong Kong: Government Printer.

ICAC (1997b) "Annual report 1996", www.icac.org.hk/filemanager/en/Content_27/1996.pdf.

ICAC (1998) "Annual report 1997", www.icac.org.hk/filemanager/en/Content_27/1997.pdf.

ICAC (2001) "Annual report 2000", www.icac.org.hk/filemanager/tc/Content_27/2000.pdf.

ICAC (2006) "Annual report 2005", https://www.icac.org.hk/filemanager/tc/Content_27/2005.pdf.

ICAC (2018) "Annual report 2017", www.icac.org.hk/filemanager/en/content_27/2017.pdf.

Independent Review Committee (2012) "Report of the Independent Review Committee for the prevention and handling of conflicts of interest", www.legco.gov.hk/yr11-12/english/panels/ca/papers/ca0604-rpt20120531-e.pdf.

Independent Review Committee (2013) "Report of the Independent Review Committee on ICAC's regulatory systems and procedures for handling official entertainment, gifts and duty visits", www.gov.hk.

Kpundeh, Sahr J. (1998) "Political will in fighting corruption" in Sahr J. Kpundeh and Irene Hors (eds.) *Corruption and integrity development initiatives*. New York: UNDP: 91-110.

Lai, Alan N. (2001) "Keeping Hong Kong clean: Experiences of fighting corruption post 1997", *Harvard Asia Pacific Review*, 5(2): 51–54.

Lau, Chris (2015) "Former Hong Kong leader Donald Tsang out on bail after court hears misconduct charges over Shenzhen flat rental", *South China Morning Post*, 5 October, www.scmp.com/news/hong-kong/law-crime/article/1864267/former-hong-kong-leader-donald-tsang-released-bail-court.

Lau, Chris (2017) "How a small team of graft-busters tightened the net in Hong Kong's most explosive corruption case", *South China Morning Post*, 7 August, www.scmp.com/news/hong-kong/law-crime/article/2105628/how-small-team-graft-busters-tightened-net-hong-kongs-most.

Legislative Council (1997) "Report of the select committee into the circumstances surrounding the departure of Mr. Leung Ming-yin from the government and related issues", http://ebook.lib.hku.hk/HKG/B36226270V1.pdf.

Legislative Council (2008) "Report of the Bills Committee on the Prevention of Bribery (Amendment Bill) 2007, LC Paper No. CB (2)2365/07–08", 19 June.

Legislative Council, House Committee (2014) "Minutes of the 2nd meeting: LC Paper No. CB (2) 124/14–15", 17 October.

Legislative Council Secretariat (2017) *Information note: The UGL incident*, 23 February, www.legco.gov.hk/research-publications/english/1617in03-the-ugl-incident-20170223-e.pdf.

Manion, Melanie (2004) *Corruption by design: Building clean government in Mainland China and Hong Kong*. Cambridge, MA: Harvard University Press.

O'Clery, Conor (1997) "Departure of 'a little civil servant' casts doubt on open policy", *Irish Times*, 14 January, www.irishtimes.com/news/departure-of-a-little-civil-servant-casts-doubt-on-open-policy-1.21666.

Oriental Daily News (2012) "Donald Tsang runs away from a casino reception in Macau to avoid media reports", http://orientaldaily.on.cc/cnt/news/20120220/00174_001.html.

Persson, Anna and Martin Sjöstedt (2012) "Responsive and responsible leaders: A matter of political will", *Perspectives on Politics*, 10(3): 617–632.

Quah, Jon S.T. (2013) *Curbing corruption in Asian countries: An impossible dream?* Singapore: ISEAS Publishing.

Quah, Jon S.T. (2015) "The critical importance of political will in combating corruption in Asian countries", *Public Administration and Policy*, 18(2): 12–23.

Quah, Jon S.T. (2017) "Controlling corruption in Asian countries: The elusive search for success" in Ting Gong and Ian Scott (eds.) *Routledge handbook of corruption in Asia*. London: Routledge: 241–261.

Rotberg, Robert I. (2017) *The corruption cure: How leaders and citizens can combat graft*. Princeton: Princeton University Press.

Scott, Ian (2000) "The public service in transition: Sustaining administrative capacity and political neutrality" in Robert Ash, Peter Ferdinand, Brian Hook and Robin Porter (eds.) *Hong Kong in transition: The handover years*. Basingstoke: Macmillan: 154–174.

Scott, Ian (2014) "Political scandals and the accountability of the Chief Executive in Hong Kong", *Asian Survey*, 54(5): 966–986.

Scott, Ian (2017) "The challenge of preserving a successful anti-corruption agency", *Asian Education and Development Studies*, 6(3): 227–237.

Siu, Jasmine (2016) "Hong Kong radio host convicted over plan to pay localists to win votes in district council elections", *South China Morning Post*, 24 October, www.scmp.com/news/hong-kong/law-crime/article/2039644/hong-kong-waiter-convicted-over-plan-pay-localists-win.

South China Morning Post (2017) "Weigh pros and cons before giving ICAC extra powers", *South China Morning Post* editorial, 17 August, www.scmp.com/comment/insight-opinion/article/2107114/weigh-pros-and-cons-giving-icac-extra-powers.U4 Anti-Corruption Resource Centre (2010) "Unpacking the concept of political will to confront corruption", www.u4.no/publications/unpacking-the-concept-of-political-will-to-confront-corruption/.

5 Organising for success

An ACA's success is predicated on its ability to construct and maintain an effective and independent organisation. For the organisation to be effective, it must have adequate resources, an institutional design which is congruent with the approach that it intends to pursue, personnel of high integrity and ability, experience provided by long-serving staff, and continuity in its methods. Any effective public organisation might be presumed to possess the same characteristics. For an ACA, however, there are often expectations of reduced corruption and the prosecution of the corrupt from the moment of its creation. Unlike many public organisations, an ACA often has high visibility and a critical society-wide constituency which follows its efforts with some interest. In addition, if it is to be successful, it is expected to undertake its task impartially and independently of government, exercising strong powers to combat corruption yet still remaining accountable to the public for its actions. As an ICAC review committee put it:

> the establishment of special institutions to tackle corruption creates dilemmas that are not easy to resolve. On the one hand, the organisation needs sufficient powers and independence to deal with the problem effectively. On the other, these powers must be circumscribed and the organisation made sufficiently accountable so that it cannot abuse its special position.
>
> (Independent Review Committee 1994: 25)

The organisational criteria are so challenging that even successful ACAs rarely have blemish-free records. Unsuccessful ACAs very often fail to reach the starting line and founder in a morass of poor funding, inadequately trained personnel sometimes lacking in integrity, unclear lines of authority and compromised or conflictual relationships with other agencies, particularly the police. In this chapter, we describe and analyse the structure of the ICAC, its recruitment and retention procedures, and the question of how accountability and integrity can be managed in an organisation with strong and relatively unchecked powers.

Structure and functions of the ICAC departments

It is a tribute to the foresight of the creators of the ICAC that the structure that they devised in a few short months in 1973 and 1974 has stood the test of time. From the outset, there was awareness that if the goal was to achieve zero tolerance of corruption in every sphere, then the ICAC had to be organised appropriately to play a comprehensive role (Hong Kong Hansard 1973: 17–18). The notion of a three-pronged approach, involving enforcement, prevention by improving procedures, and public education, was reflected in the establishment of an Operations Department (OD), a Corruption Prevention Department (CPD) and a Community Relations Department (CRD) with an Administration Branch in support (see Figure 5.1). As the Commission has evolved, it has acquired additional functions but these have been integrated within the existing framework with no fundamental change to the basic structure. It is also important that the Commission was created as a single powerful organisation. In Taiwan and Korea, for example, the powers to investigate corruption have been divided between different organisations, resulting in jurisdictional disputes and confused lines of authority (Ko *et al* 2015; Quah 2017). In Hong Kong, the ICAC's extensive remit has remained clearly understood since it overcame the initial challenges to the scope of its jurisdiction (see Ch. 3).

The ICAC Commissioner heads the organisation and is given considerable powers under both the *Independent Commission Against Corruption Ordinance (ICACO)* and *The Prevention of Bribery Ordinance (POBO)*. Under the *ICACO*, the Commissioner is responsible for the administration of the Commission and "shall not be subject to the direction or control of any person other than the Chief Executive" (Sections 5.1 and 5.2). He may terminate officers after consulting with the Advisory Committee on Corruption and may vary the terms under which they are employed. He has responsibility for receiving and considering complaints alleging corrupt practices and for authorising arrests without warrant and the actions of his officers for a wide range of offences under the *POBO* and the *Elections (Corrupt and Illegal Conduct) Ordinance* (see Ch. 6). These are formidable discretionary powers but ICAC annual survey reports suggest that they have strong public backing (ICAC 2018b).

Between 1974 and 2017, fifteen people (thirteen men and two women) held the office of Commissioner. All but four were drawn from the administrative grade of the Hong Kong government. Of those who were not, one was previously head of the civil division of the Legal Department, another was a former Solicitor General, and two were Directors of Immigration. There is no history of promoting anyone directly from within the organisation to the post of Commissioner although at least one Commissioner had previously worked for the ICAC. During colonial times, the administrative officers who served as Commissioner were normally coming toward the end of their careers which was thought to be desirable because they would not seek further positions and could then act impartially toward the government. After 1997, however, there was greater flexibility, and some controversy, over appointments. In 2006, Fanny Law Fan Chiu-fun was appointed Commissioner but resigned after eight months in office when a Commission of Inquiry found that, in her previous role as Permanent Secretary of the Education Bureau, she had improperly interfered with the academic freedom of two scholars (Yeung and Lee 2007: I, 74–95). The government, the Legislative Council and the ICAC itself launched investigations into the actions

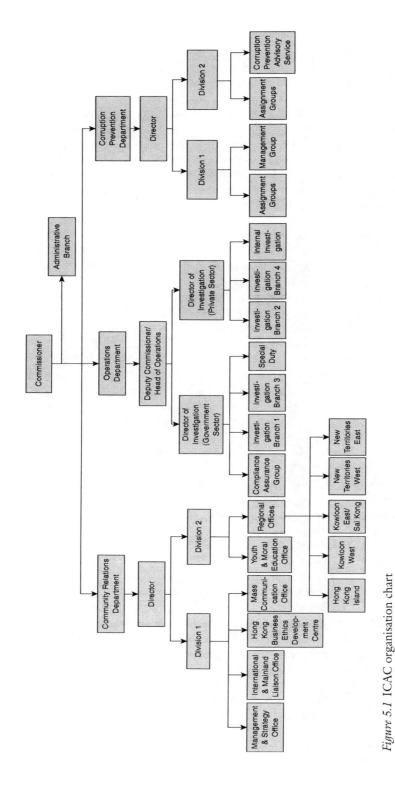

Figure 5.1 ICAC organisation chart

Source: Adapted from the ICAC Annual Report (2017): 99

of her successor, Timothy Tong Hin-ming, when it was discovered that he had over-spent on duty visits, gifts and entertainment (Independent Review Committee 2013; Legislative Council 2013, 2014).

The Director of the OD serves as Deputy Commissioner and is responsible for investigations and the enforcement work of the Commission. The OD is by far the largest of the ICAC's departments, with an establishment of 1060 and a strength of 1005 in 2017 (ICAC 2018a: 26). It oversees a process that begins with reports lodged by the public or provided by paid informers, which are processed through a Report Centre, then considered by daily meetings of the directorate officers in the OD, and finally classified on the basis of whether they can be investigated and, if so, by the type of suspected offence. Corruption reports which are to be investigated are then assigned to particular specialised sections of the Department. OD personnel may build expertise in particular areas over the course of their careers and may deal, for example, with corruption reports about the police or in private sector areas such as insurance. All investigations are compartmentalised within the various sections of the OD and confidentiality is maintained on a "need to know" basis within the section (ICAC 2015b: 14).

The OD does not comment on cases under investigation but it does occasionally provide information on its methods after cases are concluded. In the major case of Rafael Hui Si-yan, the former Chief Secretary for Administration, and Thomas Kwok Ping-kwong of Sun Hung Kai Properties, both of whom eventually received lengthy prison sentences, it took six years of investigation before the case could be brought to court (Lau 2017). The case began with an anonymous tip-off that Hui had received a flat at no cost from Kwok, but it seemed to the small team of ICAC investigators that the suspects had an adequate explanation. As they delved deeper, however, there was more evidence to support a prosecution on the grounds that Hui had been offered a "sweetener" by Kwok. In the end, the case involved 120 witnesses, an analysis of 230 bank accounts and the involvement of more than 20 ICAC investigators (Lau 2017). Not all ICAC cases, of course, require such exhaustive investigations. Some complaints are frivolous, malicious, *ultra vires* or too general to be investigated; in election years, many minor complaints are made about the behaviour of political party campaigners and candidates. In 2017, excluding election-related cases, the ICAC received 2835 complaints, of which 2129 were pursuable (ICAC 2018a: 16; ICAC 2018f: 12). Of the complaints received, 66 per cent were concerned with the private sector, 27 per cent were related to the public sector and 7 per cent were about public bodies. In 2016, of the 90 cases that went to trial, 141 people were convicted, a success rate of 74 per cent (ICAC 2017a: 10).

The CRD was clearly in MacLehose's mind from the outset. His reasoning for establishing the Department was almost identical to that of Frederick May's plea for more public education nearly seventy years earlier. MacLehose said that there should be

> a civil unit whose main task will lie in educating the public as to the evils of corruption not only from the point of view of the recipient but also of

the giver. It will also critically examine administrative procedures which lead themselves to corrupt practices.

(Hong Kong Hansard 1973: 18)

These functions were subsequently split between the CRD and CPD. At the end of 2017, the CRD had an establishment of 185 and a strength of 174 (ICAC 2018a: 26). The establishment reached a high of over 300 in the wake of the police amnesty in the late 1970s when it was seeking to generate public support for the Commission (see Ch. 3). Subsequent campaigns have been more modest. In 2016, however, the CRD was heavily involved in a Hong Kong–wide "All for Integrity" campaign, which included the introduction of a Facebook page, web interviews with young athletes to promote public values, a book fair and an ICAC TV drama series which proved very popular on both sides of the border (ICAC 2017a: 31). The CRD has responsibility for publicity and also houses the Business Ethics Development Centre, which was established in 1995 to foster business and professional ethics (ICAC 2018a: 74). The Centre seeks to develop strategic alliances with business to prevent corruption and to offer various services, such as corporate "health checks", advice to companies on system control, and a training package on business ethics for listed companies (ICAC n.d.). It has also produced guidelines for codes of conduct and a corruption prevention guide for small and medium enterprises operating in Guangdong, Hong Kong and Macao (ICAC 2008, 2012).

The CRD deploys five regional officers to supervise the work of the seven regional ICAC offices (see Figure 5.1). Each regional office has responsibility for two or more districts. The regional offices play an important part in dealing with corruption issues and in conducting corruption-awareness campaigns at the local level. They were originally established to provide a direct connection with the community and to encourage reluctant citizens to report corruption. While they still serve an important role in passing local corruption complaints to the central Report Centre – some 17 per cent of all corruption reports were made directly to regional offices in 2017 (ICAC 2018a: 72) – reports are now more frequently made by telephone or email than they were in the past. The regional offices are responsible for liaison with district organisations and develop annual plans for anti-corruption activities, and an annual joint project, in conjunction with the District Councils. The work plans integrate central programmes, such as the "All for Integrity" campaign, with local activities, including visits, talks and special projects within the district. In 2017, for example, the Hong Kong West/Islands office drew up a plan which involved 650 activities and 26 special projects with the aim of reaching 73,000 people (ICAC Regional Office 2017: 4). Overall, in 2017, the CRD's efforts were supported by 820 organisations and the department estimated that it reached nearly 820,000 people (ICAC 2018a: 81). Our interviews with regional officers revealed that they use a wide range of contacts at the district level, relying particularly on a close relationship with the District Councils which are normally very supportive of their work (Scott 2013b).

Regional officers also, unusually, each take on the responsibility for formulating anti-corruption policies which have Hong Kong–wide applications. For example, the New Territories regional office drafts policies to control electoral corruption for the whole of Hong Kong; the Hong Kong East regional office has responsibility for building management policies; and Kowloon East focuses on public sector integrity management. Regional officers, who may be transferred within the organisation, sometimes take the functional area for which they are responsible with them in order to ensure continuity. This wide range of functions reflects the "universalist" strategy of the Commission and is designed to keep the ICAC in touch with the public sentiment, to liaise with local organisations and District Councils, to act as a conduit through which local issues may be transmitted to headquarters and to produce community relations policies which are common throughout Hong Kong.

The CPD is the smallest of the departments. In 2017, it had an establishment of seventy-one and a strength of sixty-seven (ICAC 2018a: 26). The CPD's mandate, according to a former Director, is to "prevent corruption within organisations by examining their internal operations and proposing corruption-resistant management and administration systems" (Chan 2001: 367). This is reflected in the CPD assignment studies which are conducted within the client organisation and with the assistance and support of its personnel. The department's work in the past has been mainly focused on the public sector, but since the 1980s, it has also had an advisory service for the private sector (ICAC 2018d). In recent years, its work in the private sector and for public bodies has increased. Of the sixty-nine assignments conducted in 2017, sixty-three were for government departments and public bodies and six were for the private sector (ICAC 2018a: 61).

Priorities are determined in consultation with senior officials in the client organisations. Past ICAC corruption cases, in particular, are likely to trigger an examination of procedures but assignments also stem from the CPD's own perceptions of urgent issues and from the advice of the Corruption Prevention Advisory Committee. Once an assignment has been agreed, CPD officers then work with client organisations to come up with recommendations for improving practices. Most assignments follow guidelines which sequentially consider relevant laws, interviews with relevant officials, examination of files, an assessment of the adequacy and clarity of procedures, accountability, openness, fairness and transparency, feedback, and preventive and detection control measures (Mok n.d.: 6–7). In addition to its work on assignments, the CPD has become increasingly involved in assessing and developing codes of conduct for both public and private organisations, providing advice on corruption-free procedures and on integrity issues (ICAC 2015c).

The three-pronged strategy of enforcement, education and prevention is consistent with a zero-tolerance and universalist approach to controlling corruption. The structure and functions of the ICAC departments are congruent with this approach because they reflect an attempt to ensure that there are comprehensive checks and remedies for any corruption-prone areas. In the ideal sequential formulation of anti-corruption measures, this approach would see the CRD encouraging and facilitating public corruption complaints, the OD investigating and prosecuting suspected cases and the CPD introducing procedures to prevent the offence from re-occurring. In reality, there may be more need for horizontal coordination than this model assumes. It is quite possible that information obtained in one department could be useful in dealing with corruption problems in another. However, the tendency toward compartmentalisation of information between departments and within the OD is a potential obstacle. In 2006, in an attempt to encourage greater appreciation of the role of the different departments in achieving effective corruption prevention, the ICAC announced a "One Commission" policy. The policy presaged a new system whereby officers could be transferred from one department to another; previously, officers had tended to spend all their careers within one department. There has always been coordination at the pinnacle of the organisation with regular meetings between the Commissioner and the Directors of the departments, but further integration and coordination of work in the field may prevent some duplication of effort.

Recruitment and selection of personnel

Every ACA must attempt to ensure that its personnel have high standards of integrity and are the best available for the job. The ICAC addresses these issues in the selection process and through subsequent training. Applicants are required to pass examinations in Chinese, English and the Basic Law, attend an interview, and show good knowledge of Hong Kong. If selected, there are two entry points to the Commission at the officer level: Assistant Commission Against Corruption Officer and Commission Against Corruption Officer (Middle/Lower). In most cases, new recruits would enter on the bottom rungs of the grade structure shown in Table 5.1 which cover the two entry ranks. There is intense competition for positions; in 2016, for example, there were 4200 applications for 35 investigative officers at the Assistant Commission Against Corruption level (Yau 2017). The Commission normally takes fresh graduates for the OD and the CRD although high school graduates are also eligible to apply (ICAC 2015d). Candidates for positions in the OD undergo fitness and psychometric tests. The CPD does not employ fresh graduates because it requires specialists. It recruits at the Commission Against Corruption Officer (Middle/Lower) level and pays a relatively higher salary based on experience and qualifications. New recruits undertake an induction course which varies according to the needs of the department. OD recruits, for example, are trained in the use of firearms and investigatory and interviewing techniques and participate in mock trials (ICAC 2015b; Yau 2017).

About 76 per cent of the Commission's staff are on the ICAC pay scale (see Table 5.1) with the remainder, mainly administrative staff, on the civil service master pay scale. The ICAC pays well in comparison with similar positions in the Hong Kong civil service. The entry salary for an Assistant Commission Against Corruption Officer as a graduate is higher than that of new recruits in the civil service aside from the administrative grade or equivalent ranks in the disciplinary services. ICAC officers are employed on contract and receive a bonus of 25 per cent of their total salary after two and a half years of service. Contracts are renewable, and many ICAC officers remain with the Commission for their entire careers. The contract system enables the ICAC to dismiss unsuitable officers

Table 5.1 ICAC grade structure: career path and pay scale, 2018

ICAC pay scale point	Pay scale (per month)	Operations Department	Corruption Prevention Department	Community Relations Department
48	$232,750–$247,050	Head of Operations	Not applicable	Not applicable
47	$199,050–$217,300	Director of Investigations	Director	Director
45–46	$148,400–$187,150	Assistant Directors	Assistant Directors	Assistant Directors
43–44a	$130,775–$140,560	Principal Investigator	Principal Corruption Prevention Officer	Regional Officer
36–42	$97,575–$125,515	Chief Investigator	Chief Corruption Prevention Officer	Deputy Regional Officer
29–35	$72,770–$93,760	Senior Investigator	Senior Corruption Prevention Officer	Senior Community Relations Officer
18–28	$45,035–$70,210	Investigator	Corruption Prevention Officer	Community Relations Officer
4–14	$21,890–$39,045	Assistant Investigator	Not applicable	Assistant Community Relations Officer

Sources: Adapted from ICAC (2018c); Civil Service Bureau (2018)

Note: US$1 = HK$7.80.

more easily than if tenured positions were granted after a successful probationary period, as is the case in the Hong Kong civil service. There is no evidence that the system has caused any major organisational instability or a rapid turnover in personnel. ACAs need stability in their organisations because effective corruption control requires learning on the job. Experience in investigations, knowledge of control systems that help check corruption, ability to produce eye-catching publicity and familiarity with civil society organisations are valuable assets for any ACA but these skills can only be acquired through lengthy exposure to different situations. Over the entire span of its history, the ICAC has been fortunate to retain an able and experienced workforce, well-versed in the many forms that corruption may take and in the ways of preventing it from occurring.

Accountability and integrity

The integrity of employees is critically important for ACAs. Any adverse publicity which suggests that ACA personnel are corrupt or act in unethical ways seriously compromises effectiveness. In the three major cases that have raised public concerns about the ICAC, which we consider below, integrity and accountability have been closely linked. Underlying the relationship between them has been the assumption that organisations which are accountable are more likely to show integrity than those which are not. Since the ICAC has strong discretionary powers, it is not surprising that legislators have asked questions, set up select committees and conducted debates about the Commission's accountability whenever integrity issues have arisen. We consider, first, the meaning attached to accountability and the mechanisms which have been used to try to ensure that the powers exercised by the ICAC are not abused. Second, we examine the cases that have caused concern and the actions taken to resolve contentious issues.

The accountability of the ICAC

The various definitions of accountability have been at the heart of important controversies concerning the ICAC. In its weaker meaning, accountability is sometimes defined as answerability (reporting to), which need not necessarily imply that some subsequent action will be taken (Blatz 1972). In its stronger sense, accountability may mean "responsible to", implying that reforms may be imposed on the subordinate organisation or sanctions on the accountable person by a superior organisation (Schedler 1999; Burns 2004: 157–158). In the case of the ICAC, Article 57 of the Basic Law simply states that it "shall function independently and be accountable to the Chief Executive". The *ICACO*, however, stipulates that the ICAC Commissioner is "subject to the orders and control" of the Chief Executive (Section 5.1) and to no one else and holds office on such terms and conditions as the Chief Executive thinks fit (Section 5.3). These provisions seem to contradict Article 57 of the Basic Law because the ICAC cannot act independently and also be subject to the direction of the Chief Executive. In practice, the ICAC does act independently, and it would be improper for the Chief Executive to intervene directly in the investigation of any case. It would be even more improper if the matter concerned the Chief Executive himself, as was alleged in the Rebecca Li Bo-lan case (Yiu 2017).

Aside from the Chief Executive, there are other accountability mechanisms which are designed to check on the ICAC's performance and to make suggestions for improving corruption control. A code of ethics requires that ICAC officers should, *inter alia*, uphold the law, adhere to the principles of integrity and fair play, and carry out their duties without fear or favour, prejudice or ill will and maintain confidentiality (ICAC 2018e). The ICAC also has a system of advisory committees, drawing their unofficial membership from government, business and the community. The advisory committee for the ICAC as a whole is composed of six external members, the three heads of the advisory committees of the ICAC departments and three ICAC officials. The Committee reports annually to the Chief Executive on the state of corruption and, if necessary, makes recommendations or reports its views on matters affecting the Commission (ICAC 2018f: 8).

There is also an advisory committee for each of the ICAC departments which also report to the Chief Executive. The Operations Review Committee monitors the handling of major investigations, cases under investigation for over twelve months and persons on ICAC bail for over six months. The Committee is composed of sixteen members drawn largely from the community but including the Secretary of Justice and the Commissioner of Police or their representatives and an ICAC official. The Head of the OD is not a member but is always invited to the meeting. The Committee has a wide remit including the right to draw the Chief Executive's attention to any aspect of the work of the OD that requires remedial action.

The CRD's Citizens' Advisory Committee has seventeen members, including the ICAC Commissioner *ex officio*, and comprises two sub-committees which focus respectively on its publicity and the media role and on its preventive education and public engagement role (ICAC 2018f: 37). The CPD's Advisory Committee is composed of twelve professional members with qualifications in such fields as accountancy, medicine, insurance and quantity surveying, and three official members. The Committee considers recommendations arising from CPD assignments and monitors their implementation (ICAC 2018f: 23).

The ICAC points to the advisory committees as evidence of "checks and balances" on its work (ICAC 2017b). The majority of the unofficial members are drawn from business and the professions, while the remainder are former civil servants, academics and Legislative Councillors. They are respected figures in the community, and it is their reputations rather than their representativeness which provides assurance that matters of probity or failure to observe the rules will be taken seriously. By themselves, the committees are insufficient to meet demands for more transparency in the ICAC's work which has been a particular concern of the pan-democrats in the Legislative Council.

The Legislative Council, the courts and the media are usually alert to serious problems relating to a perceived lack of integrity in the Commission or to issues which they think need investigation. The relationship between the Council and the ICAC is not based on a constitutional requirement of accountability but rather on a convention that the Commission should periodically report on the state of corruption and what is being done to prevent it. At various times, the Council has pressed for greater answerability although both the executive and the ICAC itself have been reluctant to go beyond the present arrangements. In common with the government's disciplined services, the ICAC reports to the Legislative Council's Panel on Security which meets regularly with the Commissioner and senior officers. The principal purpose of the meetings is to review the current corruption scene and for the Commissioner to alert the Panel to new ICAC initiatives. The Panel on Security has a large remit and it does not have the resources or the time to undertake detailed scrutiny of what the ICAC is doing unless there is a specific issue which needs to be investigated such as the Tsui case (see below). The Legislative Council as a whole has taken up issues relating to the ICAC when civil liberties issues have been involved or when there have been suspected scandals involving the Commission.

The ICAC is also subject to the provisions of the *Interception of Communications and Surveillance Ordinance* (Cap 589). Prior to 2006, the courts expressed some concern about invasions of privacy and the ICAC's cavalier use of wire-tapping (Young 2013). In 2006, the new ordinance required that any law-enforcement agency, including the ICAC, would have to seek permission in writing from a panel judge to conduct interception or surveillance other than audible conversations or other direct observations of a targeted person (Hong Kong Government 2016: 7–8). The Office of Commissioner on Interception and Surveillance is charged with overseeing the compliance of the four law-enforcement agencies with the ordinance. According to the Commissioner, the agencies have become "careless or not vigilant enough" about meeting the requirements of the ordinance (Legislative Council, Panel on Security 2017: 11). Whether this applies to the ICAC is not clear because the Commissioner's report does not distinguish between the law-enforcement agencies. It is clear, however, that the *POBO* offence of offering and accepting an advantage in both the public and private sectors and the common law offence of misconduct in public office constitute major categories of applications to panel judges for surveillance permission (Hong Kong Government 2017: 69).

The courts have provided an important check on the work of the ICAC, particularly on how its powers and the laws on corruption are to be interpreted and how it collects evidence for prosecutions. Shortly before 1997, the courts expressed concerns about the ICAC's violation of the rule of law in deliberate breaches of the right to confidential legal advice, a concern which has again been recently raised by the Commissioner on Interception and Surveillance (Hong Kong Government 2017: 32–45). There has also been concern about coaching of witnesses (Young 2013). Court cases serve to establish the boundaries of what the ICAC can and cannot do and, in that respect, help hold it accountable.

Finally, the media has had a consuming interest in the work of the ICAC and in corruption in general. This is important dimension of accountability and, in addition, helps reduce corruption. In a study of 157 countries, Starke *et al* (2016) found that corruption was significantly reduced in those countries which had a free media. In Hong Kong, some important incidents, such as the transgressions of the former Chief Executive, Donald Tsang Yam-kuen, have been revealed by the press. Although there are justifiable concerns over the future of a free media in Hong Kong, there are still usually full reports on all major accountability and integrity cases including those to which we now turn.

The Tsui case and civil liberties

In 1991, in the wake of the Tiananmen Square protests, the Legislative Council passed a Bill of Rights which provided that the International Covenant on Civil and Political Liberties should become part of Hong Kong law. The passage of the *Hong Kong Bill of Rights Ordinance* was an important milestone amid increasing concern that civil liberties might be violated after the resumption of Chinese sovereignty in 1997. The ICAC came under scrutiny because some of its own provisions were potentially in conflict with the provisions of the ordinance (Ng 1992; Cook Liu 1992).

At the end of 1993, the ICAC Commissioner, acting under the Section 8(2) of the *ICACO*, dismissed Alex Tsui Ka-kit, the Senior Assistant Director of the OD, without, as he was entitled to do, giving an explanation (Legislative Council

1994: 1). Legislative Councillors wanted to understand what had happened, especially since Tsui, who was the most senior Chinese officer in the ICAC, alleged that he was a victim of racial discrimination. On the grounds that the anti-corruption legislation did not excuse the ICAC from public accountability, Legislative Councillors voted against the government to set up a Panel on Security investigation into the case (Hong Kong Hansard 1993: 1195). The Panel found that the Commissioner was justified in dismissing Tsui because he had associated with people of dubious moral character which led to a loss of confidence in his integrity (Legislative Council 1994: 24; Chan 1997: 114–117). The Panel also pointed out, however, the importance of the government's (and implicitly the ICAC's) accountability and regretted that it had not provided "a timely explanation of the dismissal" (Legislative Council 1994: 25).

There remained concerns about the powers of the ICAC which one Legislative Councillor described as "anachronistic" (Hong Kong Hansard 1994: 2128). In January 1994, a Legislative Councillor, Christine Loh, introduced a motion calling on the government (subsequently amended to "a broad-based committee") to conduct a review of the powers of the ICAC "to ensure that there is proper public accountability, taking into consideration any changes in social circumstances which may have taken place in Hong Kong since its establishment" (Hong Kong Hansard 1994: 2121). The government then announced that it would set up an independent committee to recommend whether the ICAC's powers and system of accountability needed to be modified.

The Review Committee did not recommend radical changes. Rather, it sought to improve communication with the Legislative Council and the police and to strengthen the advisory committee system. It considered whether the Commission's powers to obtain information were too wide and recommended that the *POBO* should be amended to provide greater protection for the innocent during ICAC investigations (Independent Review Committee 1994: 49–50). It believed that the Commissioner's direct accountability to the Governor should be retained but preferred that the courts rather than the Commissioner should approve the use of some powers. The Committee also raised the possibility of stricter controls on electronic surveillance. Other proposed measures were that the Commission should exercise its powers only in relation to corruption offences and not include other criminal matters (Independent Review Committee 1994: 105). The Committee also thought that the Commissioner should retain the power to dismiss ICAC staff but that reasons should be given for termination and that the officers concerned should have an opportunity to state their cases (Independent Review Committee 1994: 94–95). In 1996, amendments were made to the ordinance to permit the press to report cases that were being investigated and to repeal Section 25 of the *POBO* which had been superceded by the *Hong Kong Bill of Rights Ordinance* and Section 26, which was no longer thought to be useful (see also p. 96). As Lo and Yu (2000) remark, the amendments had no negative impact on the ICAC's effectiveness and may even have helped increase its legitimacy.

The Tsui case brought the issue of the ICAC's powers and accountability to public debate for the first time. By 1996, opinion on what these powers should be was much more divided than it had been two decades before. There was an informed community which, while it did not want to diminish the role of the ICAC, was concerned that its powers should not be exercised at the expense of civil liberties and that it should be accountable for any errors or infringements of the law.

The Tong case

Timothy Tong Hin-ming was the ICAC Commissioner between 2007 and 2012. In March 2013, the Director of Audit noted irregularities in two official dinners which he had hosted as Commissioner and recommended that the ICAC should tighten its financial control on entertainment (Director of Audit 2013: 51). Over the next month, there were many more media reports of excessive expenditure on gifts and duty trips and some twenty receptions for Chinese liaison officials (Cheung *et al* 2013). Lam Cheuk-ting, a former ICAC officer, lodged a complaint with the Commission, alleging misconduct and possible breach of the *POBO*. In May 2013, the government appointed an independent committee to investigate and review ICAC expenditure and practices on entertainment, gifts and duty visits (Independent Review Committee 2013). The ICAC itself set up an Internal Audit Unit under the CPD to investigate the charges. The Legislative Council set up a Select Committee and also considered the issues raised by the Director of Audit in the Public Accounts Committee (Legislative Council 2013; Legislative Council 2014).

The Independent Review Committee was mainly concerned with building a more robust financial control system (Independent Review Committee 2013: 50–53). The Public Accounts Committee and the Select Committee, in contrast, sought to hold Tong to account. They found that expenditure on 37 per cent of the 206 official lunches and dinners had exceeded the official limit, that there had also been over-spending on hard liquor and gifts, and that Tong had made 35 overseas duty trips during his tenure as Commissioner amounting to a total of 146 days of his time in office (Legislative Council 2013: 67, 76; Legislative Council 2014: 30–45, 66–78). The Public Accounts Committee concluded that Tong had tarnished the image of Hong Kong and the ICAC's reputation and credibility and undermined the effectiveness of the work of the CRD by using its funds for entertainment and gifts (Legislative Council 2013: 76). The Select Committee reiterated those points and went further claiming that Tong had used entertainment as a means to further his post-ICAC career and that his "unduly close contact with Mainland officials would shake confidence in the impartiality of himself as Commissioner of the ICAC" (Legislative Council 2014: para 8, 99–100).

Tong said that he was an honest man and claimed that over-spending "was not a sin" (Chong 2014). The Select Committee thought that he was an evasive witness and that he might be charged with misconduct in public office, but the Secretary for Justice, on legal advice from the Director of Public Prosecutions, said that there was no evidence of a corrupt motive and no charges were laid (Lee *et al* 2016). The combined efforts of the Director of Audit, the Public

Accounts Committee and the Select Committee tightened the ICAC's financial control system, but morale in the Commission and public confidence were less easily restored. Corruption reports, excluding election reports, fell by nearly 40 per cent from 3932 in 2012 to 2362 in 2014 (ICAC 2013: 14, 2015a: 36). The Tong case shows that the external accountability mechanisms – in this case, the Director of Audit, the press and the Legislative Council – were in place although it took some time before the case came to light.

The Li case

In July 2016, the ICAC Commissioner, Simon Peh Yun-lu, reverted the Acting Head of the OD, Rebecca Li Bo-lan, to her substantive position of Assistant Director. Immediately after her reversion, Li, who was a well-respected officer of high integrity, promptly resigned. Another senior investigator soon followed her and 70 per cent of the ICAC staff were reported to have boycotted an annual dinner (Tse and Pankhurst 2016). Ricky Lau, later to succeed Li as Acting Head of the OD, initially resigned but later rescinded his resignation (ICAC Post 2016). The suspicion, repeatedly expressed in the Legislative Council, was that Peh had acted at the behest of the Chief Executive, Leung Chun-ying, because Li had been heading an investigation into Leung's relationship with the Australian firm UGL (Chan 2016; Forsythe 2016; *Ming Pao* 2016; see p. 64). The ICAC Commissioner said that the decision had been made on the basis of her performance and the Chief Executive denied that he played any part in making the decision (Ng 2016; Siu 2016).

The Li case resulted in sharp reactions within the community amid concerns that if political interference were proven, it would ham-string the ICAC and undermine its independence with serious consequences for Hong Kong (Ewing 2016). The veteran democrat Emily Lau, for example, said that "If the ICAC is finished, Hong Kong is also finished" (Forsythe 2016). In the Legislative Council, the democrats, as they had done in the Tong case, tabled a motion to set up a select committee to investigate the circumstances surrounding Li's resignation. Their case revolved around whether there was a link between Li's reversion to her substantive position and the ICAC's investigation of Leung's involvement with UGL. There was no immediate evidence to support the link but the democrats argued that, in the interests of the future impartiality and effectiveness of the ICAC, the matter should be clarified and resolved (Hong Kong Hansard 9 November 2016: 351ff). On the government side, the Chief Secretary for Administration, Carrie Lam Yuet-ngor, later to succeed Leung as Chief Executive, argued that Li's reversion was purely a personnel matter on which the Commissioner had every right to decide (Hong Kong Hansard 9 November 2016: 357). After two days of heated debate, in which there were calls for the ICAC to be removed from the Chief Executive's control, the motion to set up a select committee was voted down (Hong Kong Hansard 10 November 2016: 539). A committee of investigation was later set up but, as it had no powers to order witnesses to attend its hearings, it did not make much progress.

There were similarities in the Tsui and the Li cases. In both cases, personnel matters, conducted with limited transparency, took on another life when they were linked with wider political issues. In the Tsui case, possible political implications of the transfer of sovereignty were evident in the Legislative Council's attempts to make the ICAC more accountable. In the Li case, it was difficult for the ICAC to respond to the various allegations without compromising its own investigative processes. But by not saying very much, it tended to fuel conspiracy theories. However, even though both the Tsui and Li cases generated considerable political heat and much interest from the media, they did not noticeably affect public support for the ICAC. The institutionalisation of the ICAC's structures and processes may have helped build social trust to the point where there was confidence that the Commission had taken the right course of action. The Tong case was rather different. He was an ex-Commissioner and the evidence of over-spending did not sit well with the ICAC's image of probity. Tong's excessive expenditure and an inadequate financial control system seem to have been the cause of a sharp drop in corruption reports, usually taken as a proxy for confidence in the Commission. In this case, the public seems to have taken the integrity of the ICAC itself as the issue at stake, whereas the Tsui and Li cases were largely regarded as internal personnel issues.

The cases that we have considered were aberrations but they serve to show that issues of accountability and integrity are never far away when contentious politics meets powerful organisations. The ICAC, constrained by the confidentiality of its processes and unwilling to enter the political arena, has had difficulty in defending itself when such issues emerge. Wherever possible, it is important that ACAs remain above politics, because once they are dragged into the maelstrom, their own impartiality and integrity are likely to be called into question. Even successful ACAs need strong political support at such times, but clearly it is best that problems should be avoided by having effective accountability mechanisms at work in the first place.

Over the course of its history, concerns about the integrity of the ICAC have been rare. ICAC surveys have consistently shown that the public has respect for its impartiality and does not believe that officers abuse their powers. The organisational structure has been fit for purpose and the checks and balances, both internal and external, have worked well to ensure that the pursuit of the corrupt is generally not conducted with a disregard for the law and the rights of citizens.

References

Blatz, Charles V. (1972) "Accountability and answerability", *Journal for the Theory of Social Behaviour*, 2(2): 101–120.

Burns, John P. (2004) *Government capacity and the Hong Kong civil service*. Hong Kong: Oxford University Press.

Chan, Anson (2016) "ICAC: We must keep our advantage", *Voice of Hong Kong*, 16 August, www.vohk.hk/2016/08/15/icac-we-must-keep-our-advantage.

Chan, Kin-man (1997) "Combating corruption and the ICAC" in Joseph Y.S. Cheng (ed.) *The other Hong Kong report, 1997*. Hong Kong: The Chinese University Press: 101–121.

Chan, Thomas (2001) "Corruption prevention-the Hong Kong experience", *UNA-FEI, Resource material series No. 56*, 365–377, www.unafei.or.jp/publications/Resource_Material_56.htm.

Cheung, Simpson, Johnny Tam and Colleen Lee (2013) "Ex-ICAC boss faces graft probe for allegedly dining out on public money", *South China Morning Post*, 26 April, www.scmp.com/news/hong-kong/article/1223227/ex-icac-boss-faces-graft-probe-allegedly-dining-out-public-money.

Chong, Tanna (2014) "Overspending 'was not a sin', Timothy Tong Hin-ming tells select committee", *South China Morning Post*, 26 January, www.scmp.com/news/hong-kong/article/1413780/overspending-was-not-sin-timothy-tong-hin-ming-tells-select-committee.

Civil Service Bureau (2018) "Independent Commission Against Corruption pay scale", www.csb.gov.hk/print/english/admin/pay/54.html.

Cook Liu, Bernadette Sau-fong (1992) *Civil liberties and the ICAC: An evaluative study*. Unpublished M. Soc. Sc. dissertation, Department of Political Science, University of Hong Kong.

Director of Audit (2013) "Report No. 60 – Chapter 7", www.gov.hk.

Elections (Corrupt and Illegal Conduct) Ordinance (ECICO) (Cap 554).

Ewing, Kent (2016) "Decadence and decline at Hong Kong's once proud anti-corruption agency", *Hong Kong Free Press*, 14 July, www.hongkongfp.com/2016/07/14/decadence-and-decline-at-hong-kong-once-proud-anti-corruption-agency/.

Forsythe, Michael (2016) "Hong Kong graft-buster's exit stirs fears over agency independence", *New York Times*, 26 July, www.nytimes.com/2016/07/27/world/asia/hong-kong-corruption-icac-china.html.

Hong Kong Bill of Rights Ordinance (Cap 383).

Hong Kong Government (2016) "Code of practice (issued pursuant to Section 63 of the Interception of Communications and Surveillance Ordinance)", www.sb.gov.hk/eng/special/sciocs/2016/ICSO%20CoP%20-%20June%202016%20(E).pdf.

Hong Kong Government (2017) "Annual report to the Chief Executive by the Commissioner on Interceptions of Communications and Surveillance, 2016", www.info.gov.hk/info/sciocs/en/pdf/Annual_Report_2016.pdf, accessed 17 December.

Hong Kong Hansard 17 October 1973; 1 December 1993; 26 January 1994; 9, 10 November 2016.

ICAC (2008) "Defining and developing an effective code of conduct for organizations", www.hkbedc.icac.hk/english/publications/practical_guides.php.

ICAC (2012) "Business success: Integrity legal compliance: Corruption prevention guide for SMEs in Guangdong, Hong Kong and Macao", www.hkbedc.icac.hk/english/files/publications/1._Eng.pdf.

ICAC (2013) "Annual report 2012", www.icac.org.hk/filemanager/en/content_27/2012.pdf.

ICAC (2015a) "Annual report 2014", www.icac.org.hk/filemanager/en/content_27/2014.pdf.

ICAC (2015b) "40 years in the Operations Department (1974–2014): Fighting corruption with the community", www.icac.org.hk/filemanager/en/content_28/ops2014.pdf.

ICAC (2015c) "Integrity and corruption prevention guide on managing relationships with public servants", www.icac.org.hk/filemanager/en/Content_216/ps.pdf.

ICAC (2015d) *Vacancy for Assistant Commission Against Corruption Officer (Ref. 1/2015)*. Hong Kong: mimeo.

ICAC (2017a) "Annual report 2016", www.icac.org.hk/filemanager/en/content_27/2016.pdf.

ICAC (2017b) "Checks and balances", www.icac.org.hk/en/check/balance/index. html.

ICAC (2018a) "Annual report 2017", www.icac.org.hk/filemanager/en/content_ 27/2016.pdf.

ICAC (2018b) "Annual survey 2017", www.icac.org.hk/filemanager/en/content_ 176/survey2017.pdf.

ICAC (2018c) "Career in ICAC", www.icac.org.hk/en/job/grade/index.html.

ICAC (2018d) "Corruption prevention advisory service", https://cpas.icac.hk/ EN/.

ICAC (2018e) "Mission and pledges", www.icac.org.hk/en/about/mission/index. html.

ICAC (2018f) "Reports of ICAC advisory committees", www.icac.org.hk/fileman ager/en/content_27/2017.pdf.

ICAC (n.d.) "Hong Kong business ethics development centre", www.hkbedc.icac.hk.

ICAC Post (2016) "Interview with Acting Head of Operations", October, www.icac. org.hk/en/resource/post/index.html.

ICAC Regional Office (2017) "Hong Kong West/Islands work plan, 2017–2018", www. districtcouncils.gov.hk/island/doc/2016_209/en/committee_meetings_doc/ CACRC/11475/CACRC_2017_25_EN.pdf.

Independent Review Committee (1994) *Report of the ICAC review committee*. Hong Kong: Government Printer.

Independent Review Committee (2013) "Report of the Independent Review Committee on ICAC's regulatory systems and procedures for handling official entertainment, gifts and duty visits", www.gov.hk.

Interception of Communications and Surveillance Ordinance (Cap 589).

Ko, Ernie, Yu-chang Su and Chilik Yu (2015) "Sibling rivalry among anti-corruption agencies in Taiwan: Is redundancy doomed to failure?" *Asian Education and Development Studies*, 4(1): 101–124.

Lau, Chris (2017) "How a small team of graft-busters tightened the net in Hong Kong's most explosive corruption case", *South China Morning Post*, 7 August, www. scmp.com/news/hong-kong/law-crime/article/2105628/how-small-team-graft-busters-tightened-net-hong-kongs-most.

Lee, Eddie, Stuart Lau and Chris Lau (2016) "Former Hong Kong anti-corruption commissioner Timothy Tong Hin-ming to face no further criminal probe", *South China Morning Post*, 27 January, www.scmp.com/news/hong-kong/law-crime/ article/1905876/former-hong-kong-anti-corruption-commissioner-timothy-tong.

Legislative Council (2014) "Report on matters relating to Mr Timothy Tong's duty visits, entertainment, and bestowing and receipt of gifts during his tenure as Commissioner of the Independent Commission Against Corruption, Hong Kong", www.gov.hk.

Legislative Council, Panel on Security (1994) *Enquiry into the circumstances surrounding the termination of the employment of Mr. Alex Tsui Ka-kit, former Senior Assistant Director of the Independent Commission Against Corruption*. Hong Kong: mimeo.

Legislative Council, Panel on Security (2017) "Report of the Panel on Security", www. legco.gov.hk/yr16-17/english/panels/se/reports/se20170705cb2-1752-e.pdf.

Legislative Council, Public Accounts Committee (2013) "Report 60A-part 4: Preventive education and enlisting public support against corruption", www.legco.gov. hk/yr12-13/english/pac/reports/60a/60a_rpt.pdf.

Legislative Council Secretariat (2017) "Information note: The UGL incident", 23 February, www.legco.gov.hk/research-publications/english/1617in03-the-ugl-incident-20170223-e.pdf.

Lo, T. Wing and Ricky C.C. Yu (2000) "Curbing draconian powers: The effects on Hong Kong's graft-fighter", *The International Journal of Human Rights*, 4(1): 54–73.

Ming Pao (2016) "ICAC earthquake: The only reason for Rebecca Li-Bo-lan's resignation", *Ming Pao*, 14 July, https://news.mingpao.com/ins/instantnews/web_tc/article/20160714/s00022/1468455919832.

Mok, W.H. (n.d.) "Corruption prevention in public organizations–the Hong Kong experience", http://unpan1.un.org/intradoc/groups/public/documents/un-dpadm/unpan049657.pdf.

Ng, Joyce (2016) "ICAC chief claims he alone, and not C.Y. Leung, made decision to remove deputy", *South China Morning Post*, 16 July, www.scmp.com/news/hong-kong/law-crime/article/1988466/icac-chief-claims-he-alone-and-not-cy-leung-made-decision.

Ng, Margaret (1992) "ICAC powers: Is it time to look at the investigators?" *South China Morning Post*, 23 February.

Quah, Jon S.T. (2017) "Learning from Singapore's effective anti-corruption strategy: Policy recommendations for South Korea", *Asian Education and Development Studies*, 6(1): 17–29.

Schedler, Andreas (1999) "Conceptualising accountability" in Andreas Schedler, Larry Diamond and Marc F. Plattner (eds.) *The self-restraining state: Power and accountability in new democracies*. Boulder, CO: Lynne Reiner: 13–28.

Scott, Ian (2013) "Engaging the public: Hong Kong's Independent Commission Against Corruption's Community relations strategy" in Jon S.T. Quah (ed.) *Different paths to curbing corruption: Lessons from Denmark, Finland, Hong Kong, New Zealand and Singapore*. Bingley: Emerald: 79–108.

Siu, Phila (2016) "C.Y. Leung insists he did not take any part in decision-making to remove ICAC's Rebecca Li", *South China Morning Post*, 12 July, www.scmp.com/news/hong-kong/law-crime/article/1988806/cy-leung-insists-he-did-not-take-any-part-decision-making.

Starke, Christopher, Teresa K. Naab and Helmut Scherer (2016) "Free to expose corruption: The impact of media, internet access and government online service delivery on corruption", *Journal of International Communication*, 10: 4702–4722.

Tse, Crystal and Paul Pankhurst (2016) "Graft-busters' dinner plans touch a nerve in anxious Hong Kong", *Bloomberg*, 15 July, www.bloomberg.com/news/articles/2016-07-15/graft-busters-dinner-plans-touch-a-nerve-in-anxious-hong-kong.

Yau, Ching Man (2017) "ICAC recruits: Tips for interviews written tests and physical assessment of assistant investigative officers; most important is integrity", *Hong Kong 01*, 12 December, www.hk01.com/article/140251.

Yeung, Chun Kuen and Lee Jark Pui (2007) "Report of the Commission of Inquiry on allegations relating to the Hong Kong Institute of Education", www.commissionofinquiry.gov.hk/pdf/Commission%20Report_e.pdf.

Yiu, Enoch (2017) "ICAC's former operations head joins private investigative firm", *South China Morning Post*, 3 April, www.scmp.com/business/companies/article/2084165/icacs-former-acting-operations-head-joins-private-investigative.

Young, Simon N.M. (2013) "Prosecuting bribery in Hong Kong's human rights environment" in Jeremy Horder and Peter Alldridge (eds.) *Modern bribery law*. Cambridge: Cambridge University Press: 267–293.

6   Enforcing the law

The institutionalisation of ACAs is critically dependent on the enforcement of effective anti-corruption laws and the perception that the agency is making a significant difference. Yet the speed with which the corrupt can seize upon new opportunities and exploit loopholes in the law generally means that legislation lags behind changes in the type and level of corruption. Effective anti-corruption laws are consequently continual works-in-progress. Ideally, if the law were appropriate for the corruption offences being committed, if the penalties did serve as deterrents, if citizens were fully aware of what the law meant, and if there was evidence that the corrupt were being caught and justly punished, there would be no need for debate because the corruption laws would be fit for purpose. In practice, to achieve any one of these goals is difficult and to ensure that they are synchronised with each other is even more problematic. Still, the ideals of a compliance-based integrity system are goals which every successful ACA must aspire to achieve. If an ACA's anti-corruption enforcement is not effective, the chances of its institutionalisation are remote.

In Hong Kong, the anti-corruption laws were mostly ineffectual until the 1970s. The law did not adequately cover the scope of the offence, the prescribed penalties were not a deterrent, the public were not sufficiently informed of the nature of the offence and the corrupt quite frequently escaped punishment (see Ch. 2). The *POBO* did not entirely resolve these problems and required further amendment, but it was a considerable improvement over previous anti-corruption laws. Other legislation, the *ICACO*, was introduced to supplement the *POBO* and new functions were added with the passage of the *Elections (Corrupt and Illegal Conduct) Ordinance (ECICO)* in 2000. As the nature of corruption in Hong Kong changed so, too, did the nature of the offence. More use was made of the common law offence of misconduct in public office which was gradually developed into an effective tool for combating serious conflicts of interest. In this chapter, we examine the evolution of the anti-corruption laws in Hong Kong against the background of survey evidence on public knowledge of the legislation and efforts to sustain the integrity of a process which attempted to bring the corrupt to book from initial corruption report to conviction in the courts.

Statutory offences and forms of corruption

The effect of the *POBO* and the *ICACO* on changes in the forms of corruption over time appears to have been substantial. We cannot conclude, however, that the enforcement of the ordinances was the sole reason for the sharp decline in bribery offences, the emergence of a clean public service or the shift to less easily detectable forms of corruption. The efforts of the CRD to change social attitudes through effective publicity and on-the-ground liaison work were also important. In the public sector, the CPD's recommendations resulted in tighter corruption-proof control systems. What the *POBO* and the *ICACO* did achieve was to link the statutory offences with bribery, the then-prevalent type of corruption, and to provide sufficient deterrents to discourage any potential future offenders who might be tempted to solicit, offer or accept bribes. Backing the legislation were efficient investigators armed with strong powers to uncover malfeasance.

The decline in bribery offences

The principal offences listed in the *POBO* relate to the solicitation or acceptance of an advantage without permission of the Chief Executive in the public sector or the principal in the private sector (Sections 3, 4.1 and 9.2). Offering any advantage to a public servant to perform or not to perform public duties and offering bribes to aid or hinder business transactions are equally culpable offences (Sections 4.1, 8 and 9.2). The offences of soliciting or accepting or of offering bribes constituted by far the greatest number of prosecutions in the early years of the ICAC. For example, in 1974, 81 of 108 prosecutions and, in 1975, 136 of 218 prosecutions were directly concerned with bribery (ICAC 1975: Appendix XIV; ICAC 1976: Appendix: XIV). Gradually, the pattern of prosecutions changed as more of the accused were charged under other offences detected in the course of investigations or under specific offences listed in Section 10(5) of the *ICACO*, such as obstructing and perverting the course of justice, blackmail, theft, fraud, obtaining a pecuniary advantage by deception and conspiracy to commit any of these offences (see Table 6.1).

By 1980, of 509 prosecutions, 184 were for bribery offences, 181 were offences listed under Section 10(5) of the *ICACO* and 125 were other offences detected in the course of investigations (ICAC 1981: Appendix XVI). Prosecutions under *ICACO* offences reflected the beginning of a shift away from bribery but it is also probable that investigators and prosecutors were seeking convictions and would look for charges that were most likely to succeed in the courts. The novel *POBO* offence of possessing unexplained assets (Section 10), for example, was not much used after the 1970s, which may reflect better concealment on the part of the corrupt and/or more certainty of conviction under another charge.

While, for these reasons, it is necessary to be cautious in using prosecutions as the sole indicator of changing patterns of corruption, viewed over the life of the ICAC, they do illustrate some significant changes in the form of corruption.

Table 6.1 Number of persons prosecuted for corruption and related offences, selected years

Offence	1976	1986	1996	2006	2016
Soliciting/accepting a bribe[1]	97(51)[2]	52(10)	75(29)	54(7)	29(1)
Offering a bribe[3]	77(20)	40(34)	87(52)	48(9)	26(0)
Unexplained assets[4]	9(9)	–	–	–	–
Offences connected with or facilitated by corruption[5]	47(11)	75(40)	36(13)	51(19)	20(10)
Offences listed in *ICACO* S.10(5)	18(12)	108(34)	135(28)	161(51)	118(22)
Other (excluding election offences)	11(4)	1(0)	10(0)	27(9)	4(0)
Total	259	276	343	341	197

Sources: Adapted from ICAC (1977): Appendix XIV; ICAC (1987): Appendix 17; ICAC (1997): Appendix 8; ICAC (2007): Appendix 11; 1CAC (2017): Appendix 9

Notes:
[1] *POBO* Sections 3, 4(2), 9(1).
[2] Figures in brackets are public sector prosecutions or private individuals charged with offences concerning government departments.
[3] *POBO* Sections 3, 4(2), 9(1).
[4] *POBO* Sections 4(1), 8, 9(2).
[5] *ICACO* Section 10(2).

By 1986, bribery in government was on the wane. In Table 6.1, the numbers in brackets are public sector prosecutions. After the 1970s, these cases were almost entirely prosecutions of private individuals soliciting or offering a bribe to civil servants rather than civil servants seeking bribes.

Although the figures show an increase in public sector prosecutions in 1996, every one of the fifty-two public sector prosecutions for offering a bribe were charges against private individuals (ICAC 1997: 30). By 2016, even this form of corruption had nearly disappeared from the public sector, although the *POBO* was still used to pursue private sector bribery cases. Corruption offences in the public sector were no longer about simple bribery. They were much more likely to be complex dealings involving other crimes or serious conflicts of interest. Increasingly, corruption in the public sector was prosecuted under Section 10 of the *ICACO* or under the common law offence of misconduct in public office.

Public knowledge of the POBO

Surveys conducted by the ICAC's Community Research Unit in the 1970s and 1980s show significant changes in public attitudes toward bribery and more extensive knowledge of the provisions of the *POBO*. In its first survey in 1977, the Unit found that although 65 per cent of respondents claimed to have heard of the *POBO*, 75 per cent of those did not know its details (ICAC 1979: 22). Since 31 per cent of respondents also believed that ignorance of the law was a reasonable excuse for bribery, this prompted the Unit to recommend that for publicity purposes the law should be reduced to its simple essentials (ICAC 1979: 64). The CRD subsequently focused its publicity on what was not acceptable under the law. By 1990, 82 per cent of respondents had heard of the *POBO* and, although most still claimed not to know its details, 58 per cent got five or more questions correct on an eight-question simplified test (ICAC 1990: 121). By the 1990s, the ICAC annual survey no longer specifically asked questions about the *POBO* but instead asked whether the Commission's powers were too great, too little, or appropriate; in 2009, the last year the question was used, 77 per cent of respondents considered that the powers were appropriate, 2 per cent thought the powers were too large and 12 per cent thought that they were too small (ICAC 2010: XII). Thereafter, the survey used scenarios to ask respondents whether certain actions were ethically acceptable and legal (see Ch. 7).

Powers and penalties

Under the *ICACO* (Section 10A), the Commission's officers have similar powers of arrest and detention to the police force. Originally, the powers of arrest extended only to corruption offences covered under the *POBO* and the *Corrupt and Illegal Practices Ordinance*. In the course of investigations, other offences were often discovered and in February 1976 the *ICACO* was amended to extend the powers of arrest to those offences (Hong Kong Hansard 1976: 463). The *POBO* had already given extensive investigatory powers to the ICAC. On the authorisation of the Commissioner, officers may inspect bank and other financial accounts and documents, obtain tax information, order travel documents to be surrendered, and require any person with knowledge of a suspected corruption case to divulge that knowledge (*POBO* Sections 13, 14 and 17). They may also access all government records, books and other documents relevant to suspected offences in the public service (*ICACO* Section 13(2)). Both the *POBO* (Section 17) and the *ICACO* (Section 10B) provide the Commission with the power to search premises on production of a court warrant. In the courts, the presumption of innocence does not always rest with the defendant. Section 24 of the *POBO* states that "[I]n any proceedings against a person for an offence under this Ordinance, the burden of proving a defence of lawful authority or reasonable excuse shall lie upon the accused". Failure to prove lawful authority for accepting an advantage or inability to explain assets disproportionate to income results in a guilty verdict (McWalters *et al* 2015: 400–402). It is not a defence to show that providing an advantage "is customary in any profession, trade, vocation or calling" (*POBO* Section 19).

Penalties for offences under the *POBO* (Section 12) have gradually risen. In 2017, on conviction on indictment, offences under Sections 5 and 6 (bribery relating to contracts and tenders) and Section 10 (unexplained property) were set at a maximum of HK$1 million fine and ten years imprisonment, with conviction on all other offences leading to sentences of up to seven years and fines of HK$500,000. There are also various offences that relate to the investigation of corruption and related offences under the *ICACO* and to electoral offences under the *ECICO*.

Attempts to amend the POBO

By the 1990s, with the decline in bribery, questions were being asked in the Legislative Council and elsewhere about whether the ICAC needed the considerable powers which had been granted to it (Ng 1992). There were also growing concerns about possible conflicts between the ICAC's powers and the *Hong Kong Bill of Rights Ordinance* (Cap 383), which had been passed in 1991, and the fear of abuse of civil liberties after the handover in 1997. Differences of opinion were clearly apparent in two court cases and in a debate in the Legislative Council (Chan 1997: 112–114; Cheung 1997: 128; Lo and Yu 2000). In 1995, a district court judge ruled that Section 10 of the *POBO* was in conflict with the Bill of Rights. The Court of Appeal overruled the decision, arguing that the offence was necessary in the public interest (*Attorney-General v Hui Kin-hong* 1995). A further challenge was mounted against Section 30 of the *POBO* when the newspaper, *Ming Pao*, was accused of disclosing information on a case under investigation. The newspaper argued that it had not reported the names of the suspects and the Privy Council agreed that it was entitled to report on the investigation although it also found that Section 30 was consistent with the Bill of Rights. In July 1996, the ICAC Commissioner attempted to tighten the legislation to ensure that cases under investigation could not be reported. Legislative Councillors declined to support his proposals and instead supported an amendment allowing the press to report cases where the suspect was not identified (Hong Kong Hansard 1996: 170–202). At the same meeting, the Council debated the recommendations of the review committee on the ICAC's powers arising from the Tsui case (see Ch. 5) and repealed two sections of the *POBO* (Sections 25 and 26) which were thought to have little value (Independent Review Committee 1994: 84; Hong Kong Hansard 1996: 150–170).

The amendments to the *POBO* in 1996 liberalised the provisions under which the ICAC operated, but they did not significantly reduce its powers of investigation or effectiveness. As the ICAC saw it, the reforms promoted "greater transparency and accountability and increased involvement of the courts in the exercise of powers under the legislation" (ICAC 1997: 27). The tension between effective legislation and protection of suspects under the rule of law was evident in the Legislative Council debate but the government's appeal to the importance of stamping out corruption, particularly at a time when corruption reports were rising, overrode any major changes to the investigatory process (Independent Review Committee 1994: 25–29; Hong Kong Hansard 1996: 184–185).

In the period under the Tsang and Leung administrations (2005–2017), the major issue relating to the amendment of the *POBO* was the inclusion of the Chief Executive under Sections 3 and 8 (see pp. 62–63). The government refused to amend Sections 3 and 8, arguing that the Chief Executive was already liable to prosecution under the common law offence of bribery and was subject to Sections 4 and 10 of the *POBO* which had been amended in 2008. Leaving aside the political conflict that resulted (see pp. 64–65), the failure to amend the law to include the Chief Executive left the ICAC with more limited powers of investigation than it may have needed. When the transgressions of the former Chief Executive, Donald Tsang Yam-kuen, were revealed, it was widely observed that had he been a civil servant, he could have been charged under Section 3 of the *POBO*. As it was, in 2015, he was charged on two counts of misconduct in public office (Lau 2015). The investigation took well over three years, possibly because the misconduct in public office charge meant that the ICAC had to use the weaker common law powers of investigation rather than the stronger powers provided under the *POBO*. Leung Chun-ying's promise that reforms, including the amendments of Sections 3 and 8, would be introduced "as soon as possible" after he became Chief Executive never materialised. In 2017, the incoming Chief Executive, Carrie Lam Yuet-ngor, said that she wanted to resolve the problem so that Sections 3 and 8 would be extended to include the Chief Executive (Hong Kong Government 2017: para 29).

Despite the highly contentious debates over the amendments to the *POBO*, the ordinance, coupled with concerted efforts to change public attitudes toward corruption and tighter anti-corruption control systems within government, has been a very effective instrument in achieving what it was originally intended to do. At the outset, its principal purpose was to reduce bribery in the public sector, but the ordinance also covers private sector corruption offences which have become increasingly important over the years. Neoh (2010: 231–232) has calculated that between 1974 and 2007, complaints about corruption in the public sector declined by 65 per cent, from 2745 to 975 complaints, while complaints about private sector corruption increased by 471 per cent from 416 to 2376. By 2017, public sector complaints had dropped even further to 950 reports, but there had also been a decline in private sector corruption complaints to 1885 (ICAC 2018: Table 4.1). The *POBO* continues to be central to the anti-corruption effort in Hong Kong, remaining relevant for the pursuit of private sector corruption and as the locus of the powers which are necessary for the ICAC to pursue its investigations. But, by the end of the 1990s, corruption in the public sector had shifted away from simple bribery. Much more sophisticated forms of corruption required the development of new legal weapons to which we now turn.

Misconduct in public office

Misconduct in public office is a common law offence which has been used for centuries in England to prosecute those who fail to perform their official duties, alter records or abuse their powers. In 1979, Lord Widgery laid down conditions under which misconduct in public office could be regarded either as an act of commission or of omission (*R v Dytham* 1979), but there has been much subsequent legal argument about the nature of the offence (Lusty 2014). Hong Kong prosecutors began to use misconduct in public office for corruption offences from 1998 onward in cases, which were thought unlikely to lead to convictions under the *POBO*. The first three cases resulted in acquittals or in the case being withdrawn, but thereafter there were some successful and legally important prosecutions involving serious conflicts of interest.

The first major case of misconduct in public office which secured a conviction was that of Shum Kwok-sher, the government's Chief Property Manager (*Shum Kwok-sher v HKSAR* 2002; McWalters *et al* 2015: 673–676). He was accused of awarding contracts worth more than HK$150 million to companies controlled by relatives (for further details of the offences committed, see p. 184). The prosecutors evidently felt that it would be difficult to show that Shum himself had received an advantage and prosecuted him under the misconduct in public office offence rather than the provisions of the *POBO*. On appeal, his defence lawyers made a case for regarding misconduct in public office as an invalid offence because it was not part of the common law and was inconsistent with rights guaranteed under the *Hong Kong Bill of Rights Ordinance*. The Court of Final Appeal judges rejected this defence and went on to observe that

> the receipt of a bribe or an advantage is not an essential ingredient of corruption in the broad and general sense. A deviation from fidelity in the discharge of a person's duty can amount to corruption.
>
> (*Shum Kwok-sher v HKSAR* 2002)

The Court also sought to clarify further the nature of the offence. Sir Anthony Mason said that misconduct in public office occurs when "(1) a public official; (2) who in the course of or in relation to his public office; (3) wilfully and intentionally; (4) culpably misconducts himself" (*Shum Kwok-sher v HKSAR* 2002). The Shum case extended misconduct in public office to include cases where there was an improper motive: that the accused intended the consequences that resulted and was therefore guilty of an act of commission, not simply of omission (McWalters *et al* 2015: 675–676). In *Sin Kam-wah and Another* v *HKSAR* 2005, the Court of Final Appeal further defined the nature of the offence, noting that the misconduct must be "serious, not trivial, having regard to the responsibilities of the office and the officeholder, the importance of the public objects which they serve and the nature and extent of the departure from these responsibilities".

Armed with these new powers, the Director of Public Prosecutions laid some forty-three charges of misconduct in public office in thirty-nine cases between 1998 and 2010. Of the forty-three persons who were prosecuted, thirty were convicted. There were nine acquittals; two cases were withdrawn; and in two other cases no evidence was offered. The prosecutions covered different kinds of transgressions. The largest number were concerned with contracts and procurements (seventeen prosecutions) and law enforcement (eight prosecutions). Most of those prosecuted were civil servants, although eleven other public officers, including three Legislative and District Councillors, were also charged. While the prosecutions show a rise in serious conflicts of interest, it should be noted that the civil service was engaged in much more outsourcing of contracts in the 2000s than previously, which provided more opportunities for corrupt practices (Scott and Leung 2012).

The offence had a potentially very wide application, and civil servants were concerned that they might not know if they were committing a corruption offence (Scott and Leung 2012). In *HKSAR v Ho Mi-mi and Cheng Sai-man*, two Education Officers split a contract – unacceptable under the civil service regulations – to complete a job on time. Although the judge recognised that they had no improper motive, that no corruption was involved, that they had blameless previous records and that the contract had been completed on time, the accused were nonetheless found guilty of the offence and received a suspended sentence. In a similar case, a public officer attempted to bend the rules to increase the salary of two contract staff by making additional payments into their relatives' bank accounts (*HKSAR v Tsang Yip-fat* 2002). The judge took the view that there had been a serious infringement of the rules and, although there was no benefit to Tsang personally, he was sentenced to a suspended sentence of four months' imprisonment.

It was clearly unsatisfactory to use the offence both for violations of civil service regulations where no corrupt motive was involved and for serious conflict of interests in which corrupt motives were evident. The issue first came before the courts in 2010 in the case of *HKSAR v Wong Lin Kay*. On appeal, a judge dismissed a charge of misconduct in public office against a driver in the Agricultural and Fisheries Department who had failed to inform the department that he had lost his licence as a result of a drink driving charge. The judge found that the driver had been appropriately convicted and sentenced for driving without a licence but dismissed the misconduct in public office charge. His reasoning was that

> defendants charged as public officers . . . were invariably individuals who had some form of authority or power arising from a public trust or duty placed upon them, whereby the exercise of that authority or power directly or indirectly affected the public interest.

In the judge's opinion, the driver was simply a truck driver and did not fall into this category. When the case reached the Court of Final Appeal, Ribeiro PJ agreed with this finding and concluded that the offence

> does not arise merely on the basis of some wrongdoing occurring within the confines of the employer/employee relationship even where the employer is a government or public body. It requires misconduct by a public officer in relation to powers and duties exercisable by him for the public benefit.
>
> (*HKSAR v Wong Lin Kay* 2012)

This served to clarify the offence without robbing the ICAC of a valuable weapon for combating serious conflicts of interest. In the following years, two high-profile public figures, Rafael Hui Si-yan, the former Chief Secretary for Administration and Donald Tsang Yam-kuen, the former Chief Executive, were brought before the courts on misconduct in public office charges (*HKSAR v Rafael Hui Si-yan and Others 2014*; Lau 2015).

There have been suggestions that misconduct in public office should be made a statutory offence, not only in Hong Kong but also in Singapore and in England.

Difficulties of definition have so far posed problems, although in Hong Kong the political climate may also have been unfavourably disposed toward change. The advantage of making misconduct in public office a statutory offence is that it would enable the Commission to use the powers granted to it under the *POBO* and *ICACO*. At present, if the investigation begins as a misconduct in public office offence, then the ICAC cannot use those powers to obtain evidence. Misconduct in public office has been an innovative way of adapting to significant changes in the pattern of corruption in Hong Kong, providing the flexibility in serious conflict of interest cases which the *POBO* does not have. But it may need to be made a statutory offence to increase its effectiveness in conflict of interest corruption cases, which have become increasingly complex in recent years.

Enhancing integrity

The introduction of the offence of misconduct in public office coincided with a Hong Kong government initiative to enhance the integrity of its officers and to address their concerns about the wide scope of the offence. The initiative was also intended as a partial response to the increasing number of corruption reports at the time of the handover. Enhancing the integrity of public servants supplemented the compliance-based approach centred on the *POBO* with more value-based elements. It placed, at least in theory, a greater emphasis on individual responsibility and moral reasoning rather than on reliance on knowledge of the rules which had characterised the approach to corruption prevention until that time (Scott and Leung 2012; Scott 2013a; Brewer *et al* 2015).

In 1998, the Chief Secretary for Administration, Anson Chan, held a conference of her most senior civil servants on the theme of maintaining integrity in the civil service. She spoke of the need for public servants to have shared values – commitment to the rule of law, honesty and integrity above private interests, accountability and openness, political neutrality, impartiality, dedication and diligence – and of the importance of "embedding a culture of probity" in the civil service (Chan 1998). After the conference, corruption was more broadly, if implicitly, defined to extend beyond bribery to include conflicts of interest and unethical behaviour. The role of the ICAC was also expanded to include the positive dimension of promoting integrity in the public service.

In 1999, the government's Civil Service Bureau published *The Civil Servants' Guide to Good Practices*, which stressed the core values laid down by Anson Chan and covered such issues as the acceptance of advantages and entertainment, conflict of interest, post-public employment, upholding integrity and misconduct in public office (Civil Service Bureau 2005). Together with the ICAC, the Civil Service Bureau also subsequently published *Ethical Leadership in Action*, a handbook for senior managers in the public service (ICAC and Civil Service Bureau 2008). It recommended the establishment of integrity promotion committees, headed by a senior civil servant, in each department; stressed the need for junior public servants to be aware of the integrity issues associated with offers of gifts and entertainment, "sweeteners", loans, indebtedness and conflicts of interest; and provided checklists by which managers could identify problems among their staff.

In 2002, with the introduction of an integrity enhancement programme, the Civil Service Bureau and the ICAC began to look at ways in which integrity might be introduced into training programmes. With the exception of the police force, which launched a successful value-based programme in 1996, training had been almost exclusively focused on the evils of corruption and penalties which might be incurred for offences under the *POBO*. It had also been organised centrally by the ICAC and the Civil Service Bureau. The new integrity enhancement programme was delegated to departments which were expected to develop their own integrity training programmes and report to the Civil Service Bureau on an annual basis. A pilot programme on integrity management was organised in public works departments where there were problems in relationships between civil servants and contractors and with tenders and contracts (Legislative Council, Panel on Public Service 2008: 3).

The pilot programme proved successful, and in 2006, the ethical leadership programme was extended to the whole civil service. Ethics Officers are selected from among the directorate-level staff in each bureau and department, and are supported by Assistant Ethics Officers, who are also senior officers and often hold the post of Departmental Secretary. They are the "focal point for all integrity-related activities and . . . [are] responsible for mapping out the strategy and work plan" of the bureaus and departments (Legislative Council, Panel on Public Service 2008: 4) and are required to submit regular reports to the Civil Service Bureau on their integrity management and promotion efforts. They are expected to review corruption prevention assignment studies and future areas which may require attention; to follow up on disciplinary cases when the ICAC refers cases back to the bureaus and departments for potential disciplinary action; to review the department's code on conduct and discipline; to communicate ethical standards to staff; and to review awareness of corruption and the need to avoid conflicts of interest (ICAC and Civil Service Bureau 2008). Although this seems a formidable list, most departmental ethics officers, aside from the police force, which has a permanent branch devoted to integrity management, reported that they spent less than 10 per cent of their time on the ethical leadership programme (Brewer *et al* 2015).

The Ethics Officers discuss their plans at annual departmental or bureau committee meetings at which an ICAC CPD officer is also present. The committee identifies areas in which the CPD will conduct assignment studies, if necessary, and also approves the training programme. Despite the thrust toward including more value-added elements in these programmes, about one-third of departments, especially those with large numbers of junior staff, still concentrate their training programmes almost exclusively on compliance-based issues (Scott 2013a). With the exception of the police force, where there has been a focused effort and considerable resources devoted to enhancing the values of junior officers, most disciplinary departments, such as Correctional Services, Customs, Immigration, and Fire Services, have been primarily concerned with teaching the rules. In the remaining departments, the stress on value-based elements has been mainly directed at middle level and senior staff.

The ethical leadership programme gained impetus in the 2000s from two incidents which increased public interest in ethical standards in government (Scott and Leung 2008). In 2005, Elaine Chung, a former senior civil servant, was implicitly accused of lobbying her former department. She denied the charges and, although her position was eventually accepted, it raised issues in the Legislative Council and in the media about whether the rules were too lenient (Scott and Leung 2008). Three years later, the former Director of Housing, Leung Chin-man, was employed by a property developer with which he had previous contractual dealings when in government. The incident aroused public anger and the Legislative Council set up a select committee to investigate (Legislative Council Select Committee 2010). Although Leung resigned, the issue remained politically contentious. The government was faced with some pressure from its own senior civil servants not to tighten the post-service employment rules. The Civil Service Bureau did widen the conditions under which it would grant permission for civil servants to take up post-service employment, but it also said that former senior civil servants themselves should be aware of the danger of bringing the government into disrepute (Review Committee 2009; Secretary for the Civil Service 2011).

The logical outcome of Anson Chan's belief in the need to identify and promote shared values found expression in the promulgation of a Civil Service Code in 2009 (Civil Service Bureau 2009). The ICAC subsequently advised many departments and public bodies on their own codes which usually begin with the core values and then includes other specific departmental values. Aside from the initial statement of values, the sample codes of conduct tend to be rule-based, focusing on the provisions of the *POBO* and emphasising good behaviour – avoiding acceptance of entertainment, abuse of office, gambling and indebtedness (ICAC Corruption Prevention Department 2014). Both the CPD and the Hong Kong Business Ethics Development Centre also offer free advice to business organisations on the development of codes of ethics and other corruption prevention issues (ICAC n.d.; ICAC Hong Kong Business Ethics Development Centre 2017).

The ICAC has undertaken a considerable amount of work in alerting civil servants to the dangers of misconduct in public office. In 2017, its website listed seventeen publications relating to conflicts of interest, financial management, codes of conduct, integrity management and good governance (ICAC and Civil Service Bureau 2017). In addition, it provided seminars and training videos which warn of the dangers of "sweeteners", nepotism in awarding contracts and deferred advantages (ICAC n.d.; Gong and Scott 2015). Over the past two decades, there can be little doubt that civil servants have been much more exposed to value dilemmas than they were previously. Yet the material is still presented within a predominantly rule-based framework in which individual moral reasoning on ethical issues is not strongly encouraged (Brewer *et al* 2015). The Civil Service Code (Civil Service Bureau 2009: para 3.4), for example, specifies that if civil servants think that they have conflicts of interest, their first action should be to contact a superior officer who then takes responsibility for reaching a decision on what should be done. The consequence is that civil servants mostly remain under organisational protection if they follow procedures on ethical issues and, as some ICAC investigations have shown, may only face misconduct in public office investigations if they have clearly not complied with those procedures (Fung and Wong 2014).

The integrity of the system

At every stage in the process from investigation to prosecution, the public should have confidence in the integrity and impartiality of the ACA and of the criminal justice system. In Hong Kong, the process follows well-established procedures, which begins when the OD receives a corruption report, decides whether the complaint is pursuable and, if so, investigates. If it considers that there is sufficient evidence to warrant a prosecution, the evidence is then passed to the Director of Public Prosecutions who in turn makes a judgement on whether the prosecution should be initiated. The permission of the Secretary for Justice is then required for prosecutions under the *POBO* (Section 31), although arrests may be made without the consent of the Secretary provided that subsequent approval is obtained within three days. The annual numbers prosecuted have ranged between approximately 200 and 600 over the period between 1975 and 2016 (see Figure 6.1). The conviction rate is high. In each of the four years between 2013 and 2017, more than 80 per cent of cases that went to trial resulted in convictions (Legislative Council, Panel on Security 2016; ICAC 2018: Appendix 8).

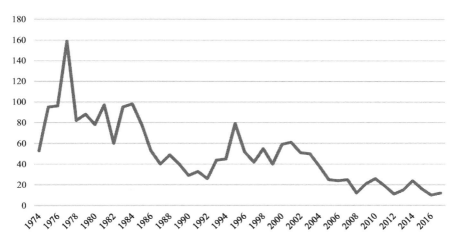

Figure 6.1 Number of persons prosecuted for corruption offences, 1974–2017

Source: ICAC Annual Reports (1975–2017)

Note: The chart excludes those prosecuted for election offences which distort the figures during years in which elections were held.

In most cases, the system works well, but in politically sensitive cases, there are two sets of circumstances in which the integrity of the process may be called into question:

- whenever there are suspicions or complaints that the ICAC is initiating an investigation on political instructions; and
- whenever there are suspicions or complaints that the Secretary for Justice is politically biased in deciding whether or not to prosecute.

Complaints about ICAC investigations

The intense public interest in whether or not the ICAC is actively pursuing a high-profile case was exacerbated by the fractious political circumstances prevailing during Leung Chun-ying's tenure as Chief Executive. Leung's comments suggested that he thought that the Commission's legal requirement to investigate all corruption reports was being abused (*Ming Pao* 2013). His media adviser also reportedly claimed that the Commission was persecuting senior officials in the administration (Leung 2016). Leung's administration was blighted by the ICAC investigation of his involvement with UGL, and there were repeated calls from legislators for more clarity on the issue (see p. 64; Hong Kong Hansard 2016: 351ff; Legislative Council Select Committee 2016; Legislative Council Secretariat 2017). Three of Leung's senior advisers were also investigated. After only twelve days in office, the Secretary for Development, Mak Chai-kwong, was arrested by the ICAC for allegedly defrauding the government. He was convicted in the lower courts before winning his appeal in the Supreme Court. Two Executive Councillors, Franklin Lam Fan-keung and Barry Cheung Chun-yuen, were also investigated but were cleared of any malfeasance (Scott 2017).

In another case, Lew Mon-hung (Dream Bear), a member of the Chinese People's Political Consultative Conference, claimed that Leung had promised him an Executive Council seat for his assistance during the 2012 Chief Executive campaign, but had later reneged on his promise. If true, this would have been a violation of the electoral rules but the ICAC found insufficient evidence to support the allegation. Subsequently, however, it investigated Lew's company, leading to charges of fraud and money laundering. A jury unanimously acquitted Lew in March 2015, although a year later he was imprisoned for attempting to pervert the course of justice by writing threatening letters to the Chief Executive and the ICAC Commissioner (*HKSAR v Lew Mon-hung* 2013).

There were also allegations that Leung had interfered with the ICAC's investigation of cases. The ICAC Commissioner's decision to revert Rebecca Li Bo-lan from Acting Head of Operations to her substantive position of Assistant Director of Operations in July 2016 caused an outcry (see p. 87). There were widespread allegations of links between Li's reversion and the ICAC investigation of Leung's involvement with UGL and questions about whether the method used by the Commissioner to bring about a change of personnel were appropriate (Chan 2016; Hong Kong Hansard 2016: 351ff). The Commissioner told the press that

Li's performance had not been up to the standard required of the Head of the OD and that the decision had been taken by himself alone (Ng 2016). In the 2016 annual report, he said that the decision was in accordance with government and ICAC regulations and that "the ICAC's investigative work could never be interfered (sic) by any person, nor would it deviate from the normal path because of any personnel movement" (ICAC 2017: 18–19). Leung Chun-ying said that he had no part in the decision (Siu 2016).

In dealing with complaints emanating from this politically charged environment, the ICAC has attempted to remain as distant as possible from the fray. It notes that it is obliged to investigate every complaint and re-affirms, as the Commissioner indicated in the annual report, that its investigations are impartial and independent. The outcomes of its investigations, and whether or not there is a subsequent prosecution, are clearly not always going to please the political participants. More seriously, if perceptions of the impartiality and independence of investigations are affected by political "noise", the integrity of the system and its outcomes may be compromised in the public mind.

Complaints about decisions on prosecutions

There have also been political problems associated with the decisions of the Secretary of Justice on whether or not to prosecute. The Department of Justice is bound by the Prosecution Code which notes that two questions must be answered before a prosecution is considered:

> First, is the evidence sufficient to justify instituting or continuing proceedings? Second, if it is, does the public interest require a prosecution to be pursued?
>
> (Department of Justice 2015)

There is clearly room for differences of opinion on both matters. In 1998, a newspaper proprietor, Sally Aw Sian, was named as a co-conspirator in a case in which three of her executives were jailed for deceiving advertisers on sales numbers. In November 2013, Grenville Cross, who had been Director of Public Prosecutions at the time of the Aw case, revealed that he had wanted to start proceedings against her but had been overruled by the Secretary for Justice (Buddle 2013). The case attracted considerable public attention because Aw had been a business partner of the then Chief Executive and was also a member of the Chinese People's Political Consultative Conference.

In another case, an Executive Councillor, Franklin Lam Fan-keung, was investigated by the ICAC for putting four flats up for sale just before the government was about to introduce cooling measures in the property market. When the ICAC presented the evidence to the Department of Justice, the Secretary for Justice declared that he had a conflict of interest because Lam was a colleague on the Executive Council. He then delegated the case to the Director of Public Prosecutions, who found that Lam had put the flats up for sale in the month before the issue was discussed in the Executive Council. He advised that Lam should not be prosecuted. The Department of Justice's explanation of why it did not prosecute is a model of transparency, which goes through the evidence carefully and relates it to offences under the law. It said that it did so to ensure "that the public are fully and properly informed about this case which has been the subject of public concern" (Department of Justice 2013). However, the Department does not always give reasons why it decides not to prosecute.

Leung Chun-ying's period in office was characterised by the intensification of the political divide between the democrats and the pro-government establishment. The Occupy Central civil disobedience movement between September and December 2014 subsequently resulted in many court cases which were themselves seen as political battles. The actions taken by the Department of Justice were subject to intense scrutiny, particularly when it decided to appeal community service orders which had been deemed fit punishment for two separate groups of protesters. In August 2017, the Court of Appeal handed down jail terms to both groups which meant that student leaders were banned from running for public office for five years (Siu 2017). Tens of thousands rallied in the streets in support of the jailed student leaders, claiming political persecution (Lam 2017). The Department of Justice said that it had followed the Prosecution Code, that there could not be "any suggestion of political motivation whatsoever" and that the student leaders were convicted on "objective evidence" (Department of Justice 2017). The convictions were subsequently over-turned but the student leaders found themselves back in jail in January 2018 for contempt of court (Lau 2018).

The convictions of the demonstrators and public reactions to them raise the same issues for prosecutions of politically sensitive corruption cases. The assurances of the Department of Justice that proper procedures are being followed is important but the public perceptions of whether issues are being handled fairly and without political bias is equally important. What the public thinks about the prosecutorial role affects the integrity of the system and their belief in the efficacy of anti-corruption efforts. The process needs not only to be fair but also to be seen to be fair.

What might be done to improve this situation? After Grenville Cross left office in 2009, he argued that the Director of Public Prosecutions should be independent which would free the office from the evident political conflicts of interest that a Secretary for Justice, as a political appointee, might have in such circumstances (Cross 2011). The proposal was considered, but rejected, by the government in 2011 (Legislative Council Panel on Administration of Justice 2011). Cross returned to the issue in 2016, noting that independent Directors of Public Prosecutions were in place in other common law jurisdictions. Although he affirmed the independence of the Hong Kong system, Cross said "many people do not believe this, and they will certainly not change their minds as long as a political appointee exercises ultimate authority over prosecutions" (Cross 2016). An independent Director of Public Prosecutions would be one way to try to improve the current situation. Other ways would be for the Secretary of Justice to delegate full authority to the Director of Public Prosecutions in political cases and to provide more transparency on the reasons for a decision, as was done in the Franklin

Lam case and also for the ICAC investigation of Leung Chun-ying (Legislative Council Secretariat 2017).

Aside from the questions raised by the politically sensitive cases, ICAC corruption investigations and Department of Justice prosecutions have functioned smoothly. It has been important that investigations have proceeded in a linear manner for reasons of efficiency and because it increases public confidence in the process. In some countries, other organisations become involved in the investigation and classification of complaints and political bias and self-interest affect the impartiality of the process with seriously detrimental consequences. ICAC surveys suggest that the public see the Commission as impartial and that its methods of investigations have been regarded as appropriate. The integrity of the system has been maintained and reinforced by the evident exercise of due process over time and the strongly held belief that the enforcement of effective laws has contributed to a cleaner Hong Kong.

The evolution of the corruption laws in Hong Kong illustrates the need for ACAs to be adaptable to the changing environment. As corruption takes new forms and as unethical behaviour becomes a greater public concern, old ways of dealing with conventional corruption problems become outdated. The *POBO* served Hong Kong well when bribery was the primary offence, but it presently cannot consistently capture complex conflicts of interest, cases where it is difficult to show that an advantage has been obtained, or corruption in which there is no immediate beneficiary. The offence of misconduct in public office, which was successfully used to supplement the *POBO*, has itself faced problems of interpretation and the need for further refinement. Its intent nonetheless has been well supported by integrity management programmes which explain the nature of misconduct in public office offences and how they might be avoided. There remain problems of ensuring that politically sensitive cases do not undermine faith in the integrity of the criminal justice process and that public confidence in the Commission remains at its traditionally high level.

References

Attorney-General v Hui Kin-hong (1995) HKCLR 227.

Brewer, Brian, Joan Y.H. Leung and Ian Scott (2015) "Value-based integrity management and bureaucratic organizations: Changing the mix", *International Public Management Journal*, 18(3): 390–410.

Buddle, Cliff (2013) "Ex-DPP tells of split over news tycoon prosecution", *Sunday Morning Post*, 17 November, www.scmp.com/news/hong-kong/article/1358155/former-dpp-grenville-cross-reveals-split-over-sally-aw-sian.

Chan, Anson (1998) "Maintaining integrity in the civil service", *Daily Information Bulletin*, 21 May, www.info.gov.hk/gia/general/199805/21/0521069.htm.

Chan, Anson (2016) "ICAC: We must keep our advantage", *Voice of Hong Kong*, 16 August, www.vohk.hk/2016/08/15/icac-we-must-keep-our-advantage.

Chan, Kin-man (1997) "Combating corruption and the ICAC" in Joseph Y.S. Cheng (ed.) *The other Hong Kong report, 1997*. Hong Kong: The Chinese University Press: 101–121.

Cheung, Arthur K.C. (1997) "Bill of rights – hotbed of challenge" in Joseph Y.S. Cheng (ed.) *The other Hong Kong report, 1997*. Hong Kong: The Chinese University Press: 123–135.

Civil Service Bureau (2005) *Civil servants' guide to good practices*. 2nd edition. Hong Kong: mimeo.

Civil Service Bureau (2009) "Civil service code", www.csb.gov.hk/english/admin/conduct/1751.html.

Cross, Grenville (2011) "Free to decide", *South China Morning Post*, 10 February.

Cross, Grenville (2016) "Time to get serious on prosecutorial independence in Hong Kong", *South China Morning Post*, 1 August, www.scmp.com/news/hong-kong/law-crime/article/1997722/time-get-serious-prosecutorial-independence-hong-kong.

Department of Justice (2013) "DPP's statement on Mr. Franklin Lam Fan-keung's case", 1 August, www.doj.gov.hk/eng/public/pr/20130801_pr2.html.

Department of Justice (2015) "Prosecution code", www.doj.gov.hk/eng/public/pubsoppaptoc.html.

Department of Justice (2017) "Statement by Department of Justice", Press Release, 17 August.

Elections (Corrupt and Illegal Conduct) Ordinance (ECICO) (Cap 554)

Fung, Fanny and Olga Wong (2014) "Declaration of interest row after Lands official bought 13 plots", *South China Morning Post*, 14 April, www.scmp.com/news/hong-kong/article/1567858/row-over-officials-property-deal.

Gong, Ting and Ian Scott (2015) "Conflicts of interest and ethical decision-making: Mainland China and Hong Kong comparisons" in Alan Lawton, Leo Huberts and Zeger van der Wal (eds.) *Ethics in public policy and management; a global research companion*. London: Routledge: 257–276.

HKSAR v Ho Mi-mi and Cheng Sai-man (2002) ESCC410/2002.

HKSAR v Lew Mon-hung (2013) DCCC819/2013.

HKSAR v Rafael Hui Si-yan and Others (2014) HCCC 98/2013.

HKSAR v Tsang Yip-fat (2002) HCMA1125/2002.

HKSAR v Wong Lin Kay (2012) 2 HKLRD 898.

Hong Kong Bill of Rights Ordinance (Cap 383).

Hong Kong Government (2017) "Policy address", www.policyaddress.gov.hk/2017/eng/pdf/PA2017.pdf.

Hong Kong Hansard 11 February 1976; 10 July 1996; 9 November 2016.

ICAC (1975–2017) "Annual reports", www.icac.org.hk/en/about/report/annual/index.html.

ICAC (1975) "Annual report 1974", www.icac.org.hk/filemanager/en/Content_27/1974.pdf.

ICAC (1976) "Annual report 1975", www.icac.org.hk/filemanager/en/Content_27/1975.pdf.

ICAC (1977) "Annual report 1976", www.icac.org.hk/filemanager/en/Content_27/1976.pdf.

ICAC (1979) *Mass survey 1977 final report*. Hong Kong: mimeo.

ICAC (1981) "Annual report 1980", www.icac.org.hk/filemanager/en/Content_27/1980.pdf.

ICAC (1987) "Annual report 1986", www.icac.org.hk/filemanager/en/Content_27/1986.pdf.

ICAC (1990) *ICAC mass survey 1990*. Hong Kong: mimeo.

ICAC (1997) "Annual report 1996", www.icac.org.hk/filemanager/en/Content_27/1996.pdf.

ICAC (2007) "Annual report 2006", www.icac.org.hk/filemanager/tc/Content_27/2006.pdf.

ICAC (2010) *Annual survey 2009*. Hong Kong: mimeo.

ICAC (2017) "Annual report 2016", www.icac.org.hk/filemanager/en/content_27/2016.pdf.

ICAC (2018) "Annual report 2017", www.icac.org.hk/filemanager/en/content_27/2017.pdf.

ICAC (n.d.) "Integrity and corruption prevention guide on managing relationships with public servants", www.icac.org.hk/filemanager/en/Content_216/ps.pdf.

ICAC (n.d.) "Reference package on conflict of interest for managers in the civil service", www.icac.org.hk/en/resource/publications-and-videos/ps/index.html.

ICAC and Civil Service Bureau (2008) *Ethical leadership in action: Handbook for senior managers in the civil service*. Hong Kong: ICAC and Civil Service Bureau.

ICAC and Civil Service Bureau (2017) "Web learning portal on integrity management for civil servants", www.icac.org.hk/en/resource/publications-and-videos/ps/index.html.

ICAC Corruption Prevention Department (2014) "Sample code of conduct for employees of public bodies", www.icac.org.hk/en/resource/publications-and-videos/ps/index.html.

ICAC Hong Kong Business Ethics Development Centre (2017) "Sample code of conduct", www.hkbedc.icac.hk/english/files/publications/Sample_English.pdf.

Independent Commission Against Corruption Ordinance (ICACO) (Cap 204).

Independent Review Committee (1994) *Report of the ICAC review committee*. Hong Kong: Government Printer.

Lam, Jeffie (2017) "Protestors turn out in force against jailing of Hong Kong activists", *South China Morning Post*, 20 August, www.scmp.com/news/hong-kong/politics/article/2107529/former-hong-kong-bar-association-chief-says-jailing-three.

Lau, Chris (2015) "Former Hong Kong leader Donald Tsang out on bail after court hears misconduct charges over Shenzhen flat rental", *South China Morning Post*, 5 October, www.scmp.com/news/hong-kong/law-crime/article/1864267/former-hong-kong-leader-donald-tsang-released-bail-court.

Lau, Chris (2018) "Hong Kong Occupy activist Joshua Wong denied bail after being sentenced to three months' jail for contempt of court", *South China Morning Post*, 17 January, www.scmp.com/news/hong-kong/politics/article/2128580/hong-kong-occupy-activist-joshua-wong-jailed-three-months.

Legislative Council, Panel on Administration of Justice and Legal Services (2011) "Response to the background brief provided by the Legco Secretariat entitled 'An independent Director of Public Prosecutions'", LC Paper No. CB (20 2154/10–11(01).

Legislative Council, Panel on Public Service (2008) "Integrity enhancement initiatives for public servants", LC Paper No. CB (1) 764/07–08(05), 18 February.

Legislative Council, Panel on Security (2016) "Briefing by the Commissioner, Independent Commission Against Corruption", LC Paper No. CB (2) 654/14–15(06), 2 February.

Legislative Council Secretariat (2017) "Information note: The UGL incident", 23 February, www.legco.gov.hk/research-publications/english/1617in03-the-ugl-incident-20170223-e.pdf.

Legislative Council Select Committee (2010) "Report of the select committee to inquire into matters relating to the post-service work of Mr. Leung Chin-man", www.legco.gov.hk/yr08-09/english/sc/sc_lcm/report/lcm_rpt-e.pdf.

Legislative Council Select Committee (2016) "Select committee to inquire into matters about the agreement between Mr. Leung Chun-ying and the Australian firm UGL Limited", www.legco.gov.hk/yr16-17/english/sc/sc_lcyugl/general/sc_lcyugl.htm.

Leung, Stanley (2016) "Graft watchdog is being used to politically persecute officials, claims C.Y.'s spin doctor Andrew Fung", *Hong Kong Free Press*, 16 October, www.hongkongfp.com/2016/10/14/graft-watchdog-is-being-used-to-politically-persecute-officials-claims-cys-spin-doctor-andrew-fung/.

Lo, T. Wing and Ricky C.C. Yu (2000) "Curbing draconian powers: The effects on Hong Kong's graft-fighter", *The International Journal of Human Rights*, 4(1): 54–73.

Lusty, David (2014) "Revival of the common law offence of misconduct in public office", *Criminal Law Journal*, 38: 337–363.

McWalters, Ian, David Fitzpatrick and Andrew Bruce (2015) *Bribery and corruption law in Hong Kong*. 3rd edition. Singapore: LexisNexis.

Ming Pao (2013) "Leung demands complainants apologise", *Ming Pao*, 12 August.

Neoh, Anthony (2010) "An impartial and uncorrupted civil service: Hong Kong's fight against corruption in the past 34 years" in Christopher Forsythe, Mark Elliott, Swati Javeri, Michael Ramsden and Anne Scully Hill (eds.) *Effective judicial review: A cornerstone of good governance*. New York: Oxford University Press: 216–242.

Ng, Joyce (2016) "ICAC chief claims he alone, and not C.Y. Leung, made decision to remove deputy", *South China Morning Post*, 16 July, www.scmp.com/news/hong-kong/law-crime/article/1988466/icac-chief-claims-he-alone-and-not-cy-leung-made-decision.

Ng, Margaret (1992) "ICAC powers: Is it time to look at the investigators?" *South China Morning Post*, 23 February.

Prevention of Bribery Ordinance (POBO) (Cap 201).

R v Dytham (1979) 2QB 722.

Review Committee (2009) "Review of post-service outside work for directorate civil servants", www.dcspostservice-review.org.hk.

Scott, Ian (2013) "Institutional design and corruption prevention in Hong Kong", *Journal of Contemporary China*, 22(79): 77–92.

Scott, Ian (2017) "The challenge of preserving a successful anti-corruption agency", *Asian Education and Development Studies*, 6(3): 227–237.

Scott, Ian and Joan Y.H. Leung (2008) "Managing integrity: The regulation of post public employment in Britain and Hong Kong", *Public Organization Review*, 8(4) (October): 365–380.

Scott, Ian and Joan Y.H. Leung (2012) "Integrity management in post-1997 Hong Kong: Challenges for a rule-based system", *Crime, Law and Social Change*, 58(1): 39–52.

Secretary for the Civil Service (2011) "Remarks by the SCS on the review of post-service outside work for directorate civil servants", *Press Release*, 22 July.

Shum Kwok-sher v HKSAR (2002) 5 HKCFAR 381.

Sin Kam-wah and Another v HKSAR (2005) 8HKCFAR 192.

Siu, Jasmine (2017) "Joshua Wong and other Hong Kong student leaders see political careers halted", *South China Morning Post*, 17 August, www.scmp.com/

news/hong-kong/politics/article/2107216/occupy-activists-joshua-wong-and-nathan-law-jailed-hong-kong.

Siu, Phila (2016) "C.Y. Leung insists he did not take any part in decision-making to remove ICAC's Rebecca Li", *South China Morning Post*, 12 July, www.scmp.com/news/hong-kong/law-crime/article/1988806/cy-leung-insists-he-did-not-take-any-part-decision-making.

7   Changing perceptions of corruption

What the public thinks about corruption can be an important element in devising an effective preventive strategy. Positive perceptions – for example, the belief that corruption is unacceptable or that it can be controlled – will provide public support for an ACA. Negative perceptions – for example, beliefs that corruption is inevitable, part of the culture, or intrinsic in economic transactions – may lead to, or be based upon, social attitudes which obstruct anti-corruption policies. If resources are to be allocated to changing negative perceptions, a first step is to find out what they are. The common means of doing so is to conduct a survey, but it is important to establish that the purpose of the survey is to determine what the public thinks, not to attempt to estimate the level of corruption. Perceptions are often used as proxies for measuring corruption which pose methodological and empirical problems because corruption is difficult, if not impossible, to measure and because perceptions are simply a reflection of what people think and may have little to do with the prevalence of corruption (Galtung 2006; Heywood and Rose 2014; Rose 2015; Yu 2017). Transparency International's Corruption Perceptions Index, for example, is widely taken to be representative of the level of corruption in countries around the world, whereas it is actually only a report on the findings of perception surveys. Whether those findings match the actual level of corruption in any country is unknown. In this chapter, the findings which we report and analyse are attempts to measure perceptions of corruption, not the level of corruption itself.

In its first report on survey research into public perceptions of corruption published in 1979, the ICAC's Community Research Unit laid down three objectives which have remained at the heart of the surveys conducted on behalf of the ICAC by independent companies, bi-annually in the 1970s and 1980s and annually since 1992. The Unit said that the aim was, first, "to measure public perceptions of and attitudes towards corrupt behaviour" and to determine changes over time; second, to assess the "public response to the activities of the Commission"; and, third, to develop and plan activities which were "most conducive to the proper development . . . of the public education programmes for fostering more positive, healthier social values in Hong Kong" (ICAC 1979a: I). Underlying these objectives were some initial assumptions about how the public perceived corruption and how their perceptions and attitudes might need to be changed.

MacLehose himself had talked about "deeply ingrained attitudes" toward corruption and the need for public education (Hong Kong Hansard 1973: 18). The ICAC started from the position that the CRD would have to make major efforts to ensure that public values were generally consistent with the Commission's zero-tolerance approach to corruption and that it would need public support to overcome syndicates and to ensure that corruption was reported. This required a social engineering campaign which was orchestrated by the CRD with much enthusiasm and great success in the ICAC's first decade and continued thereafter through both Hong Kong–wide efforts and specific programmes aimed at those who were thought to be "at risk" (McDonald 1994).

In this chapter, we consider, first, the CRD's approach to changing perceptions through its anti-corruption publicity and liaison work; second, the kinds of public perceptions that the CRD tried to change (notably, perceptions of corruption as a social evil, levels of tolerance of corruption, the social acceptability of some forms of corruption and the willingness of the public to report corruption); and, finally, what the public thinks of the ICAC and how this relates to institutionalisation of its anti-corruption efforts.

The CRD's publicity and liaison work

The ICAC's universal model is designed to ensure that corruption has no place in the government, the private sector or in society. This implies attention to any situation in which values inimical to a zero-tolerance approach might arise, where opportunities for corruption might develop or where actual corruption occurs. Although Hong Kong is a relatively small place, implementation of the model has still required a large ICAC staff and a substantial budget. Even though the Commission has been well supported, it is still necessary that its resources should be used strategically and economically, based on judgements of where it is likely to get the best returns.

Publicity

The first significant strategic decision that the ICAC had to make on gaining public support and changing public perceptions was whether it should concentrate its activities on publicity or on liaison work. The problems over funding regional offices (see Ch. 3) meant that it was not possible to open some regional offices to conduct liaison work at a level and as widely as the CRD wanted (ICAC 1977: 35–36). Some funding, originally intended for liaison work, was consequently diverted into publicity and used, in particular, for publicity on the importance of reporting corruption. The CRD was able to make rapid progress in publicising the moral position of the ICAC and its activities. It received support from government radio and television services and from the community, including well-known actors, who sometimes offered free services. It also recruited very able staff. Ann Hui, later to become one of Hong Kong's most famous film producers and directors, worked for the ICAC during this early period, producing six documentaries, although two were considered too controversial to be shown at the time.

By 1976, the ICAC already had a five-minute weekly ICAC spot on television; was making regular announcements of public interest (APIs), such as where and how to report corruption; and had begun a thirteen half-hour drama series, which was intended to carry a strong anti-corruption message (ICAC 1977: 36). The drama series has been a continuing success. Originally called *The Quiet Revolution* (later *ICAC Investigators*), successive series over the years have been widely watched not only in Hong Kong but also in southern China. The episodes are professionally produced, based on real ICAC cases, and always end with the moral lesson that corruption does not pay (Donald 2013: 80–84). In 2016, the five episodes involved election bribery, bribing tour guides to take their clients to retail establishments, bribing a bank executive to approve a home loan, drug trafficking and falsified financial statements. The series attracted 9.5 million viewers.

ICAC publicity covers all kinds of media and is aimed at all kinds of people. The importance of moral values in the education of youth has been a recurrent theme, but there are also television programmes for adults and a variety of targeted messages for specific groups in the community. For young people, a flying rabbit (*Gee-dor-dor*) appears on YouTube cartoons, on worksheets for kindergarten students and on an internet game for teens, illustrating the concept of fairness (ICAC 2018a). Other comics deal with topical issues based on actual cases. The ICAC has also made increasing use of the internet and has a website for teens. Since March 2016, it has been on Facebook, where it publicises the Commission's activities and features egames and competitions. It is also on Weibo. Its YouTube channel has 1300 videos available for downloading, and its websites receive some four million visits every year (Peh 2015). The ICAC's main advertising campaign consists of TV and radio APIs and posters which are changed every two to three years. The posters are carefully designed to reflect the current theme which the Commission wishes to emphasise and are widely displayed throughout Hong Kong. Supplementing the visual media, there are many written guides, pamphlets and instruction manuals on ethical behaviour, conflicts of interest, elections, and best practices in business. There is also a bi-annual ICAC newsletter, *ICAC Post*, which covers larger issues of anti-corruption policy as well as updates on the number of corruption reports and interesting court cases (ICAC 2018e).

The ICAC's publicity has changed over time in response to different needs. The changes are often generated by evident changes in patterns of social behaviour, such as a drop in the number of corruption reports. The annual perception surveys have also proved to be a source of new initiatives. An early concern was that the public were unwilling or frightened to report corruption and that when they did report, they wanted to remain anonymous. In 1975, the first API campaign was entitled "Report Corruption in Person" and gave directions about where to make complaints and assurances that all information would be treated in confidence. In the 1980s and 1990s, the CRD ran a territory-wide programme called "Toward a Fuller Life" emphasising that a zero-tolerance policy toward corruption could achieve a clean society and a better lifestyle. Later, in the 1990s, the focus changed again as posters were used to attempt to allay fears that the ICAC would become less effective after the resumption of Chinese sovereignty. More recently, the "All for Integrity" campaign, which began in 2016, is designed to sustain and entrench a culture of probity (ICAC 2018b: 81).

Since 1995, when the Hong Kong Business Ethics Development Centre was established within the CRD, considerable attention has been paid to the promotion of business ethics (ICAC 2018b: 74). The Centre, advised by the ten major chambers of commerce, concentrates on promoting information, courses, best practices and changes in the law to professional bodies and specific trade organisations. The broader aim is to communicate the message that everyone is better off if economic transactions are legal and if investment and job creation are conducted on a level playing field. A similar sentiment – that corruption-free practices makes life better for everyone – underpins a host of other publicity initiatives which focus on appropriate behaviour for particular groups, such as business directors and SMEs operating in China, or for elections (ICAC Hong Kong Business Ethics Development Centre 2018; ICAC 2018d).

Much of the ICAC's publicity is produced by in-house production teams but it is distributed by chambers of commerce for their members, the Hong Kong Monetary Authority for the integrity issues relating to bank staff, the Electoral Affairs Commission for clean elections, the Hong Kong Trade Development Council for trading companies, and the District Councils for their constituents and other organisations. This partnership programme means that the ambitious aim of saturating the population with the anti-corruption message has been relatively inexpensive. The cost of publicity was HK$17.87 million for the 2015–2016 financial year and was expected to decline to HK$15.58 million in the 2017–2018 financial year (Hong Kong Government 2017: 629). The CRD's Mass Communication Office, which is responsible for the design and production of ICAC products, employs less than 20 personnel although some projects are contracted out.

The ICAC's publicity reaches a large percentage of the population. In 2017, 76 per cent of the respondents to the annual survey said that they had received information from the ICAC in the past year, 22 per cent said that they had not and about 3 per cent were not sure whether they had or had not (ICAC 2018c: 12). The main means of receiving information was through television (93 per cent), followed by newspapers (31 per cent) and the internet (26 per cent) (ICAC 2018c: 12). When asked which message impressed them most, the two highest ranking categories were "don't bribe" and "report corruption" (ICAC 2018c: 12). A striking finding from the 2017 annual survey was that although some 75 per cent of respondents who had lived in Hong Kong for more than seven years had received information about the ICAC in the past year, only 46 per cent of those who had lived in Hong Kong for less than five years had done so (ICAC 2017: 89). This suggests that new migrants from China are not yet sufficiently integrated into the ICAC's information network or are not as aware of its message as longer-term residents.

It is generally thought that the ICAC's publicity does have an impact on perceptions of corruption (Donald 2013: 84) but the ways in which perceptions and attitudes might be affected are not well understood. The problem is that changing perceptions may be a consequence of many different factors other than publicity. For example, the ICAC attributed the increased number of corruption reports in 2015 to more publicity on the need to report corruption (ICAC 2016: 14, 75). While that may be a factor, it is also possible that there was simply more corruption in 2015 than there had been previously. Nonetheless, the ICAC does appear to have used information more strategically than other ACAs. In Fritzen and Basu's (2011) study of five ACAs (Hong Kong, South Korea, New South Wales, India and Singapore), only the ICAC is rated as "well-developed" in the strategic use of information. Although the study was not a specific analysis of publicity, it does show that information has been used effectively as an anti-corruption tool and that the CRD has always been aware of the importance of publicity in supporting its stance. Unlike many ACAs, where publicity is largely a rhetorical exercise warning the public of the ethical and punitive consequences of corrupt behaviour, the Commission has used it as an arm of an integrated policy which is evidence-based, drawing on the feedback received from regional offices, programme coordinators, survey research and discussions between ICAC departments on the latest corruption trends (Scott and Gong 2015). In this respect, its publicity is more targeted and cost-effective than many other ACAs and has made a vital contribution to the Commission's overall success.

Liaison work

In the aftermath of the partial police amnesty in 1997, the CRD's liaison work was of vital importance in re-gaining public confidence in the Commission, in propagating the vision of a corruption-free society, and in sustaining the belief that corruption could and would be controlled. Once confidence had been restored, the role of liaison work changed. There were still concerns about what people thought about corruption but the task gradually became rather more than a general exercise aimed at changing perceptions. First, there was a focus on influencing the development of perceptions in particular groups, especially youths and new migrants. Second, efforts were made to support and maintain existing perceptions of the importance of a zero-tolerance approach to corruption. Third, the CRD sought to address trouble-spots where there was evidence of corrupt or dubious ethical behaviour and where there was thought to be a need to strengthen the anti-corruption message and to address perceptions accordingly. We consider each of these areas in turn.

Perceptions of youth and new migrants toward corruption

The CRD has always stressed the importance of the development of integrity in youth in the expectation that acquired attitudes will be maintained in adulthood. The means of achieving this objective has changed, however. In the early days, the CRD sent its officers to give talks in schools and universities. With the arrival of the internet, more attention was given to websites and to other means of communicating integrity messages. The focus also changed from talks on corruption prevention to other forms of communication such as interactive drama performances. An ICAC ambassador programme has been established in 19 tertiary institutions with 140 ambassadors and 220 "buddies", creating programmes featuring integrity issues for their fellow students (ICAC 2018b: 77). The equivalent at the secondary school level is the iTeen leadership programme which organises promotional activities and visits to the ICAC (ICAC 2018b: 78).

There have been major concerns about youth perceptions of corruption and integrity which, at various times, have shown greater tolerance of corruption than other sectors of the population. In 1997, for example, a survey of 529 youths revealed that up to 10 per cent would be willing to use a bribe to solve a problem (Hong Kong Federation of Youth Groups 1997; Gomomo 2001: 461). The survey caused considerable alarm among legislators at a time when corruption reports were rising (see Ch. 4). More recently, the 2016 ICAC annual survey shows that there is a gap in intolerance of corruption between youth between the ages of fifteen and twenty-four (66 per cent) and those twenty-five and older (82 per cent) (ICAC 2017: 9).

It is not entirely clear how these figures can be explained. One possible explanation is that it has become more difficult for the CRD to provide comprehensive coverage of integrity programmes for youth. The talks in schools and universities, which used to be the principal feature of the ICAC's liaison work, have been replaced by a greater reliance on the internet and other activities. Schools have also been less willing to provide time for ICAC officers. Over the period 2007 to 2012, for example, the Director of Audit found that the CRD had been able to give talks or interactive drama performances at 310 schools but had not been able to contact or had its requests to give talks or performances rejected by 45 schools (Director of Audit 2013: 29). There may, of course, be many factors other than coverage which explain differences in attitudes toward corruption between young people and their seniors. Gong *et al* (2015), in their survey of Hong Kong and Chinese university students' attitudes toward corruption, note that Hong Kong students are more inclined to place their trust in institutions, such as the ICAC, than their Chinese counterparts. One consequence of this is that they seem to be less personally involved (and perhaps less interested) in the need to combat corruption and are willing to leave such matters to the ICAC.

The corruption perceptions of new migrants are also a source of concern. Between July 1997 and November 2016, some 860,000 Mainland immigrants came to live in Hong Kong on family re-union one-way permits (Hong Kong Hansard 2016: 1494). There is a quota of 150 new migrants per day under the scheme. Many of the new immigrants were poorly educated and some spoke neither Cantonese nor English. Their integration into Hong Kong has posed problems, particularly when the new migrants have been disproportionately isolated in satellite towns, such as Tin Shui Wai, with low levels of social cohesion (Rochelle 2015). The fear has been that the new migrants will bring with them attitudes toward corruption that are acceptable in Mainland China but might be illegal in Hong Kong. In 2012, we undertook a survey with 207 respondents in two districts of Hong Kong with high proportions of migrants to see if we could detect any significant differences between the attitudes of Hong Kong residents and new migrants toward corruption. We did find some differences between those with less than four years' residence in attitudes toward the use of government property for personal purposes, the failure of officials to report financial interests, and post-service employment of public servants with companies which had dealings with government. Immigrant respondents thought these practices were acceptable but longer-term Hong Kong residents did not. After four years' residence, there was little difference in attitudes toward corruption in the two groups (Scott 2013b: 99–101).

The ICAC has been sensitive to the political concern that it might be treating new migrants separately from other Hong Kong citizens and has not devoted much resources to them as a group. It contracts out some of its corruption prevention work for new migrants to International Social Service (ISS), an NGO which receives almost all its funding from the Hong Kong government. ISS is responsible for providing support services and induction courses while the ICAC provides anti-corruption videos and some liaison work. Although there is no evidence to suggest that new migrants are more involved in most areas of corruption than any other group in the society, vote-rigging has been a matter of concern (Hong Kong Hansard 2016: 1499). Survey research has shown that new migrants tend to vote for pro-establishment parties rather than democrats and there appear to have been attempts to register them before they are qualified to vote (Wong *et al* 2016). In addition, the ICAC (2017: 89) annual survey finding that more than half of new migrants had not heard from the ICAC in the previous year suggests that many are not yet fully aware of the anti-corruption message.

Maintenance of the zero-tolerance approach

Much of the ICAC's liaison work is preaching to the converted. It believes that it is important to sustain a zero-tolerance approach to corruption, and it does so by organising events which enable its officials to speak to specific groups or show videos which emphasise the dangers of corruption to the social fabric, often coupled with warnings that reduced vigilance could result in a return to the bad old days of the 1960s. The extent of the ICAC's coverage and network of contacts is remarkable. CRD campaigns reach many hundreds of thousands of people and involve hundreds of different organisations. In 2017, staff gave talks to 69,000 secondary and tertiary students, ran 660 seminars for 26,000 civil servants and held a further 200 seminars for 9000 members of public bodies (ICAC 2018b: 73, 78). The Hong Kong Business Ethics Development Centre maintains contact with over seventy banks and seventy trade organisations (ICAC 2018b: 73, 75). At the local level, the regional offices are in close contact with the District Councils and organise annual events. It is estimated that the regional offices have contacts with over 1600 district-level organisations (ICAC 2018b: 81).

These figures suggest that the original objective to embed the ICAC in the community has been achieved (Lee 2006). Although the activities which the

ICAC organises vary from year to year, they are designed to reinforce the same anti-corruption values that have been part of the ICAC's message since its inception. New organisations and new members may become involved in the activities but the underlying theme has always been that the zero-tolerance approach to corruption remains in force. Community activities serve as an affirmation of that determination and of its expectation that citizens should support effective corruption prevention in the broader public interest.

Dealing with trouble-spots

Despite the ICAC's best efforts, corruption does occur in Hong Kong. The Commission's reactions depend on the circumstances. If an individual, working alone or with one or two other persons, is investigated, charged and convicted of a corrupt offence, the ICAC might congratulate itself on the effectiveness of its anti-corruption system. If, on the other hand, there is evidence of wide collusion within an organisation, there is a possibility that syndicated corruption might be emerging or might even be present. At that point, the organisation or the sector may become a target for increased liaison work and CPD assignment studies.

In the public sector, the CRD has guidelines on where and to what extent liaison work has priority. Bureaus and departments in the disciplined services, those which are related to construction, those which have large workforces and those which top the list of corruption complaints are supposed to take precedence over other parts of the civil service (Director of Audit 2013: 20). In 2013, the Director of Audit, reviewing the period between 2008 and 2012, was critical of the extent to which the ICAC was following these guidelines. He noted that there had been requests from the Police, the Housing Department and the Buildings Department for more liaison work from the CRD which had been provided. However, other departments which fell within the top ten departments in terms of the ICAC's criteria had received less coverage, and fourteen of seventy-nine bureaus and departments had received no coverage at all (Director of Audit 2013: 24). Whether blanket coverage is more important than dealing with trouble spots is a moot point, but eleven of the fourteen bureaus and departments which had not been contacted had an average of seven corruption complaints per year and should have fallen within the guidelines.

Two private sector areas which have caused perennial problems of corruption control have been owners' corporations and banks. Private apartment buildings in Hong Kong are usually run by owners' corporations which employ estate managers to run them and contractors to maintain or renovate the property. Bid-rigging occurs when contractors collude with each other or with the estate manager or with the owners' corporation to raise the price of a tender. Various kinds of fraud and misappropriation of funds can occur and, if there is no corrupt element involved, it falls outside the ICAC's purview (Competition Commission 2016). Private estates are large, and bid-rigging may involve many different parties and result in large costs to the owners. In one case, a sub-contractor confessed to a conspiracy on a renovation contract worth more than HK$250 million.

The conspiracy involved the chairman of the owners' corporation, the executive directors of the estate company and architectural and engineering firms (Lau 2015). The chairman of the owners' corporation was allegedly offered a bribe of HK$26 million. Although collusion of this kind is difficult to detect, the ICAC has made great efforts through its liaison work to raise awareness of the responsibilities of the owners' corporations and to inform them of the provisions of the *POBO*, potential corruption-prone areas and effective preventive measures. It has also sought to enlist the support of the District Offices in raising awareness. In 2016, the CRD contacted 620 owners' corporations through visits, talks and seminars to 3600 people (ICAC 2017: 74; ICAC n.d.).

Banks also present perennial problems of collusion, partly because any significant amount of dirty money probably has to go somewhere in the banking system and partly because banks are involved in many business activities where there are opportunities for corruption (Global Witness 2015: 4, 16–19). Although the banking system in Hong Kong is sound, a legacy of failed banks and the problems of the Bank Bumiputra Malaysia Berhad in the Carrian case have concerned the ICAC and influenced its liaison work accordingly. It has formed partnerships over many years with the Hong Kong Monetary Authority, the Hong Kong Institute of Bankers and the Hong Kong Association of Banks, which jointly provide leadership training programmes with the ICAC (ICAC *et al* n.d.). Nonetheless, problems still arise. In December 2016, for example, the ICAC arrested twenty-nine bank officials from four banks on charges of alleged bribery connected with obtaining confidential customer information to market personal loans (Bloomberg 2016).

With the corruption opportunities that owners' corporations and banks present, the ICAC's liaison work can only serve to alert managers and employees to common problems that may need attention. It is one aspect of an approach that also needs to ensure that good practices and financial checks are in place and that the chances of being caught outweigh the benefits of subverting the system.

Perceptions of corruption

For many ACAs, their anti-corruption message is designed principally to serve as a rhetorical injunction not to be corrupt, usually coupled with a warning of dire consequences if the injunction is ignored. The ICAC has approached the issue of changing perceptions of corruption rather differently. Publicity and liaison work have been used as means to change public perceptions about corruption to coincide with those of the Commission itself. From the outset, the ICAC wanted the public to share its view:

- that corruption was a social evil which had strongly detrimental effects on the cost and delivery of public goods and social services and adversely affected economic growth;
- that anti-corruption policies should be based on zero-tolerance of corruption and that corruption was equally socially unacceptable whether it was in

the public or private sectors, whether the corrupt were highly or lowly paid, and whether the parties offered or accepted bribes; and

- that it was necessary to report corruption to enable the ICAC to deal with it.

In the mid-1970s, it was not known what proportion of the public held these views; the ICAC had first to discover how the public saw its approach to corruption prevention. The Community Research Unit, which was part of the CRD, took on the task of devising questionnaires, which were then administered by an independent company. The Unit's aim was to study perceptions of corruption which could be used to provide benchmarks to assess the effects of publicity and liaison work, and to make recommendations for approaches in areas which had raised problems.

We examine each of the major areas in which the survey findings influenced the focus and content of the CRD's publicity and liaison work.

Corruption as a social evil

In many places, the public regards corruption as a nuisance rather than a social evil at least when compared with other major problems, such as disease, crime, high unemployment and inadequate or non-existent social services. It has also been argued that corruption is a part of the culture, a means to get things done, and that to try to change it represents an unwarranted intrusion on a way of life (Zerilli 2005; Kanekane 2007). ACAs, by definition, take the opposite standpoint, although most of them are not as interventionist as the ICAC.

In 1971, the Social Research Centre of the Chinese University of Hong Kong conducted a survey of 1065 randomly selected household heads and found that only 29 per cent regarded corruption as a serious social problem. Older and less well-educated respondents were less likely to see corruption as a problem (Lee 1981a). The percentage who regarded corruption as a serious social problem is low in the context of the subsequent portrayal of Hong Kong as a place where, before the creation of the ICAC, corruption was endemic, exploitative and widely resented. Lee (1981a) argues that the perceptual gap between official views of the need to control corruption and the lack of public concern can be explained by differences between the bureaucratic values of impersonality and demonstrated fairness for all and the Chinese social value of strong personal relationships, which could be seen as approving and promoting corrupt practices.

The Community Relations Unit's first survey found that the perception of corruption as a serious social evil was even lower than that reported by the Social Research Centre. In the 1977 survey, only 6 per cent of respondents regarded corruption as a serious social problem in relation to other problems such as crime (72 per cent), housing (43 per cent) and transportation and traffic (30 per cent) (ICAC 1979a: 16). When asked about serious social problems in Hong Kong, less than 2 per cent independently mentioned corruption (ICAC 1979b: 10). The Unit was convinced that this was because corruption did not regularly affect people's livelihood and survival and was seen as a "soft" crime (ICAC 1979b: 2).

In consequence, it recommended that the ICAC should strongly stress the causal relationship between corruption and other social problems in both its publicity and liaison work.

The issue became intertwined with the declining rate of corruption in the public sector. The 1980 survey found a correlation between perceptions of corruption in the public sector and perceptions of whether corruption was a serious social issue. The lower the number of respondents who felt that corruption was declining in the public sector, the lower the percentage who felt that corruption was a serious social issue and vice versa (ICAC 1981: 16). By 1986, this perception had changed significantly. About 13 per cent of the sample thought that corruption was a very serious issue, and 58 per cent thought that it was a serious issue (ICAC 1986: Ch. 3: 15). Respondents who thought that it was a very serious issue were middle-aged and predominantly worked in the private sector in sales, service or transport, or in public bodies providing utilities. Those who thought it was only one of many serious issues were younger and came mainly from the lower levels of the civil service or were in financial services and manufacturing (ICAC 1986: 3–2). The implication was that, by 1986, respondents saw corruption in the public sector as under control but were still concerned about the private sector and public bodies.

What the ICAC wanted to achieve – and has subsequently achieved – was the perception that corruption was a very serious social issue in the abstract but one which did not affect Hong Kong because the Commission had effectively reduced it to minimal levels. In consequence, the Unit's recommendation that the link between social issues and corruption should be strongly stressed has remained an integral part of the CRD's community relations strategy and is implicit in the long-used slogan "Hong Kong's advantage: you and the ICAC".

Social acceptability and tolerance of corruption

The zero-tolerance approach means that the ICAC cannot accept differences in social attitudes toward particular kinds of corruption. Yet, if we construct a profile of respondents based on the Community Research Unit surveys of the late 1970s, prevalent beliefs and social attitudes were clearly some distance from where the ICAC wanted them to be. A common position was that corruption in the civil service (including, in particular, the police) was unacceptable but that some lower-paid civil servants could be tipped; that corruption was more acceptable in the private sector where it was difficult, if not impossible, to control and detect; and that the person offering the bribe was less guilty than the person accepting it (ICAC 1979a; ICAC 1979b; ICAC 1981).

The ICAC sought to address these issues by stressing that corruption was an offence in both public and private sectors, that lower-paid civil servants who solicited for tips would be prosecuted, and that both the person offering and the person accepting a bribe were guilty of an offence. Progress in changing perceptions differed considerably. Even by 1996, the ICAC's annual survey found that respondents were almost equally divided between those who were intolerant of all corruption and those who were more intolerant of corruption in the public than in the private sector (ICAC 1997: VII). By 2012, although over 80 per cent of the public were totally intolerant of corruption in both the public and private sectors, there remained a strong belief that the ability to detect private sector corruption, such as illegal commissions, was much lower than in the closely monitored control systems in the civil service (Scott and Gong 2015). In 2017, while there were high levels of absolute intolerance for corruption, public concern about major areas of corruption still included the civil service (although there were few cases by that stage), construction and engineering, and real estate (ICAC 2018b: 10). More rapid progress was made in changing perceptions on tipping lower-level civil servants. In 1977, the Community Research Unit found that tipping was a widely shared community norm, regardless of age, education, sex, income or occupation (ICAC 1979a: 25). By 1986, almost all respondents knew that tipping civil servants was illegal, compared with only 32 per cent in 1977 (ICAC 1986: Table 5.9).

The perception that a bribe was less morally reprehensible if offered than if accepted was seemingly common in Hong Kong in the early years of the twentieth century and was confirmed as still prevalent in the Community Research Unit's 1977 report (ICAC 1979a: III). It is possible that the perception stems from the belief that the offer of a bribe is a payment for a service and that, having made the payment, the person offering the bribe is then thought to be excused from the moral and legal consequences of the action. If the potential recipient of the bribe refused the offer, the surveys found that there was far less likelihood that he or she would report the incident. Although willingness to report corruption if asked to pay a bribe (soliciting) increased from 59 per cent in 1977 to 83 per cent in 1990, willingness to report corruption if offered a bribe dropped from 44 per cent to 25 per cent over the same period (ICAC 1979a: 55; ICAC 1990: 127). Knowledge of the law gradually increased but may not necessarily have influenced behaviour. In 1988, the Unit presented a scenario in which a health inspector accepted a bottle of cognac from the manager of a restaurant and asked respondents if an offence had been committed. Some 65 per cent of respondents knew that both the person offering and the person accepting the cognac were guilty of an offence (ICAC 1988: Table 5–4e). The respondents had doubts, however, about whether penalties continued to apply to gift-giving (ICAC 1988: Ch. 5: 5).

By 1986, the Unit was beginning to speculate that the ICAC might have "bottomed out" in terms of the progress it could make in changing perceptions of corruption (ICAC 1986: Ch. 7: 1). It acknowledged that significant change had been achieved, notably in people's thinking about the use of bribes, and that there was a much greater congruence between public values and the ICAC's zero-tolerance approach. But there was also awareness that no matter how much publicity and liaison work was undertaken, some perceptions of corruption could not be easily changed – particularly, in respect to illegal commissions – and that other findings on perceptions did not necessarily represent how respondents would act in practice. Further, although Hong Kong citizens were increasingly well-versed in corruption law, that did not always mean that it would be respected. The Community Research Unit was integrated into other units of the CRD after its final survey report in 1990. Thereafter, surveys were contracted out on an annual basis to independent companies.

After the dissolution of the Unit, the surveys took a different approach to measuring tolerance of corruption. As Figure 7.1 shows, since 2001, perceptions of tolerance have been measured on a 0–10 scale where 0 represents absolute intolerance of corruption and 10 represents absolute tolerance. While this provides a macro-level picture, it does not adequately cover all the circumstances in which respondents might be faced with potentially corrupt situations. To capture specific situations, the surveys provide scenarios which ask respondents for their ethical positions on particular issues and whether they think that they are legal. Generally, the respondents score above 90 per cent on both the ethical course of action and awareness of the law, but occasional scenarios appear to cause some uncertainty. In 2016, one scenario was "A District Council election candidate asks his/her voters to vote for him/her when providing the service of blood pressure checking free of charge". When asked whether this was acceptable/legal, 18 per cent thought that it was acceptable and 22 per cent thought that it was legal. Most of those who thought that it was acceptable argued that there was no need to vote for the candidate. Under the law, the blood pressure service would be seen as an inducement to persuade the voter to cast a vote for the candidate.

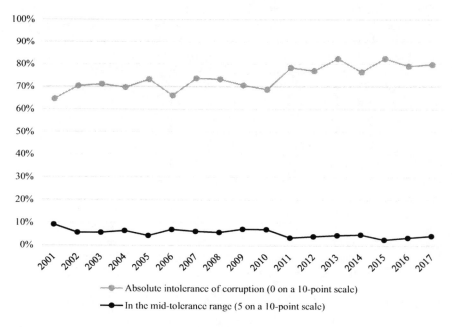

Figure 7.1 Tolerance of corruption (in per cent)
Source: ICAC Annual Surveys (2001–2017)

Answers to the scenarios usually correspond with the high percentage of respondents who are absolutely intolerant of corruption.

Most of the respondents to the annual surveys are not likely to be involved in the complex conflicts of interest that occasionally beset civil servants and politicians. In these cases, what corruption means and what may be tolerated is usually more nuanced than simple bribery situations and can lead to very different conclusions. There is enough evidence to suggest that some politicians are not as aware of the need to avoid conflicts of interest as they should be (see p. 142; Gong and Scott 2015). This has created a gap between a public which regards itself as morally righteous and is mostly absolutely intolerant of corruption and members of the political elite who are perceived to have violated strongly held social norms.

Willingness to report corruption

From the outset, the CRD made a concerted effort to increase willingness to report corruption because the Commission could not function properly unless it received reports and also because it associated a higher propensity to report with a lower tolerance of corruption in the community (Gong and Xiao 2017b). In 1977, the first survey report identified the major reasons behind the relatively low reporting rate. First, if asked to pay a bribe by a government employee, only 47 per cent would report it; the majority said that they had no time or that procedures were too cumbersome. Second, respondents were less willing to report corruption in the private sector than in the public sector. Third, respondents saw no point in reporting corruption if it was victimless; only 27 per cent said they would report corruption if they were offered a bribe and refused it. Fourth, although 90 per cent of respondents said that they would provide names and addresses when they lodged a complaint, only 51 per cent of complainants actually did so in 1977 (ICAC 1979a: 55, 57). The complainants' unwillingness to identify themselves made it more difficult to investigate cases.

The CRD gave high priority to encouraging the public to report corruption. Publicity in the early years and whenever corruption reports dropped was strongly focused on reporting corruption; liaison work almost invariably linked the importance of reporting to the ICAC's mission; regional offices were designed so that complaints could be made in person but as anonymously as possible; and a hotline telephone number was set up and given such widespread publicity that, in 1990, more than 48 per cent of respondents knew exactly what the number was. Despite these considerable efforts, it appears that changing attitudes toward reporting corruption was also closely related to the ICAC's success in pursuing and prosecuting the corrupt (Gong and Xiao 2017b). Once the Commission had begun to show that it could get results, the number of complaints began to rise and respondents to the surveys indicated an increased willingness to report.

As Figure 7.2 shows, in 2017, about 78 per cent of respondents were willing to report corruption, about 14 per cent said that it depended on the circumstances and about 6 per cent said that they would not report corruption. The

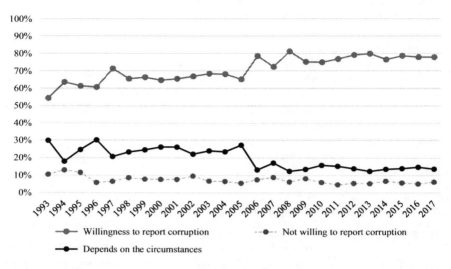

Figure 7.2 Willingness to report corruption (in per cent), 1993–2017
Source: ICAC Annual Surveys (1993–2017)

main reasons given for unwillingness to report were lack of time, that the matter did not concern them, or fear of reprisals. Those who would report depending on the circumstances said that self-interest, public interest and the possibility of adverse effects on relatives were the principal reasons (ICAC 2018c: 3). Willingness to report has also been shown to be sensitive to ethical issues such as the Tong incident, after which corruption complaints dropped by almost 40 per cent. Although respondents did not give the incident as a reason for unwillingness to report, it seems unlikely that the usual reasons for not reporting would have increased so rapidly in such a short period. Motivation for reporting corruption is, moreover, largely based on what the respondents would do in a hypothetical situation; in 2017, only 1 per cent of respondents said that they had actually experienced corruption (ICAC 2018c: 14). The ICAC seems satisfied if corruption reports remain within the "normal" range of 2000 to 3000 complaints per year, if willingness to report corruption remains around or above 80 per cent, if complainants are mostly willing to provide names and addresses and if absolute intolerance of corruption remains at similar levels to those willing to report.

The ICAC's efforts to change perceptions of corruption have been largely successful in bringing public values and social attitudes into line with its zero-tolerance approach. The public perceptions that corruption is a social evil which adversely affects many dimensions of life, that corruption should be regarded as absolutely intolerable, and that it is necessary to report corruption have provided support for the ICAC and enhanced its capabilities.

Perceptions of the ICAC

The principal survey questions with which the ICAC seeks to determine public sentiment toward it are "Does the ICAC deserve your support?" and "Do you consider the ICAC's anti-corruption work is effective?" In 2017, 97 per cent of respondents answered positively to the first question and 79 per cent thought that the ICAC's anti-corruption work was either very effective or quite effective (ICAC 2018c: 11). These responses have not changed significantly over the last decade and reflect the high regard with which the ICAC is held in the community. However, the responses do pose the issue of whether this support is unequivocal and ingrained and, if so, for what reasons and relates to the wider question of the ways support and institutionalisation affects the ICAC's capabilities.

The questions are closely linked because when the surveys break down the reasons why the ICAC deserves the support, the main reason in one form or another is that the ICAC has been effective in preventing corruption. Thus, in 2017, those who thought the ICAC deserved their support said that it had maintained a corruption-free society (26 per cent), that "fairness and justice had been upheld" (23 per cent) and that it had "a successful cracking/high detection rate of cases" (ICAC 2018c: 11). Breaking down the reasons why respondents thought the ICAC was effective suggests that some were influenced by media reports (24 per cent), some by a record of successful arrest and prosecution (18 per cent) and others because it served as a strong deterrent (ICAC 2018c: 11).

While there is little doubt that most Hong Kong citizens greatly value the ICAC and that it is institutionalised, it is important to determine how public evaluations of its role relate to support for the Commission and views on its performance over time. We believe that Hong Kong citizens regard the ICAC as a *necessary* component in maintaining the lifestyle and economy, which has brought them prosperity. The Commission's reputation is the result of hard work to change perceptions of corruption; memories of the "bad old days" kept fresh by the ICAC's publicity; persistent investigations and prosecutions of the corrupt; networks of support; and, ultimately, the ability to produce highly desired outcomes. When respondents were asked, for example, whether a corruption-free society was important to the overall development of Hong Kong, 99 per cent responded positively (Hong Kong Government 2017: 625).

The public's past experience of the ICAC is critically important in determining this perception, and it means that the public is prepared to forgive, if not to accept, circumstances where the ICAC does not live up to its own high standards. As a pro-establishment Legislative Councillor, Chung Kwok-pan, put it,

> Who can we trust if we do not trust the ICAC? If even the ICAC wavers, I believe Hong Kong will come to its demise. Thus . . . I have full trust in the ICAC . . . if it takes over the investigation [of Leung Chun-ying], it should be allowed to do so.
>
> (Hong Kong Hansard 2014: 1687)

The *South China Morning Post* (2013) has called the ICAC an "institutional pillar". Institutional pillars, particularly those concerned with corruption, do not simply appear. They are built on the provision of a service that is thought to be necessary and which the Commission has performed well in the past.

The support for the ICAC may thus be said to be ingrained but it is not unequivocal. Hong Kong legislators and citizens have often been critical of the ICAC, especially when there have been doubts about its ethical behaviour or when there have been concerns about its autonomy. The lesson usually drawn is that the ICAC should return to the principles on which its reputation was built. Anson Chan, the former Chief Secretary for Administration, captured that mood well in an article which was very critical of the behaviour of the ICAC Commissioner in the Li Bo-lan incident. She wrote:

> We must keep our [ICAC] advantage, at all costs, and we must not hesitate to speak up and to take whatever steps are necessary . . . to put the ICAC's house in order, re-establish its reputation for transparency, accountability and integrity and restore staff morale.
>
> (Chan 2016)

During Leung Chun-ying's tenure in office and the continuing investigation into the UGL incident, there were many others who were critical of the role played by the ICAC. To what extent does ingrained institutionalisation provide insulation from doubts about its short-term capacity and effectiveness? We explore this question in the following chapter.

References

Bloomberg (2016) "Hong Kong officials arrest 29 in bank corruption investigation", *South China Morning Post*, 15 December, www.scmp.com/news/hong-kong/law-crime/article/2054111/hong-kong-arrests-29-corruption-investigation.

Chan, Anson (2016) "ICAC: We must keep our advantage", *Voice of Hong Kong*, 16 August, www.vohk.hk/2016/08/15/icac-we-must-keep-our-advantage.

Competition Commission (2016) "Fighting bid-rigging", www.compcomm.hk/en/media/press/files/Press_release_Fighting_bid_rigging_kick_off_ceremony_e.pdf.

Director of Audit (2013) "Report No. 60", Ch. 7, 28 March, www.aud.gov.hk/eng/pubpr_arpt/rpt_60.htm.

Donald, David C. (2013) "Countering corrupting conflicts of interest: The example of Hong Kong" in Jeremy Horder and Peter Allridge (eds.) *Modern bribery law*. Cambridge: Cambridge University Press: 66–94.

Fritzen, Scott A. and Sherya Basu (2011) "The strategic use of public information in anti-corruption agencies: Evidence from the Asia-Pacific region", *International Journal of Public Administration*, 31(14): 893–904.

Galtung, Frederik (2006) "Measuring the immeasurable: Boundaries and functions of (macro) corruption indices" in Charles Sampford, Arthur Shacklock, Carmel Connors and Frederik Galtung (eds.) *Measuring corruption*. Aldershot: Ashgate: 101–130.

Global Witness (2015) "Banks and dirty money", www.globalwitness.org/en-gb/campaigns/corruption-and-money-laundering/banks-and-dirty-money/.

Gomomo, Nceba (2001) "Community participation: A 'sine qua non' for an effective anti-corruption strategy" in Joseph Rotblat (ed.) *Confronting the challenges of the 21st century*. Singapore: World Scientific: 456–468.

Gong, Ting and Hanyu Xiao (2017) "Socially embedded anti-corruption governance: Evidence from Hong Kong", *Public Administration and Development*, 17(3): 176–190.

Gong, Ting and Ian Scott (2015) "Conflicts of interest and ethical decision-making: Mainland China and Hong Kong comparisons" in Alan Lawton, Leo Huberts and Zeger van der Wal (eds.) *Ethics in public policy and management; a global research companion*. London: Routledge: 257–276.

Gong, Ting, Shiru Wang and Jianming Ren (2015) "Corruption in the eye of the beholder: Survey evidence from Mainland China and Hong Kong", *International Public Management Journal*, 18(1): 458–482.

Heywood, Paul and Jonathan Rose (2014) "Close but no cigar: The measurement of corruption", *Journal of Public Policy*, 34(3): 507–529.

Hong Kong Federation of Youth Groups (1997) *Youth opinion polls: No.41: Young people's outlook on life*. Hong Kong: Hong Kong Federation of Youth Groups.

Hong Kong Government (2017) "The 2017–18 budget, Head 72", www.budget.gov.hk/2017/eng/pdf/head072.pdf.

Hong Kong Hansard 17 October 1973; 6 November 2014; 20 November 2016.

ICAC (1977) "Annual report 1976", www.icac.org.hk/filemanager/en/Content_27/1976.pdf.

ICAC (1979a) *Mass survey 1977 final report*. Hong Kong: Community Research Unit, February.

ICAC (1979b) *Mass survey 1978 final report*. Hong Kong: Community Research Unit, November.

ICAC (1981) *Final report of the 1980 mass survey*. Hong Kong: Community Research Unit.

ICAC (1986) *ICAC mass survey 1986*. Hong Kong: Community Research Unit.

ICAC (1988) *ICAC mass survey 1988*. Hong Kong: mimeo.

ICAC (1990) *ICAC mass survey 1990*. Hong Kong: mimeo.

ICAC (1993–2017) *Annual surveys*. Hong Kong: mimeo.

ICAC (1997) *Annual survey 1996*. Hong Kong: mimeo.

ICAC (2016) "Annual report 2015", www.icac.org.hk/filemanager/en/content_27/2015.pdf.

ICAC (2017) *Annual survey 2016*.Hong Kong: mimeo.

ICAC (2018a) "All for integrity", *Gee-dor-dor party on fairness*, https://iteencamp.icac.hk/GameView/Details/955.

ICAC (2018b) "Annual report 2017", www.icac.org.hk/filemanager/en/content_27/2017.pdf.

ICAC (2018c) "Annual survey 2017", www.icac.org.hk/filemanager/en/content_176/survey2017.pdf.

ICAC (2018d) "Anti-corruption resources: Clean elections", www.icac.org.hk/en/resource/publications-and-videos/ps/index.html.

ICAC (2018e) "ICAC post", www.icac.org.hk/en/resource/post/index.html.

ICAC (n.d.) "Building maintenance toolkit", www.bm.icac.hk/en/education_and_publicity_materials/education_and_publicity_materials.aspx.

ICAC Hong Kong Business Ethics Development Centre (2018) "Publications and resources", www.hkbedc.icac.hk/eindex.html#panel1-3.

ICAC, Hong Kong Monetary Authority, Hong Kong Association of Banks, the DTC Association, the Hong Kong Institute of Bankers (n.d.) "Bank on integrity: A practical guide for bank managers", http://cpas.icac.hk/UPloadImages/InfoFile/cate_43/2016/194ad8e4-d904-4a24-b992-aa0f6812a2e9.pdf.

Kanekane, Joe (2007) "Tolerance of corruption in contemporary Papua New Guinea" in Albert Ayius and Ronald J. May (eds.) *Corruption in Papua New Guinea: An understanding of the issues.* Port Moresby: NRI.

Lau, Chris (2015) "'One small step': Hong Kong residents of alleged bid-rigging estate see subcontractor as winning pivot in war with management", *South China Morning Post,* 29 October, www.scmp.com/news/hong-kong/law-crime/article/1873518/one-small-step-hong-kong-residents-alleged-bid-rigging.

Lee, Ambrose (2006) "The public as our partner in the fight against corruption" in Charles Sampford, Arthur Shacklock, Carmel Connors and Frederik Galtung (eds.) *Measuring corruption.* Aldershot: Ashgate: 221–232.

Lee, Rance P.L. (1981) "The folklore of corruption in Hong Kong", *Asian Survey,* 21(3): 355–368.

McDonald, Gael M. (1994) "Value modification strategies on a national scale" in W. Michael Hoffman, Judith Brown Kamm and Robert E. Frederick (eds.) *Emerging global business ethics.* London: Quorum: 14–35.

Peh, Simon Yun-lu (2015) "Culture building and systemic prevention – a twin pillar anti-corruption strategy of Hong Kong", Paper delivered to the 8th Annual Conference and General Meeting of IAACA, 31 October, www.icac.org.hk/filemanager/en/content_77/c-iaaca-2015.pdf.

Rochelle, Tina L. (2015) "Diversity and trust in Hong Kong: An examination of Tin Shui Wai, Hong Kong's city of sadness", *Social Research Indicators,* 120(2): 437–435.

Rose, Jonathan (2015) "Corruption and the problem of perception" in Paul Heywood (ed.) *Routledge handbook of political corruption.* London: Routledge: 172–182.

Scott, Ian (2013) "Engaging the public: Hong Kong's Independent commission against corruption's community relations strategy" in Jon S.T. Quah (ed.) *Different paths to curbing corruption: Lessons from Denmark, Finland, Hong Kong, New Zealand and Singapore.* Bingley: Emerald: 79–108.

Scott, Ian and Ting Gong (2015) "Evidence-based policy-making for corruption prevention in Hong Kong: A bottom-up approach", *Asia Pacific Journal of Public Administration,* 37(2): 87–101.

South China Morning Post (2013) "Keep the faith in the work of the ICAC", editorial, 13 August, www.scmp.com/comment/insight-opinion/article/1296270/keep-faith-work-icac.

Wong, Hok-wui Stan, Ngok Ma and Wai-man Lam (2016) "Migrants and democratization: The political economy of Chinese immigrants in Hong Kong", *Contemporary Chinese Political Economy and Strategic Relations: An International Journal,* 2(2): 909–940.

Yu, Chilik (2017) "Measuring public perceptions of corruption in Asia" in Ting Gong and Ian Scott (eds.) *Routledge handbook of corruption in Asia.* London: Routledge: 224–238.

Zerilli, Filippo M. (2005) "Corruption, property, restitution, and Romanianness" in Dieter Haller and Cris Shore (eds.) *Corruption: Anthropological perspectives.* London: Pluto.

8   The virtuous circle

For an ACA to control corruption, it helps if a virtuous circle, comprising capacity, effectiveness, trust and institutionalisation, can be established. In Hong Kong, when the ICAC was set up and had overcome initial challenges to its powers and jurisdiction, the elements of the virtuous circle began to fall into place. The Commission was then able to

- build its organisational capacity to act against corruption; respond to social expectations and attitudes; engage with society; adapt to new forms of corruption; and facilitate changes in government, business and society, which enabled it to
- deal effectively with corruption and create positive perceptions of its work, which in turn served to
- increase trust and generate public confidence in the integrity of the organisation and to
- institutionalise its structures and processes, further strengthening its capacity.

We express this in diagrammatic form in Figure 8.1.

This is a description of an ideal model of causal relationships promoting effective corruption prevention. In practice, no ACA is likely to be able to claim unqualified success in achieving each of these elements. There is also academic debate about the causal links themselves, particularly between effectiveness and trust. Does effectiveness generate trust? Or is trust necessary to ensure effectiveness? Which way do the causal relationships run? With Mishler and Rose (1997: 420), we would argue that trust has to be "earned" and that effectiveness generates trust. A trusting society may aid the effectiveness of an ACA but we doubt whether this was a significant factor in Hong Kong because, when the ICAC was set up, there was considerable mistrust of the government. The 1966 riots were partly attributed to police corruption and the Godber scandal further inflamed public sentiment (Scott 2017). There was a history of failed anti-corruption efforts and a good deal of scepticism about the likely success and life-span of the ICAC. Under the circumstances, the Commission had to show that it was effective and impartial before it could be trusted.

The virtuous circle assumes that each element in the circle will be performed to maximum effect. But an ACA may still be valued and trusted even if it is not able

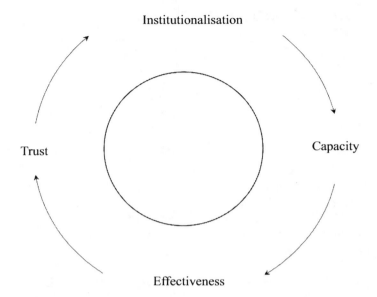

Institutionalisation

Trust

Capacity

Effectiveness

Figure 8.1 The virtuous circle

to perform to perfection. Where the problems arise are in cases which, for example, might involve government–business collusion or have cross-border implications or where corruption might constitute only one element in crimes such as money laundering or electoral fraud. These cases are difficult to investigate. Even if they are successfully resolved, they do not necessarily provide the public with convincing evidence that malpractice is under control; they may simply be taken as an indication that more misdemeanors of a similar kind lurk beneath the surface. Unlike simple bribery, where improvements in corruption prevention may be manifest on the streets or in the public's dealings with civil servants, these crimes are by their nature secretive, less easy to detect and, if revealed, may result in either positive or negative perceptions of effectiveness. Trust in the ICAC, or any ACA, may still be accompanied by doubts about whether it can deal effectively with this kind of problem despite its achievements in other areas of corruption prevention.

In this chapter, we assess the various elements in the ICAC's overall capacity to control corruption, how they relate to perceptions of effectiveness and trust and how they serve to promote institutionalisation.

Capacity

We define capacity as the organisational ability to achieve desired ends. This definition focuses on outcomes and the positive public evaluation of corruption control. However, the overall capacity of an ACA to control corruption depends on several different kinds of organisational abilities. *Ability to act* is a critical first step toward effective corruption control. If an ACA is not perceived to be able to act against corruption, the public will not report suspected corruption cases and anti-corruption efforts will probably founder. *Ability to respond* to public opinion is linked to the ability to act. Survey research into social attitudes helps refine understanding and to develop appropriate strategies. *Ability to engage* is the idea of partnership with civil society organisations to combat corruption. *Ability to adapt and change* refers to the proficiency to deal with new forms of corruption and to develop suitable tools for doing so, and the potential to induce changes in the environment by means of, for example, tighter government corruption procedures and public education. Table 8.1 provides a summary of these organisational

Table 8.1 Organisational abilities

Organisational abilities	Definition	Organisational means	Indicators
Ability to act	The agency is able to control corruption	• Autonomy • Continuity • Law enforcement • Internal coordination	• Rapidity of response • Cost-effectiveness • Continuous repetition of processes • Insulation from external influences • Number of anti-corruption investigators • Number of prosecutions • Links between ICAC departments
Ability to respond	The agency is able to respond to social expectations	• Annual survey of public perceptions and attitudes • Monitoring public opinion	• New programme initiatives to meet expectations and concerns • Evidence-based policy-making
Ability to engage	The agency is willing and able to engage with the public in its anti-corruption work	• Mobilising social resources for partnerships • Coordination with local government and NGOs	• Number of partners • Programmes with partners • Number of citizens involved
Ability to adapt and change	The agency is able to deal with new or more complex types of corruption in a changing environment and is also able to make changes for more effective corruption control	• Monitoring changing patterns of corruption • Updating skills, knowledge and external liaison • Public education • Collaboration with peak organisations	• Amending the law • Institutional reform • Adapting publicity and new technology to needs • Improved governance

Source: Authors

capacities, the means of building them and indicators of their success. In the following section, we discuss these organisational abilities in more detail.

Ability to act

In this section, we focus on specific indicators of ability to act that reflect desired organisational values: efficiency, autonomy, continuity, ability to enforce the law and internal coordination.

Efficiency

The concept of efficiency is variously defined but usually includes the notion of achieving a goal as quickly as possible at least cost but without sacrificing quality (Grossmann 2007: 259–261). The ICAC's rapidity of response can be measured by the number of completed cases within a year. Between 1995 and 2016, on average, 81 per cent of investigations were completed within six months of the same year, and 97 per cent of outstanding investigations were completed within two years (ICAC 1995–2017). In 2017, the Commission completed 90 per cent of cases within a year (Hong Kong Government 2017: 621). There is a quick response team to deal with minor cases and many cases are routine affairs which do not require complex investigation. Not all corruption reports take an equal amount of time to investigate. More complex cases, which may be the most important in influencing public opinion or creating legal precedents, may take many years to complete. The ICAC seeks to ensure that most cases are completed as quickly as possible. Completions are used as a performance measure in the annual budgetary round and the Operations Review Committee is specifically charged to receive from the Commissioner "progress reports on all investigations lasting over a year or requiring substantial resources" (ICAC Operations Review Committee 2017: 14).

A better indicator of efficiency may be the speed with which the ICAC processes new corruption reports. In 2017, the ICAC used the percentage of pursuable corruption reports in which complainants were contacted for interview within forty-eight hours as a performance indicator and reported that it had achieved its 100 per cent target (Hong Kong Government 2018: 610). In 2017, 37 per cent of corruption reports were received by phone, 24 per cent were in person, 26 per cent by letter and 5 per cent came by email or fax (ICAC 2018: 46). The Report Centre operates round-the-clock with senior OD officers meeting every morning to consider and classify the reports. The speed and manner of dealing with corruption reports is important. Some ACAs fail to handle complaints in ways which are transparent and inspire confidence. In the ICAC's case, complaints are processed in a rapid and linear fashion which has helped generate trust and respect.

Cost-effectiveness is another dimension of efficiency, but the desired output of ACAs – effective corruption control – is mostly intangible and difficult to measure. The ICAC's performance has usually been regarded as justifying its budget although there have been occasional criticisms of its expenditure. In response to the Director of Audit's critical report on preventive education in 2013, the government asked the ICAC to review the cost-effectiveness of its practices. The CRD was required to produce a five-year business plan, set out its strategic planning objectives and review all relevant performance targets and indicators (Hong Kong Hansard 2014: 7093). One journalist has called for the ICAC's budget to be cut (Van der Kamp 2016) but there has never been much public debate on the size of the budget in the legislature or in the media. Even the Tong incident, which concerned the then Commissioner's over-spending and resulted in tighter financial controls within the ICAC, did not presage a wider debate on the Commission's budget and cost-effectiveness. We conclude that, for most people, the ICAC represents value for money.

Autonomy

Autonomy may refer to either the ability of an ACA to act independently of other government institutions or to the integrity of its processes and their protection from political or other interference. Both kinds of autonomy were called into question in Hong Kong during Leung Chun-ying's administration when the ICAC was accused by both sides of political bias and when it was alleged that Li Bo-lan's reversion to her substantive position was a result of her investigation of the UGL incident (see pp. 87–88). Aside from this period – when political circumstances rather than its actual practice may have raised the issue of the Commission's autonomy and independence – the Hong Kong government has always been supportive of the ICAC's autonomy. The ICAC itself has always stressed the confidentiality of corruption reports and does not comment on ongoing investigations. The high public recognition of its role and functions supports the conclusion that there is widespread awareness of the Commission's autonomy and that the public believes that any information provided to the ICAC will be treated confidentially. In 2009, the last time a question on confidentiality was included in the ICAC annual survey, 88 per cent of respondents thought that information would be kept confidential (ICAC 2010: 72). Whether subsequent political conflict has affected perceptions of the ICAC's confidentiality and impartiality is not clear.

Continuity

The continuity of processes and recurring patterns of behaviour are important for the ability to act and the institutionalisation of any organisation (Huntington 1968: 12). ICAC directorate-level officers have usually been with the Commission for many years and share a common experience that may even go back before they were recruited. In the ICAC publication, *Forty Years in the Operations Department*, for example, there is a history of significant events that have helped shape the Commission's organisational culture (ICAC 2014). Common values and a knowledge of how past corruption problems were solved contribute to present investigations and reinforce tried and trusted procedures. The adoption of a "One Commission" policy, whereby officers can be posted to other departments, also serves to enhance understanding of the holistic aspect of ICAC work and promotes coordination.

Although most senior officers have spent many years with the Commission, there have been concerns about problems of wastage in the lower grades. In 2013, the Legislative Council Panel on Security noted that the ICAC wastage rates between 2007 and 2012 had consistently exceeded the wastage rates in the Hong Kong civil service as a whole (Legislative Council Panel on Security 2013: 12–13). The ICAC thought that the problem was that most staff were on two and a half year renewable contracts and that there were better financial offers for lower-level personnel as security officers in the private sector. In effect, the Commission was training about 10 per cent of its assistant investigators for work in the private sector. The Panel's recommendation that salaries should be increased was accepted and may have helped resolve the retention problem and attract more applicants (Yau 2017). By 2017, the annual wastage rate had declined to about 5 per cent (ICAC 2018: 26).

Law enforcement

Any successful ACA must have sufficient organisational ability to enforce the anti-corruption laws and to demonstrate that it is doing so. The indicators used to gauge the law-enforcement capacity of an ACA are usually the number of investigators employed and the number of cases that end up in successful prosecutions. These are very rough indicators which need to be treated with care. The number of investigators indicates potential ability to act but it is, of course, what they actually investigate and what outcomes they achieve that really matter. Similarly, although prosecutions make headlines, high-profile cases receive greater publicity than others. Based in part on the belief that syndicated corruption is involved, there are often public demands that the "big fish" should be caught. Arguably, however, if syndicated corruption is not involved, prosecuting many "small fish" might serve as an equally strong deterrent.

The more important question is whether the ACA serves as a deterrent. In the Hong Kong case, the large number of successful prosecutions in the early days of the Commission established its reputation as an effective deterrent force (see p. 39). This may have raised expectations which were no longer wholly appropriate once corruption had been reduced. For example, despite the prosecution of the former Chief Secretary for Administration, Rafael Hui Si-yan, and the former Chief Executive, Donald Tsang Yam-kuen, there have been complaints that the ICAC is insufficiently proactive (Van der Kamp 2016). Whether the political conflict during the Leung administration has had an impact on perceptions of the effectiveness of the ICAC as a deterrent is difficult to assess. Certainly, an ICAC investigation is still regarded as a very serious matter by most public and private sector organisations. The last time the ICAC annual survey asked whether the Commission provided a sufficient deterrent for the corrupt, 56 per cent of respondents said that it did, 30 per cent thought it was average and the remainder thought that it did not (ICAC 2010: Annex III: 5). The main reasons given by those who thought that deterrence was insufficient or very insufficient were that corruption still existed (42 per cent) or that the penalties for committing an offence were not high enough (26 per cent) (ICAC 2010: Annex III: 5).

Internal coordination

The universal model implies coverage of any area in which corruption might arise. To achieve this objective in a cost-effective manner requires attention to both horizontal coordination within the ACA and vertical coordination with its personnel at the local level. Poor coordination is expensive and often results in duplication. An underlying assumption of the ICAC's approach is that effective coordination is a continuous and sequential process. Once a case is prosecuted and closed, the CRD may step up its publicity and liaison efforts, and the CPD is likely to study the anti-corruption controls in the administrative and financial systems to look for improvements. The work of the CRD and the CPD, however, is not simply reactions to OD cases. Their programmes are designed to prevent corruption from arising in the first place, and this can potentially result in some duplication in areas such as the drafting of codes of conduct.

The CRD has also to ensure that its vertical coordination with personnel in the field is appropriate. About 40 per cent of its officers are in the headquarters office, but liaison work and the formulation and coordination of overall policies for the whole of Hong Kong in some important fields, such as youth education and elections, are undertaken at the regional level. The other two departments, OD and CPD, are centralised, although much time is spent outside the office on investigations and assignments. Effective coordination helps achieve organisational objectives supports institutionalisation. Nonetheless, there are always the perennial problems of trying to secure objectives through the best deployment of staff, appropriate information-sharing and avoiding duplication.

Ability to respond

The ability of an ACA to respond to social attitudes and perceptions of corruption prevention depends upon the quality of the information which it possesses. The best way of obtaining that information is through survey research although findings may be usefully supplemented by monitoring public opinion expressed in the media, in the publications of civil society organisations and in representative forums. Information in itself does not aid corruption prevention unless it is converted into policies which address the issues concerned. Surveys provide a basis for evidence-based policy-making, which is likely to be more targeted, more economical, and probably more feasible than policy resting on supposition. Evidence from surveys helps identify attitudes that are inimical to effective corruption prevention.

The underlying premise of the early work of the CRD was that the value of zero-tolerance of corruption should also be held by the public. To achieve this goal, the Community Research Unit of the CRD contracted out survey research with the aim of discovering social attitudes toward corruption and making policy recommendations for change. There were areas where the public remained obdurately committed to long-held beliefs, such as the impossibility of eliminating illegal business commissions. In consequence, the ICAC has not always achieved a complete correspondence between its own anti-corruption values and those of the public. Yet there has been enough common ground to ensure that a zero-tolerance policy toward corruption has been widely accepted. Many practical manifestations of unacceptable behaviour, which reflected tolerant attitudes toward corruption, have disappeared (Scott and Gong 2015).

In 2013, following the Director of Audit's report on the CRD, the government asked the ICAC to review its performance indicators. Some of those adopted were derived from the annual surveys. Table 8.2 shows some of the survey findings used as indicators for the ICAC's budgetary head in the 2018–2019 estimates.

These indicators may be useful in showing the level of support for the ICAC and perceptions of the extent of corruption but they are not always sufficient to provide guidance on policy-making. For that, perceptions have to be disaggregated to discover matters which respondents think need attention or which relate to the social attitudes of particular sectors of the population. The ICAC does ask follow-up questions on the indicators, but many answers are not particularly useful as a basis for taking policy action. For example, a near majority of those who thought that corruption was common or quite common formed that impression from the media. A smaller percentage said that they thought corruption was common in specific trades which is the kind of lead that the ICAC might pursue (ICAC 2017b: 59). The annual survey is helpful in providing an overview of perceptions but it requires more detailed follow-up questions in areas which

Table 8.2 ICAC perception indicators (in per cent)

	2014	2015	2016	2017
Respondents who perceived the ICAC as deserving their support	97	98	96	97
Respondents who considered corruption very common/quite common	28	28	30	28
Respondents who were willing to report corruption	77	79	78	78
Respondents who had not come across corruption in the past 12 months	98	98	99	100
Respondents whose relatives or friends had not come across corruption in the past 12 months	96	95	95	95
Respondents who considered keeping Hong Kong corruption-free important to overall development	99	99	99	99

Sources: Hong Kong Government (2017: 625); Hong Kong Government (2018: 614)

Note: Figures have been rounded.

have been identified in the surveys as problematic, such as government–business collusion and cross-border corruption. What the survey does provide is a picture of the evolution of perceptions over time and a disaggregation of responses by gender, income and education, which contributes to the ICAC's capacity to respond to public opinion.

While there is some danger that the ICAC may become too focused on favourable performance indicators rather than using the findings for evidence-based policy-making, there is still sufficient material in the surveys to inform policy-making and suggest new initiatives. Without the survey, there would be no reliable way of knowing what public opinion on corruption was. The CRD would be deprived of relevant policy-making information and would find it more difficult to keep its agenda abreast of public perceptions of important corruption issues.

Ability to engage

One of the ICAC's initial objectives was to embed itself in the community and to engage in partnerships with district councils, businesses and civil society organisations to control and prevent corruption. The Commission has been able to play that role for many years and has gradually expanded its contacts with various organisations and societal groups. Table 8.3 shows the indicators and targets used in the budget estimates which reflect the extent of the contact and its actual purpose. It is difficult to estimate, however, what percentage of business or civil society organisations the ICAC reaches and in what form. With government organisations, especially at the district level, coverage is extensive although some public organisations may not be contacted for a number of years (Director of Audit 2013: 25). In 2016, the CRD reached 138 government and public bodies, 2351 business organisations, 437 of 506 secondary schools, all 20 tertiary institutions and 2057 non-profit-making organisations (Hong Kong Government 2017: 613). With the government departments and public bodies, this represents a sizeable proportion of all civil servants in a given year. With business and non-profit-making organisations, the ICAC tends to work through, and with, peak organisations and some contact may occur indirectly.

Table 8.3 also shows the purpose of the engagement. Most contacts relate to corruption prevention and ethics training, various services provided by the CPD such as draft codes of conduct and advice on anti-corruption administrative systems, and instruction to candidates and agents in election years. There is also a close liaison between the regional offices and the district councils in drawing up the annual anti-corruption plan. The ICAC regional office generally takes the lead in planning and running the events which form part of the plan. In recent years, these community events have come under the umbrella of the "All for Integrity" programme, which aims "to sustain and pass on the probity culture to all citizens" (ICAC 2017a).

The capacity to engage is important if an ACA adopts a universal model. In the ICAC's case, the ability to contact and influence citizens has gradually increased as new organisations have joined in anti-corruption efforts. The entire population

Table 8.3 ICAC engagement indicators

	2015	2016	2017
Business organisations which have used the ICAC's corruption prevention service	561	594	591
Employees who have received training in corruption prevention and business ethics	43,872	42,412	45,600
Employees and members of non-profit organisations who have received training in corruption prevention	17,151	13,658	11,518
Civil servants/staff of public bodies who have received training in corruption prevention	31,118	34,821	35,891
Secondary/tertiary students who have received training in corruption prevention and ethics	77,803	74,717	69,209[1]
Election candidates/agents contacted	2572	3735	40[2]
Candidates/agents who have attended the Election Ordinance briefing	1578	550	27[2]

Source: Hong Kong Government (2016–2018)

Notes:
[1] The youth population has declined and class sizes have become smaller.
[2] There were no Legislative or District Council elections in 2017.

cannot be covered by liaison work in a year, and there are always decisions that have to be made about the effective allocation of resources. Overall, the ICAC usually has sufficient resources to sustain broad coverage and extensive contact with business and civil society organisations.

Ability to adapt and change

If ACAs cannot adapt to a changing corruption environment, they will become increasingly irrelevant to the needs of their populations. One indication of a failure to adapt is that the agenda of the ACA is not synchronised with the kinds of corruption that the public believes require attention (Gong and Scott 2017: 6–8). Aside from this kind of political pressure on an ACA, there are at least three other inter-related areas that can result in a failure to adapt. First, if the anti-corruption laws do not keep pace with changes in forms of corruption, the ACA will be left administering laws which are irrelevant or unenforceable. Second, the law may change but existing organisational rules may obstruct the intent of the reform, resulting in continuing corrupt or unethical behaviour. Third, if an ACA fails to update its technology or to re-vamp its publicity to meet new challenges, it is also likely to be out of touch with current developments. We examine the ICAC's capacity and ability to reflect public concerns in each of these areas and then consider its ability to effect change in the environment.

Law reform

Although the ICAC has the ability to act and enforce the existing law, the failure of the Leung administration to introduce amendments to the *POBO* has had some effect on the Commission. The consistent opposition to amending Sections 3 and 8 did not significantly reduce the ICAC's effectiveness. It did, however, create an unfavourable impression of the scope of the anti-corruption laws, especially since the Chief Executive himself was under investigation. Many people believed, so the government thought, that the Chief Executive could not be prosecuted at all (Hong Kong Hansard 2015: 1397). Donald Tsang Yam-kuen's subsequent prosecution may have allayed those concerns, but unless the *POBO* is amended, the Chief Executive will still not be seen as equal to other citizens under the law. Another area which requires consideration is the powers of the ICAC under the misconduct in public office offence. The Commission cannot exercise its powers under the *POBO* in investigating conflicts of interest cases because misconduct in public office is a common law offence. The cases are often complex and investigations are often quite lengthy. There is a need to give the ICAC statutory powers to investigate the offence.

The law and organisational rules

Reforms to legislation are normally undertaken on the assumption that there will be some degree of congruence between the new rules and future behaviour. Since the use of the misconduct in public office offence to deal with serious conflicts of interest was developed, the ICAC and the government have conducted training courses and provided publicity to inform public servants of the circumstances in which they might be in danger of committing an offence. Ethics Officers have also played an important role in disseminating information on conflicts of interest in bureaus and departments, and in serving as the contact point for civil servants who feel they may have a conflict. Despite these efforts, there is some evidence that the message has not penetrated throughout the civil service and the Legislative Council and that conflicts of interest have been regarded as less important than the ICAC and the government think they should be.

In 2014, an Assistant Director in the Lands Department, together with her surveyor husband, bought thirteen plots of land bordering on a proposed New Town development with the intention of building four houses on two of the plots (Fung and Wong 2014). Their application to build the houses was considered by a sub-committee of the Town Planning Board which had jurisdiction over the proposed development. The Assistant Director was a member of the sub-committee, but she recused herself, after which the sub-committee approved her application. The ICAC investigated the case but the Department of Justice found insufficient evidence to warrant a prosecution (Mok 2016). The ICAC then referred the Assistant Director to the Director of the Lands Department for disciplinary action (*Ming Pao* 2016). The committee member who laid the complaint with the ICAC thought, with some justification, that the application ought to have been heard by a third party. Equally surprising was the revelation that senior Lands Department officials were permitted to purchase land when potential conflicts of interest were so evident. Organisational and informal rules are not necessarily supportive of ethical behaviour and must be examined carefully to ensure that they do not promote conflicts of interests or support other forms of behaviour which may be antithetical to best anti-corruption practice.

Other institutions have also failed to adapt sufficiently to the need for more stringent procedures governing conflicts of interest. The ICAC has warned strongly of the dangers of "sweeteners" along the path to more serious conflicts of interest. In 2013, eight Legislative Councillors and an Executive Councillor accepted a six-day trip to Paris for themselves and a companion from Cathay Pacific Airways, supposedly to inspect a new aircraft (Chong 2013). At the time, the airline was involved in sensitive political issues relating to the possible construction of a new runway and the licencing of a budget airline. Three of the invitees were members of the Airport Authority Board. When the news broke, there was a storm of public and media criticism. Some of the legislators repaid the cost of the trip; others, seeing no conflict of interest, did not. Even within the government, there have been evident cases of conflicts of interest. In 2018, the Chair of the Communications Authority resigned after failing to disclose that he held shares in a telecom company (Cheng 2018).

Updating technology and adapting publicity

An ACA which is working without the latest technology is at a disadvantage. Corrupt individuals and syndicates have become increasingly adept at concealing their tracks especially when international dealings are involved. Effective technology enhances anti-corruption capacity and, at various times, the ICAC has made specific funding requests for additional technology. Within the OD, there is an Information Technology Management Unit which contains a Computer Forensics Section. The Section is responsible for providing support for front-line investigators and participated in 112 operations, processing 446 terabytes of data contained in the digital devices seized in 2017 (ICAC 2018: 52). It also has responsibility for liaising with international corruption prevention institutions. Other ACAs send personnel to study the Commission's methods and the ICAC also carries out continuous in-house (and some overseas) training of its own staff (Leung 2016).

For many years, the ICAC has been exemplar in its use of publicity. It has been able to relate its publicity to new forms of corruption in innovative ways which have kept pace with developments such as the advent of social media, and it has been quick to adapt publicity to changing social behaviour. A decline in the number of corruption reports has almost invariably been met by increased publicity on the importance of reporting it. But there have also been new initiatives in producing material for ethnic minorities and in publicity for the range of activities that fall under the "All for Integrity" campaign (ICAC 2018: 81).

The ability to adapt to a changing environment is a critical element of an ACA's overall capacity. If an ACA remains strictly within its remit and fails to make necessary changes to its legal and community relations policies, its agenda may not reflect what citizens consider to be necessary for effective corruption prevention. Although the ICAC has a good record of adaptability, the entrenchment of past practices, particularly in relation to conflicts of interest, suggests that formal changes to the law have to be supplemented by more stringent curbs on the continuing administrative and business practices which lead to unethical behaviour.

The ICAC was conceived of as an agent of change, but the nature of change was focused principally on investigating and prosecuting the corrupt, constructing fail-safe administrative systems and changing public attitudes. The powers provided to the Commission relate to these functions and do not extend to wider issues of good governance. Yet, in the process of accomplishing those specific objectives, the ICAC did manage to achieve broader changes, sometimes consciously, sometimes inadvertently. We consider these changes in greater detail in the following chapter.

Effectiveness

Perceptions of effectiveness are closely linked with public assessments of institutional capacity but they are not always based on objective information. They may vary over time and may be influenced by specific events, media comments on corruption, potential prosecutions and the pronouncements of leading political figures (Choi 2009; Morris and Klesner 2010). Although perceptions may be based on transitory or even inaccurate information, they are still critical in assisting or detracting from an ACA's capacity to reduce corruption. If citizens perceive that an ACA has capacity and is effective in reducing corruption and if that function cannot be provided by other organisations, the ACA will have value for citizens. Conversely, if an ACA is ineffectual and if it is perceived to be so, it will eventually become redundant. We have argued that positive public perceptions of capacity and effectiveness, based on long and continued success, have provided the ICAC with insulation from short-term fluctuations in public support. These fluctuations are nonetheless important in understanding the social constraints stemming from what it is believed that the ICAC can and cannot do.

There are two dimensions of effectiveness. The first dimension relates to organisational capacity and whether it is perceived to be sufficient for the ACA to be effective. On this dimension, effectiveness relates to the perceived characteristics of the agency: whether it has adequate powers and commitment to act, to respond effectively and efficiently to public demands, and to engage with various social groups in corruption prevention. Perceptions of effectiveness of this kind can change very rapidly if the public feel that the powers of the agency have been curtailed or that the agency itself lacks integrity. After the partial police amnesty case, there were widespread concerns that the Commission would be unable to continue its fight against corruption with the same vigour that it had previously shown (see pp. 42–44). In the Tong case, there were doubts about the moral authority of the ICAC when the former Commissioner was found to have overspent and broken the financial rules (see pp. 86–87). In both cases, corruption reports fell sharply. Once it became clear that the ICAC's capacity and integrity had not been significantly reduced as a result of the partial amnesty, and once measures had been taken to tighten financial controls and re-assure the public of the Commission's continuing integrity, corruption reports soon recovered to previous levels.

A second dimension of perceptions of effectiveness relates not to the ACA itself but to the environment within which it operates. The ACA may be constrained by factors in the political and social environment that lead to perceptions that it is unable to function effectively in certain areas. Such perceptions can also stem from entrenched public beliefs about corruption, which may not change greatly in the short term. For example, the perception that corruption would increase after the resumption of Chinese sovereignty over Hong Kong seems to have been based, at least partly, on the assumption that rampant corruption in Mainland China would be imported to Hong Kong. It was widely expected that corruption would be well beyond the ICAC's capacity to control. Despite this, on the basis of perceptions of organisational effectiveness on the first dimension, the ICAC was still perceived to be effective in dealing with traditional forms of corruption such as bribery.

The environmental dimension of perceptions of effectiveness may not directly affect people's willingness to report corruption but it may affect what they choose to report. Thus, in 1997, it was widely believed that cross-border corruption was on the rise. Whether that was so is difficult to say, but it was certainly true that cross-border corruption reports remained at very low levels. Was this because people doubted the efficacy of the ICAC in dealing with such cases? Or was it simply because that form of corruption was not as prevalent as was believed? Again, it is difficult to reach a conclusion. The environmental dimension of perceptions of effectiveness is subtle and difficult to detect because it is often embedded in broader social attitudes that go beyond corruption.

The two-dimensional approach to perceptions of effectiveness is helpful in explaining public reactions to the ICAC during the Leung administration. The seemingly almost unshakeable belief that the ICAC deserves public support is essentially a historically based reaction reflecting the public's conviction that the Commission has both the organisational resources and the intention to stamp out corruption. It is this first-dimension assessment to which the great majority of the ICAC's survey respondents have subscribed. Between 2012 and 2016, when asked "Do you think ICAC's anti-corruption work is effective?", between 61 and 63 per cent believed that the ICAC's work was effective and between 17 and 19 per cent thought that it was very effective (ICAC 2013–2016). Overall perceptions of the effectiveness of the ICAC over the period 1997 to 2017 are contained in Figure 8.2.

In 2015, the Social Science Research Centre of the University of Hong Kong administered a corruption perceptions survey of 1025 respondents for us. The questions and answers were somewhat similar to those of the ICAC annual surveys, but on the issue of effectiveness, they came up with rather different results. We asked the question, "Do you think the Hong Kong government has been effective in controlling corruption in the last year?" Only 52 per cent thought that it had been effective (44 per cent) or very effective (8 per cent). Yet the 2017 TRACE matrix placed Hong Kong fourth lowest in the world in terms of bribery risks for business in interactions with government and fifth highest in the world for the effectiveness of its anti-bribery laws (TRACE 2017).

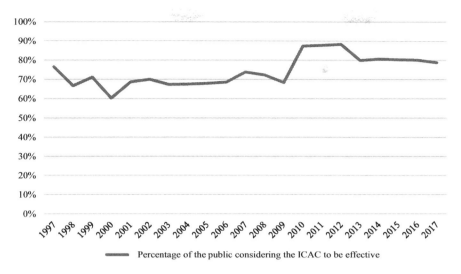

Figure 8.2 Public perceptions of the ICAC's effectiveness, 1997–2017

Source: ICAC Annual Surveys (1997–2017)

Note: The figure has to be interpreted with some caution. The ICAC changed its questionnaire in 2009, which may have resulted in more positive responses to the question on effectiveness (see ICAC 2010: XII).

How can these different results be reconciled? We suggest that for many Hong Kong citizens there is a significant difference between their perceptions of long-term and short-term performance. The ICAC survey essentially expresses the appreciation which respondents felt for the effective efforts of the Commission to control corruption, and particularly bribery, over the years. If, however, a time period is specified, as in our own survey and that of Transparency International (2017), then concerns about the current state of corruption and some second-dimension issues are more likely to emerge. In our own survey, albeit that we were asking about the government rather than specifically about the ICAC, those who thought that anti-corruption efforts had been ineffective believed that government–business collusion was the main reason. ICAC annual survey respondents who thought that the Commission was ineffective gave low detection rates as the main reason.

During the period in which these surveys were taken, the former Chief Executive had been prosecuted, and the incumbent Chief Executive was being investigated. It is possible that this was interpreted by some respondents as an indication of the effectiveness of the ICAC, but it is equally possible that many regarded it as evidence of more widespread corruption as, for example, our respondents who cited government–business collusion as a reason for ineffectiveness. Historically, there have been other issues such as illegal commissions and cross-border corruption which the ICAC has had difficulty in persuading citizens that it can control effectively (see pp. 172–173, 185). The second-dimension view of effectiveness for those respondents – that there are areas of corruption which the ICAC cannot control – does not necessarily preclude recognition of the effectiveness of the ICAC in controlling other forms of corruption, particularly bribery. Indeed, this bedrock faith in the effectiveness of the ICAC is what has helped institutionalise the Commission and to support its continuing efforts in routine corruption control.

Trust

Political trust may be defined as confidence in institutions and involves both the sense that the values of the institution are held in common with those of the community and the expectation that the future actions of the institution will be taken in accord with those values (Morris and Klesner 2010; Van De Walle and Six 2014; Uslaner 2018: 4). Trust is vital if ACAs are to be successful. They depend on the public to report corruption, to assist in investigations and to provide support for their actions in the face of opposition. In the Hong Kong case, we argue that trust developed from the perception that the ICAC had been effective in investigating, prosecuting and preventing public sector corruption. We also recognise that trust and effectiveness may be mutually reinforcing: effectiveness may generate trust but trust can also enhance effectiveness.

Trust is often linked with other social and political factors. In any society, the extent to which citizens trust each other is important in their reactions to corruption prevention (Rose-Ackerman 2017; Uslaner 2018). Hong Kong in the 1950s and 1960s had a very large immigrant population, a considerable proportion of which was not integrated into the community until a massive public housing programme was implemented. Trust in government was low. By the 1970s, Hong Kong people had begun to develop more shared community values and a pride in the economic achievements of the city. The ICAC played an important part in the emergence of this ethos. The stress that corrupt behaviour had no place in the new Hong Kong and that a corruption-free environment supported economic development helped promote the belief that people could trust their fellow citizens (see pp. 164–166).

The relationship between the ACA and governmental institutions is also important. If the ACA is part of government, then the level of trust may depend on how the government itself is perceived. It is much more likely that positive perceptions of an ACA will develop if it is independent, impartial and autonomous. The ICAC was established as an independent organisation and the public learned very quickly to distinguish its actions from those of the government. After the partial police amnesty in 1977, a survey with 858 respondents conducted for the Community Research Unit found that trust in the government's anti-corruption efforts had declined by over 20 per cent to 67 per cent since a survey taken four months previously, just before the amnesty (ICAC 1979: 16). When asked if they believed the ICAC was still sincere about fighting corruption, 78 per cent answered affirmatively (ICAC 1979: 16).

Two other features of this survey are worth noting. First, youth, defined as those between 15 and 24, tended to be more critical and less trusting of both the ICAC and the government. Their overall level of trust that the ICAC was serious in fighting corruption has remained high for over forty years, but subsequently their tolerance of corruption has appeared to increase. On the other hand, there was still a strong base of support and trust – and less tolerance of corruption – from older and less educated citizens.

A second feature of the survey was the relationship between trust and effectiveness. In the initial survey taken before the amnesty, 73 per cent thought that the ICAC's performance was very good or good. After the amnesty, 63 per cent thought that it was very good or good (ICAC 1979: 16). This roughly reflects the drop in the percentage (12 per cent) who thought that the ICAC was no longer sincere in fighting corruption (ICAC 1979: II). The Commission took this loss of confidence very seriously, seeking to emphasise that the ICAC should be judged by its overall performance rather than by the number of convictions in the courts. By the 1980s, it was evident that trust had been restored. The Commission began to receive non-corruption reports in numbers so large that they exceeded corruption reports. On investigation, it was found that the complainants lodged their complaints, despite knowing that its jurisdiction was restricted to corruption, because many trusted that the ICAC would treat them fairly (Ma Man 1988: 90).

Although effectiveness is the most important determinant of trust, it is possible for an ACA to increase the level of trust by raising its visibility even if it is not particularly effective (Baniamin and Jamil 2018). Prosecuting big cases may contribute to an increase in trust because it is often seen to be a very important measure of performance. From the outset, the ICAC benefited from high visibility but has also supplemented its conviction of prominent figures with very extensive publicity about the Commission's own role and values. Public evaluation of actual performance and effectiveness over time and over a broader cross-section of society is a key link in the virtuous circle. Positive perceptions of effectiveness may normally be expected to lead to trust in the ACA.

We do not, however, see trust as a single absolute quality but rather as a potentially volatile relationship between the public and the ACA. People's trust in the ICAC can be conceived of as a continuum. A substantial proportion of the population who have a high level of trust are at one end of the continuum. Their trust is not likely to be lost in the short term because it is essentially based on the first dimensional organisational characteristics of perceived strong capacity and effectiveness which we have considered earlier in this chapter. These people may be influenced by any sign of a loss of integrity within the ICAC itself because they see themselves as sharing the same moral values as the Commission. But other short-term failures are unlikely to damage their trust significantly. In the centre of the continuum, there is a more volatile group whose trust is more immediately related to performance. They may hold the belief that the ICAC is effective in some areas, but they are more sceptical of its ability to control corruption in the political and economic environment. At the far end of the continuum is a small group who do not trust the ICAC. In the early years, one reason given by this group was that they believed that there was corruption within the Commission itself. More recently, the main reason seems to be that they consider the ICAC to be insufficiently proactive or unable to deal with some areas where corruption is perceived to be prevalent (see Ch. 10). Overall, however, we may conclude that the ICAC has long enjoyed the trust of the great majority of the people of Hong Kong.

Institutionalisation

We come, finally, to institutionalisation. Our definition of institutionalisation contains elements which enhance capacity but usually need some time to achieve. They include the regular and continuous repetition of practices and procedures which produce effective corruption prevention outcomes; the community's endorsement of the values underlying ACA action against corruption and its sanctioning and maintenance of those practices by social norms; and the perception of the importance of anti-corruption measures for the political, economic and social structure (adapted from Abercrombie *et al* 1988: 142). These elements enhance capacity by providing the ACA with bedrock public support that stems from the perception that the ACA will act with certainty and consistency when corruption cases come to its attention. In the ICAC's case, although the platform to achieve institutionalisation and enhanced capacity was realised relatively quickly, subsequent consolidation, refinement and adaptation were still needed to enable the Commission to acquire a special status within the community. For other ACAs, the critical issue is whether there is sufficient political will to ensure that they are sufficiently well-resourced and supported to overcome the crises which they are likely to face in their initial years of operation. Many fail at this point. Even if ACAs succeed in overcoming crises, it remains important to ensure that the community's perceptions of corruption are reflected in the ACA's agenda and that there is a social climate opposed to corruption. This process requires time, patience, resources, political support, good will and community involvement. ACAs cannot be truly capable of dealing with corruption without institutionalised procedures and processes.

For the ICAC, the challenge is to maintain an already institutionalised agency. The political turmoil under the Leung administration did the Commission no favours. It called into question the practices and procedures which had been developed over many decades. It cast doubts on the role of the ICAC as a moral arbiter and as a guarantor of fairness, and raised the issue of impartiality, of whether the Commission was giving preferential treatment to one side of the political divide or the other. In an atmosphere in which conspiracy theories flourished, the ICAC had difficulty defending itself from those charges. It could only point to the fact that its practices had not changed, that it would still investigate all corruption reports fairly and that the probity of the Commission had been unaffected by political events. Perhaps its best protection was the insulation provided by the support and trust of the community. The institutionalisation of the

ICAC, the value and high regard in which it was held, and its historically significant role all served as a defence against political claims of bias and inaction. The virtuous circle, although a little dented, has remained in place.

References

Abercrombie, Nicholas, Stephen Hill and Bryan S. Turner (1988) *Dictionary of sociology*. Harmondsworth: Penguin.

Baniamin, Hassan Muhammad and Ishtiaq Jamil (2018) "Dynamics of corruption and citizens' trust in anti-corruption agencies in three South Asian countries", *Public Organization Review*, 18(3): 381–398.

Cheng, Kris (2018) "Hong Kong Communications Authority chief Huen Wong resigns", *Hong Kong Free Press*, 12 February, www.hongkongfp.com/2018/02/12/just-hong-kong-communications-authority-chief-huen-wong-resigns/.

Choi, Jin-wook (2009) "Institutional structures and the effectiveness of anti-corruption agencies: A comparative analysis of South Korea and Hong Kong", *Asian Journal of Political Science*, 17(2): 195–214.

Chong, Tanna (2013) "Lawmakers face criticism after Cathay junket to France", *South China Morning Post*, 22 August, www.scmp.com/news/hong-kong/article/1298404/lawmakers-face-criticism-after-cathay-pacific-junket-france.

Director of Audit (2013) "Report No. 60", Ch. 7, 28 March, www.aud.gov.hk/eng/pubpr_arpt/rpt_60.htm.

Fung, Fanny and Olga Wong (2014) "Declaration of interest row after Lands official bought 13 plots", *South China Morning Post*, 14 April, www.scmp.com/news/hong-kong/article/1567858/row-over-officials-property-deal.

Gong, Ting and Ian Scott (2017) "Introduction" in Gong Ting and Ian Scott (eds.) *Routledge handbook of corruption in Asia*. London: Routledge.

Grossmann, Matt (2007) "Efficiency" in Mark Bevir (ed.) *Encyclopedia of governance*. Vol. I. Thousand Oaks, CA: Sage.

Hong Kong Government (2016) "The 2016–17 budget, Head 72", www.budget.gov.hk/2016/eng/pdf/head072.pdf: 620.

Hong Kong Government (2017) "The 2017–18 budget, Head 72", www.budget.gov.hk/2017/eng/pdf/head072.pdf.

Hong Kong Government (2018) "The 2018–19 budget, Head 72", www.budget.gov.hk/2018/eng/estimates.html.

Hong Kong Hansard 19 February 2014; 11 November 2015.

Huntington, Samuel P. (1968) *Political order in changing societies*. New Haven: Yale.

ICAC (1979) *Mass survey (a sub-study 1978): Final report*. Hong Kong: mimeo.

ICAC (1995–2017) "Annual reports", www.icac.org.hk/en/about/report/annual/index.html

ICAC (1997–2017) *Annual surveys*. Hong Kong: mimeo.

ICAC (2010) *Annual survey 2009*. Hong Kong: mimeo.

ICAC (2014) "40 years in the Operations Department", www.icac.org.hk/fileman ager/en/content_28/ops2014.pdf.

ICAC (2017a) "All for integrity", www.icac.org.hk/en/twp/index.html.

ICAC (2017b) *Annual survey 2016*. Hong Kong: mimeo.

ICAC (2018) "Annual report 2017", www.icac.org.hk/filemanager/en/content_27/2017.pdf.

ICAC Operations Review Committee (2017) "Annual report 2016", www.icac.org. hk/filemanager/en/content_27/2016.pdf.

Legislative Council, Panel on Security (2013) "Background brief prepared by the Legislative Council Secretariat", LC Paper No. CB (2)696/12–13, 25 February.

Leung, Christy (2016) "Hong Kong corruption watchdog ramps up staff training to fight complex commercial crimes", *South China Morning Post*, 29 March, www.scmp. com/news/hong-kong/law-crime/article/1931348/hong-kong-corruption-watchdog-ramps-staff-training-fight.

Ma Man Su-lan, Paula (1988) *A study of the ICAC's role in handling non-corruption complaints.* Unpublished M. Soc. Sc. dissertation, Department of Political Science, University of Hong Kong.

Ming Pao (2016) "ICAC decides not to prosecute Assistant Director of Lands for purchasing land within her jurisdiction", http://news.mingpao.com/pns/dailynews/web_tc/article/20160325/s00002/1458841219346

Mishler, William and Richard Rose (1997) "Trust, distrust and skepticism: Popular evaluations of civil and political institutions in post-communist societies", *The Journal of Politics*, 59(2): 418–451.

Mok, Danny (2016) "Hong Kong ICAC drops misconduct investigation into Land Department official", *South China Morning Post*, 25 March, www.scmp.com/news/hong-kong/law-crime/article/1930555/hong-kongs-icac-drops-misconduct-investigation-lands.

Morris, Stephen D. and Joseph L. Klesner (2010) "Corruption and trust: Theoretical considerations and evidence from Mexico", *Comparative Political Studies*, 43(10): 1258–1285.

Rose-Ackerman, Susan (2017) "Corruption in Asia: Trust and economic development" in Ting Gong and Ian Scott (eds.) *Routledge handbook of corruption in Asia.* London: Routledge: 85–96.

Scott, Ian (2017) "Bridging the gap: Hong Kong senior civil servants and the 1966 riots", *Journal of Imperial and Commonwealth History*, 45(1): 131–148.

Scott, Ian and Ting Gong (2015) "Evidence-based policy-making for corruption prevention in Hong Kong: A bottom-up approach", *Asia Pacific Journal of Public Administration*, 37(2): 87–101.

TRACE (2017) "The TRACE matrix – the global business risk index for compliance professionals", www.traceinternational.org/trace-matrix.

Transparency International (2017) *People and corruption: Asia Pacific.* Berlin: Transparency International.

Uslaner, Eric M. (2018) "The study of trust" in Eric M. Uslaner (ed.) *The Oxford handbook of social and political trust.* Oxford: Oxford University Press: 3–14.

Van De Walle, Steven and Frédérique Six (2014) "Trust and distrust as distinct concepts: Why studying distrust in institutions is important", *Journal of Comparative Policy Analysis: Research and Practice*, 16(2): 158–174.

Van der Kamp, Jake (2016) "Glory days of the past do not absolve Hong Kong's ICAC from its present problems", *South China Morning Post*, 15 August, www.scmp.com/business/money/article/2004178/glory-days-past-does-not-absolve-hong-kongs-icac-its-present-problems.

Yau, Ching Man (2017) "ICAC recruits: Tips for interviews written tests and physical assessment of assistant investigative officers; most important is integrity", *Hong Kong 01*, 12 December, www.hk01.com/article/140251.

Part III

Corruption prevention and governance

9 Good governance

In what ways might effective corruption prevention enhance good governance? For major international organisations, and particularly the World Bank, the concept of good governance is largely based on the assumption that success will depend on the introduction and maintenance of appropriate values such as transparency, accountability, efficiency, legitimacy and respect for human rights and the rule of law (World Bank 1994: XIV; Lateef 2016: 2–9). In its original formulation of the concept in the 1990s, the Bank did not explicitly mention combating corruption as a good governance value, apparently because it was thought to be too political (World Bank 1994: 16; Leftwich 1994; Wolfensohn quoted in Marquette 2003: 11). While it might be inferred that embedding good governance values in institutional practices would result in corruption-free practices, how this was to be achieved was not clear. The Bank and the IMF specifically excluded the political nature of the regime from their mandates for governance reform. Even so, many national leaders saw the Bank's proposed value changes as synonymous with embracing Western democracy and/or a neoliberal agenda. Their concerns were usually focused on the more immediate problems of political and economic survival than the distant Utopia of good governance. The vaguely formulated and overly ambitious original agenda was consequently never widely adopted.

In 1996, James Wolfensohn, the then President of the World Bank, delivered a speech in which he outlined the economic costs of corruption and spoke of it as a "cancer" (World Bank 2005: 50). The IMF followed suit in 1997, specifying that it would address corruption issues only if the macro-economic performance of a country was affected (IMF 1997: 3–5). The Bank was left with the responsibility of developing a more proactive and comprehensive plan. It began, modestly, by trying to ensure that there was no corruption within its own projects, by developing partnerships with regional banks, governments and Transparency International and by conducting some anti-corruption training programmes (World Bank 1997; Marquette 2003: 79–121). Although there may have been some sympathy within the Bank for more bottom-up approaches to corruption prevention, most of its efforts were directed toward top-down attempts to facilitate greater corruption control. There was little apparent enthusiasm in the Bank or in other multi-national agencies for the support or development of ACAs as the principal means of combating corruption (Heilbrunn 2004: 2–3; UNDP 2005: 5). The most immediate impact of the Bank's new emphasis on corruption seems to have been in publicising its debilitating consequences for development at the level of international donors and governments (Marquette 2003: 80–81).

The conceptual focus did gradually change as corruption began to be perceived as an "entrenched symptom of misgovernance" (Kaufmann *et al* 2000: VIII). From this perspective, a corruption-free society may be a desirable moral end in its own right but it is also an opportunity to improve governance in other areas. Klitgard *et al* (2000: XI, 17), writing about corrupt cities, argue that corruption prevention should serve as "an orienting principle for reforming urban administration", which could help achieve the governance goals of increasing city revenues, improving services, enhancing public confidence and even winning elections. Dealing effectively with corruption is expected to have positive systemic benefits and help improve the recognition and application of such good governance values as transparency, participation and accountability (Nguyen *et al* 2017). The quality of governance may also enhance political stability, the rule of law and government effectiveness (Quah 2015). Yet, although studies convincingly show the correlation between corruption prevention and good governance, that does not necessarily mean that this constitutes a causal relationship. It is quite possible that other independent variables might simultaneously create situations in which governance improves or that some areas of governance are unaffected by effective corruption prevention.

If successful corruption prevention is a potential trigger for governance improvements, then the role of the ACA assumes a greater significance than the World Bank has acknowledged. In its refined post-1996 version of good governance strategies, there is still no guarantee that identifying corruption as a major obstacle to good governance will make any difference unless there is an effective plan to deal with it. ACAs obviously could play an important role if they were established with the genuine intent of controlling corruption and if they were to approach the task with a viable plan based on the structural, political, legal and social considerations which we have considered in previous chapters. Equally, however, it would be unrealistic to expect an ACA, or any form of effective corruption control, to deliver good governance improvements throughout the system (Peters 2010). ACAs' terms of reference do not include many aspects of constitutional, legal and political reform that require action to improve governance. As a consequence, we need to distinguish as clearly as possible between the areas in which ACAs can help improve governance and areas in which they may have little or only an indirect impact.

Although it is difficult to distinguish between the contributions that an ACA may make to good governance and changes that may be caused by government action or even economic growth (Makowski 2016), in the Hong Kong case, there is virtually unanimous agreement that the ICAC should be credited with substantial improvements in governance. It has been claimed, for example, that the zero-tolerance approach has generated respect for good governance values, resulted in a clean civil service and more positive relationships between government and the public, promoted economic development and the moral climate in which business is conducted, and increased the level of trust in the society (Klitgaard 2000; Manion 2004: 2). The Hong Kong government and survey respondents alike agree that it is the ICAC that has brought about these changes (ICAC 2018b: Table C; Hong Kong Government 2018).

In this chapter, we evaluate these claims, noting areas where there appears to be a strong causal relationship between successful corruption prevention and good governance and others in which the evidence seems to be more tenuous. In Chapter 10, we analyse areas in which the Hong Kong government and the ICAC have not been entirely successful in detecting or preventing corruption or in changing perceptions that corruption is occurring. Changes are needed in these areas to improve good governance practices.

Corruption, legitimacy and good governance

Seligson's (2002) seminal research comparing four Latin American countries shows conclusively that perceptions of high levels of corruption at the regime level are correlated with perceptions of lower levels of legitimacy. This suggests that successful corruption prevention provides an important pillar of support for regimes, although we cannot, of course, conclude that regimes with low levels of corruption are necessarily legitimate. Other factors, such as consent and legal and moral authority, are likely to be more critical in legitimating power (Beetham 1991: 12–13). Successful corruption prevention may contribute only indirectly, if at all, to increased legitimation stemming from consent or legal authority, but it may have a more direct impact in reducing legitimacy deficits relating to the moral authority of the regime to rule.

In Hong Kong, the colonial regime, by its nature, was constrained in its ability to meet Beetham's criteria of consent and legal authority (Scott 1993). Senior officials believed that they could not seek popular consent for more democratic legitimation and eventual independence that had characterised British colonial development elsewhere. The regime owed its ultimate legal authority to the "unequal treaties" of the nineteenth century, whose legality the PRC government strongly disputed. Although preservation of the rule of law (and implicitly the right of the courts to administer the law fairly) did become an important rallying point for public opinion in the 1990s, by then, China was about to resume sovereignty over Hong Kong and the colonial regime was close to ending. By default, reducing the legitimacy deficit was mainly aimed at improving the moral standing and performance of the government. For almost twenty-five years, from 1972 until the resumption of Chinese sovereignty in 1997, the cornerstone of that strategy was producing more desired goods and services and controlling corruption. The ICAC became a vital element in the attempt to convince Hong Kong citizens that their government was a good government and worthy of their support.

Once the ICAC had been created, its initial priority of controlling public sector corruption was consistent with the government's efforts to improve its moral standing. Situations in which citizens were constantly exploited by corrupt officials could hardly contribute to a positive image of government. Public sector corruption was also detrimental to attempts to improve the efficiency and responsiveness of the administrative system. The ICAC's successful prosecution of corrupt police officers and other public servants was widely applauded but did not, in itself, resolve the problem of a governance system that permitted such wrongdoing to occur. For good governance measures to be introduced, there was also a need for bureaucratic reforms to ensure that administrative practices were corruption-proof and to build upon perceptions of clean government to develop more user-friendly relationships between the civil service and the public. Efforts to achieve a clean government became a two-stage process: the investigation, prosecution and elimination of corruption within government, and the much longer, continuous refinement of administrative systems and practices to provide more checks on civil servants' behaviour and to develop a better relationship between front-line officers and the public.

As Figure 9.1 shows, the large-scale prosecution and conviction of police officers and other public servants dropped away sharply once civil servants realised that they would be arrested for what had previously been commonplace corrupt practices. The effect of the arrests on public opinion was evident in the surveys conducted by the ICAC. In 1977, of the 1974 respondents interviewed, only 1 per cent said that there was no corruption in government; 38 per cent believed that it was present in only a few government departments, while 46 per cent thought that all government departments were corrupt (ICAC 1979a: 20). The report concluded that there was "a high degree of public distrust of

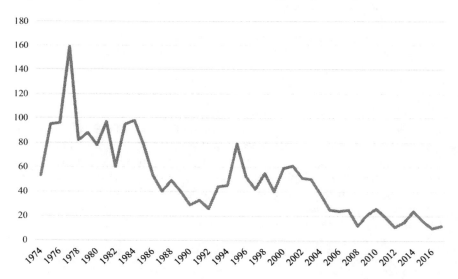

Figure 9.1 Number of civil servants prosecuted for corruption and related offences, 1974–2017

Source: ICAC Annual Reports (1974–2017)

the Government" but that "the work of the ICAC in fighting corruption should help build up a good image of clean government in Hong Kong and subsequently help restore public confidence in the Government" (ICAC 1979a: 20). By 1984, sentiment on the extent of corruption in the civil service had almost completely reversed. A survey with 1040 respondents found that only 6 per cent believed that corruption was prevalent in all government departments; 37 per cent thought that it existed in some government departments, while 13 per cent thought there was no corruption in government at all (ICAC 1984: 24–25). The departments which were thought to be most corrupt were the police, the Urban Services Department, the Housing Department, and the Medical and Health Department. With the exception of the Medical and Health Department, the findings corresponded with the highest number of corruption reports that the ICAC had received about specific departments in that year (ICAC 1984: 24).

Indirectly and inadvertently, the ICAC's elimination of bureaucratic corruption also helped change public expectations of government and the culture of relationships between government and citizens. The ICAC's extensive publicity on the need to report corruption and its call for community support represented a new development in attitudes toward the public and also, conversely, in public attitudes toward an agency. Prior to the creation of the Commission, many Hong Kong citizens sought to avoid government and other public bodies rather than to interact with them. Most probably thought that it was a waste of time to complain about maladministration. The few complaint-handling institutions that did exist were largely ineffectual and almost always found in favour of the civil servant. With the ICAC, it was soon evident that not only was it possible to make corruption complaints, but that they would be investigated and that action would be taken if necessary.

The flood of non-corruption complaints that the ICAC received in the 1980s is testimony to the public's belief in the Commission's ability to act independently and bring about positive results (Ma Man 1988). Its success in persuading the public that government could be held to account also paved the way for the establishment of other effective complaint-handling institutions in the 1990s. The strengthening of the powers of the ombudsman, the creation of the Equal Opportunities Commission, the Women's Commission, the office of the Privacy Commissioner and efforts to reform the Complaints Against the Police Office might still have been introduced because they were seen as possible administrative antidotes to fears about civil liberties under Chinese sovereignty. But their credibility would have been questioned, had the ICAC not already established that Hong Kong citizens could expect redress from maladministration and that their complaints would be treated fairly and without necessarily favouring the position of the government or its civil servants.

Another good governance development made possible by the elimination of bureaucratic corruption was the introduction of public sector reforms in the late 1980s and 1990s (Finance Branch 1989; Cheung 1996a). From 1992 onward, performance pledges were adopted in all departments. They were intended to increase responsiveness and to improve the interface between front-line officers and the public (Hong Kong Government 1995; Efficiency Unit 1996). Although some of the targets in the pledges were criticised for being too "soft", government offices were made more user-friendly and civil servants began to provide more courteous assistance to the public (Cheung 1996b). It is difficult to imagine that such changes would have been possible in the 1960s and 1970s when many providing a service would simply have seen it as an opportunity for extracting a bribe. Although the ICAC was not directly involved in these administrative reforms, it had created the conditions that made them possible.

The commitment over time to maintaining a clean civil service has been one of the most impressive features of the Hong Kong system of corruption prevention. Ensuring that corruption does not re-emerge after it has been detected or allowing it to develop in new policy initiatives is the responsibility of the ICAC's CPD. Unlike most government management services units which usually focus on achieving greater efficiencies, the CPD has a mandate to prioritise anti-corruption procedures in making recommendations for improvements. Under the *ICACO* (Sections 12d and f), the ICAC Commissioner, and by delegation the CPD, has the power "to secure the revision of methods of work or procedures which . . . may be conducive to corrupt practices" and "to advise heads of Government departments or public bodies of changes in practices and procedures . . . necessary to reduce the likelihood of the occurrence of corrupt practices". This might be interpreted as the legal power to enforce changes, although CPD recommendations and their implementation are normally reached by agreement with senior officials in the departments.

By 2015, the CPD had carried out some 3600 assignment studies with 94 per cent of its recommendations accepted and implemented (Tse 2015). The coverage of the assignment studies is very comprehensive, involving most bureaus and departments multiple times. The Constitutional and Mainland Affairs Bureau, which has only one CPD assignment study over the period 2008 to 2016, is a surprising exception (calculated from ICAC 2009–2017; see p. 179). In 2017, the CPD provided advice to departments on 610 occasions on the possible corruption consequences of new legislation and new policies and procedures (ICAC 2018a: 61). It is particularly intent on making anti-corruption recommendations on new projects involving considerable public expenditure. On projects such as the development of the cruise terminal or the expansion of the airport, the CPD has taken a synchronic approach and participates at each stage in the process from project planning to contract letting and administration. CPD staff sit as observers on the tender assessment panel and also deliver integrity talks to staff (Tse 2015).

The CPD's recommendations require a delicate balancing act, ensuring that the rule-based element of its recommendations does not affect the speed with which departmental decisions can be made, require substantial additional resources or emphasise the rules at the expense of good governance values. The CPD's recommendations may not always be the most efficient way of running a department, but they do make corruption in routine government procedures very difficult, and the overall cost-savings benefits to the Hong Kong government outweighs any loss of efficiency in a specific department. Generally, the CPD seems to favour a rule-based approach. In 2015, for example, according to its then Director, each civil servant should be aware of his/her duties and responsibilities which should always be clearly laid out in guidelines and detailed best practice manuals (Tse 2015). At the same time, the CPD attempts to provide support for good governance values. It believes that the values of fairness, accountability, simplicity and transparency (FAST) should influence its recommendations and that they may be represented by such measures as declarations of conflicts of interest, equal opportunities for all players, the expression of honest individual views and a proper appeal process (Tse 2015).

Creating a corruption-proof administrative system does not necessarily result in the development of a more ethical culture or the adherence of civil servants to good governance values on a personal level or increased individual discretion to take decisions. Despite, or perhaps because of, the success of the anti-corruption reforms, the Hong Kong public service has remained firmly rule-based. The Civil Service Code does list some personal values, such as honesty, integrity, objectivity and impartiality, which it expects civil servants to uphold. But they are framed within organisational rules which are the principal sources of guidance for appropriate behaviour for civil servants (Civil Service Bureau 2017). Departmental codes of conduct, which the ICAC is involved in drafting, stress potential corruption offences and penalties for offenders, although they also demonstrate some attempt to link values to rules. In the Customs and Excise Department, for example, where many opportunities for corruption exist, the department's seventy-seven page code of conduct notes the individual responsibilities of officers and identifies types of unacceptable behaviour and specific situations in which officers might expect to encounter attempted corruption (Customs and Excise Department 2015). The code is so detailed that it is used as a training manual for new recruits.

The government's ethical leadership programme and the introduction of Ethics Officers in all government bureaus and departments in 2006 were intended to leaven the dominance of the rule-based approach by introducing more value-based considerations. It has had some impact, particularly in increasing the stress on the importance of avoiding conflicts of interest. CPD and CRD officers give frequent lectures to civil servants and provide ample publicity on the need for public servants to be aware of "sweeteners" and to ensure that contacts outside the civil service do not degenerate into corrupt relationships. Using individual discretion and taking personal responsibility for decisions has not been encouraged. Civil servants are still required to contact their immediate superior if they think they have a potential or actual conflict of interest, a procedure that is laid down in the Civil Service Code (Civil Service Bureau 2017: Section 3.4). The rule-based system has worked successfully to keep the civil service clean and to reduce corruption cases to a few isolated instances. The careful maintenance of corruption-proof administrative systems has been at the heart of effective prevention, and the ICAC is seemingly willing to continue down this path. Value-based measures serve only as a supplement to a predominantly rule-based approach (Scott and Leung 2012).

In summary, we outline the specific benefits that clean government has brought to good governance in Hong Kong. First, although clean government is not the solution to the problems of legitimacy, which both the colonial and post-1997 regimes have faced, it has served to reduce the legitimacy deficit by strengthening the moral authority of government. The claim that government acts in the interests of the people is enhanced if citizens are treated fairly and equally. The stark contrast between the situations before and after the creation of the ICAC increased public appreciation of clean government and led to its acceptance as a core public value.

Second, clean government has reduced the cost of public goods and services by eliminating the need to pay bribes. One of the consequences of clean government has been greater willingness on the part of citizens to interact with government. Social policy programmes have come to be seen as more of an entitlement than a boon granted by a public servant. Eliminating public sector corruption can serve to improve the quality of life and the certainty that dealings with government, whether conducted by citizens or businesses, will be undertaken with integrity and impartiality.

Third, a corruption-free civil service has been the foundation on which further reforms have been built. The introduction of effective complaint-handling agencies and the "serving the community" initiative, which aimed at creating a more responsive public service, would not have been credible if the civil service had continued to be corrupt. The public/police relationship has also gradually improved to the point where reforms in the 1990s sought to change the force into a community police service.

Finally, the creation of corruption-proof administrative control systems provided civil servants with the possibility of developing a stronger ethical culture based on personal responsibility. There has been an increasing realisation within the Hong Kong government and the ICAC that rules alone cannot deal with every ethical problem which public servants may face. The attempt to introduce more value-based elements through the ethical leadership programme and through integrity training is evidence of this. Yet controlling corruption within the civil service still remains heavily dependent on the strict implementation of the rules and the maintenance of effective control systems.

The success of the ICAC in eliminating bureaucratic corruption makes a strong case for its consideration as a first priority for any ACA. The good governance benefits that stem directly or indirectly from clean government are so numerous that investment in an effective ACA focusing, at least initially, on public sector corruption repays the cost of corruption prevention many times over.

Economic development and business transactions

Governments have a responsibility to promote the economic growth and prosperity of their societies, but there has been some debate in the academic literature about whether this necessarily requires effective corruption prevention. Rapid economic growth often increases opportunities for corruption enabling entrepreneurs to take advantages of gaps in the regulations to subvert the rules. It also permits capital concentration in a few hands leading to inequalities which may further promote corruption (Rose-Ackerman 2017; You 2017). "Lubrication" theories of corruption contend that corruption may also facilitate economic growth by speeding up decision-making, avoiding unnecessary regulations, and increasing investment (Méon and Weill 2010). Asian examples present a mixed picture. Rampant corruption has not impeded, and may even have assisted, rapid economic growth in China and in South Korea, but it does not seem to have a significant effect on growth in any other part of Asia (Wedeman 2012; Huang 2016). The World Bank and the IMF believe nevertheless that corruption always has a negative impact on economic growth (Aidt 2009; Kochanova 2015; IMF 2016; World Bank 2017). The difficulty in arriving at a conclusive answer lies in the problem of making assumptions about the level of corruption. Relying on corruption perceptions surveys as a proxy for assessing changes in the level of corruption, as many analyses do, carries with it the danger of assuming that subjective impressions reflect reality. Until corruption can be accurately measured, the conditions under which it can accelerate or impede economic growth are not clear.

In Hong Kong, the ICAC is often credited with creating favourable conditions for rapid economic growth, but this direct causal link is not easily established. It is sometimes argued that capitalist systems, such as Hong Kong, gradually evolve to the point where it is necessary for continued growth to bring corruption under control and where higher wage levels reduce incentives for rent-seeking (Dzhumashev 2014). In the early 1960s and 1970s, when Hong Kong's economy was still based primarily on manufacturing, there was little need for business to become concerned about corruption and there was no pressure on government to provide more effective regulation. Prominent manufacturers could put their views to government through the Trade and Industry Advisory Board and Textiles Advisory Board and in informal meetings with senior officials. There were some concerns that this relationship was collusive because consultation was restricted to a privileged group and did not constitute a level playing field for competitors who might not have the government's ear. But the government argued that members of the advisory boards, in particular, were carefully selected and reflected their expertise (Mills 2012: 159–160). In the 1970s, the Chinese Manufacturers Association was so little concerned about corruption that it thought that the ICAC should focus only on public sector corruption and that illegal business commissions should not be regarded as an offence.

As manufacturing became increasingly less important to the Hong Kong economy and the territory began to develop as an international financial services centre, the need for effective corruption control over the private sector became more evident. There were bank failures stemming from what Li (n.d.) describes as "excessive competition under a low level of supervision in the late 1970s [which] caused over-speculation in property that reached unsustainable levels". Some senior bank executives were found to be involved in fraud and corruption. In response, the government took over the Overseas Trust Bank and subsequently, in 1986, introduced amendments to the banking ordinance, which required banks to have adequate capital and more accountable management. Government intervention and regulation also increased markedly in other fields such as trade and infrastructure, reducing the free-wheeling capitalism of the 1960s and early 1970s, which had provided many opportunities for corruption.

By the 1980s, when public sector corruption was largely under control, the ICAC began to increase its investigations into private sector corruption. In 1985, there were some large-scale investigations of corruption-related fraud, including the banks and Carrian case (ICAC 1986: 15). These types of investigations were complex and placed more strain on resources than simple bribery cases but they became increasingly central to the Commission's work. The general tightening of administrative control systems within the government reduced the incidence of corruption in government/business relationships, such as the implementation of contracts and procurement, but they did not spark any private sector initiatives to improve ethical behaviour. In 1989, the CPD conducted a survey of business-men's attitudes toward corruption and found that over half of the respondents "had no written instructions, manual of procedure or any policy on the accept-ance of advantages despite two-thirds of them agreeing that corruption preven-tion measures were desirable and necessary" (ICAC 1990: 46). In the following year, the former chairman of the Hong Kong Stock Exchange, Ronald Li, was convicted of corruption and sentenced to four years in prison.

By 1993, corruption complaints had risen by 44 per cent and there was public concern, according to the Governor, Patten, that "our business sector is becom-ing more vulnerable to corrupt practices" (Hong Kong Government 1993: para 108). He directed the ICAC to conduct a campaign in cooperation with major business associations and professional bodies to develop voluntary codes of prac-tice to prevent malpractice. The codes were expected to encourage companies "to conduct fair and open dealings" with all customers, suppliers and contrac-tors. Once they had been drafted, the ICAC was asked to invite all companies with more than 100 staff to introduce similar codes (Hong Kong Government 1993: para 110). Snell and Herndon (2000) found that, by December 1996, 1611 companies and trade associations had adopted a code. Most companies fol-lowed the ICAC's model code, making relatively minor amendments to suit their circumstances. Improving moral conduct and providing legal protection ranked about equally in business decisions to adopt a code. Only 39 per cent of those surveyed thought that it actually improved moral conduct, while 20 per cent thought that it had not (Snell and Herndon 2000).

The most important long-term outcome of the campaign was probably the creation, within the ICAC, of the Hong Kong Ethics Development Centre (later the Hong Kong Business Ethics Development Centre). In collaboration with ten major chambers of commerce, the Centre was established to formulate corporate codes of ethics, organise training courses and publish a newsletter. Subsequently, it developed a consultancy service, a resource centre and a website. In 2018, the website listed many practical guides and pamphlets, videos, articles and case stud-ies designed to assist business in promoting a more ethical culture (Hong Kong

Business Ethics Development Centre 2018). The Centre's approach tends to be one of persuasion and building best practice systems rather than stressing the penalties that would result from corrupt practices. It believes that business integrity can be achieved by ensuring that standards are clearly set out for all company employees through codes of conduct, by organising ethical training courses and by strengthening systems control (ICAC 2018c). It maintains that "good governance is good business" (ICAC 2018d).

The ICAC also stresses that it is in the best interests of business to combat corruption within the company. It points out that corruption erodes profits and that it pays to build corruption-proof systems. In 2015, the Hong Kong Stock Exchange amended its regulations for listed companies on the provision of anti-corruption policies from "recommended best practice" to "comply and explain". The ICAC's Corruption Prevention Advisory Service then produced a document which describes how a company may meet the required standards and whether further attention to anti-corruption issues may be necessary (ICAC Corruption Prevention Advisory Service 2016). The Service is on hand to provide free advice to companies, organisations and individuals, and did so on 880 occasions in 2016 (ICAC 2017: 55).

Coupled with a CRD approach which stresses that it is in the best interests of companies to put their own houses in order, the OD has developed increasingly more sophisticated means of detecting and pursuing economic crimes as they relate to corruption (Kwok 2005; Ng 2017). In 2017, of the 193 persons prosecuted for corruption, 137 were from the private sector (ICAC 2018a: 43). Most were charged under Section 9 of the *POBO*, which provides that accepting an advantage without the consent of the principal is an offence. Many cases involve corrupt or fraudulent activities, such as illegal commissions and rebates, which are small-scale and affect many different businesses. The ICAC publicises such cases in the hope that they will have a deterrent effect but, in an economy with such diverse and extensive business activities, this kind of petty corruption is difficult to control. The suspicion that grand corruption and collusion is not being detected represents a much greater public concern.

There is little doubt that the ICAC has expended a great deal of time and resources in its attempts to control private sector corruption. With what success? And with what contributions to good governance? In its relations with chambers of commerce and attempts to work with them to improve business ethics, the ICAC has followed a strategy of becoming embedded at peak levels of the business sector. Business people in Hong Kong do not now normally expect to pay bribes and transactions are usually conducted transparently. The TRACE (2017) bribery risk matrix, which employs world-wide information to assess the risk of encountering commercial bribery, rates Hong Kong very highly on three of the four domains that make up the matrix. On the likelihood of government officials asking or expecting a bribe from business people, the risk in Hong Kong is negligible; on the anti-corruption laws and their enforcement, the report concludes that they are very effective and well-enforced; and on the transparency of government regulatory functions and of financial interests, Hong Kong also scores well. Only on the fourth domain, which seeks to measure capacity for civil society oversight and includes the quality and freedom of the media, does Hong Kong drop to an average rating (TRACE International 2017).

Other surveys confirm these findings. In 2017, Transparency International's Corruption Perceptions Index, which is partly based on business surveys, ranked Hong Kong the thirteenth cleanest of 183 countries and regions (Transparency International 2018). The 2017 Global Competitiveness Index placed Hong Kong ninth lowest of 137 countries and regions in irregular payments and bribes, thirteenth lowest in favouritism in decisions of government officials and fifteenth highest in the ethical behaviour of firms (World Economic Forum 2017). A Transparency International (2017: 17) survey found that only 2 per cent of Hong Kong respondents had offered or accepted bribes, and that many of those had been parents trying to enrol their children in prestigious schools. ICAC annual surveys confirm that actual experience of soliciting or accepting bribes in both the public and the private sectors in Hong Kong is very low (ICAC 2018b: 14).

We conclude that the ICAC's efforts to reduce corruption in the business sector have been effective in increasing transparency and reducing bribery. Against this, we note that during the Leung administration, there was a marked increase in perceptions of unethical behaviour in respect to collusion and cross-border corruption. In Chapter 10, we examine these perceptions and the problems they pose for the ICAC in greater detail.

Building a trusting society

Social trust is the basis on which a more harmonious and corruption-free society can be built (Morris and Klesner 2010; Warren 2018: 83). The process of building trust is mutually reinforcing. Trusting societies help increase the level of social trust and high social trust results in more trusting societies. In a trusting society, individual transactions within and beyond social networks will be influenced by the expectation that others will behave in the same way as oneself. This, in turn, helps create exchange relationships which are governed by values which are important to building social trust such as honesty, transparency and fairness. One of the major benefits of such societies is that they are less corrupt than those in which members of the society do not trust each other (Uslaner 2008, 2017; Newton *et al* 2018: 40). Higher levels of trust also lead to a better quality of governance by providing assured public support for legitimised government action (Rothstein 2011). Once good governance is achieved, it will help increase institutional and social trust by providing certainty, fairness and policies adopted in the public interest (Hardin 2003; Rothstein and Eek 2009; Park 2017). Declining levels of institutional trust, by contrast, which may be caused by increasing levels of corruption or by significant political divisions within the polity, may lead to an even greater acceleration of corruption and to wider governance problems (Chang 2013).

Attempts to assess the levels of social and institutional trust in Hong Kong present problems because the figures on social trust differ considerably. A survey used by Uslaner (2008: 18) finds that Hong Kong has low levels of social trust. Another study of six Asia-Pacific countries and regions concludes, however, that Hong Kong is a trusting society, second only to Australia, in the level of trust in family, neighbours, foreigners and strangers (Ward *et al* 2014). A further problem in distinguishing the contribution that the ICAC has made to the development of a more trusting society is that its efforts have been accompanied by greater prosperity, a better quality of life and a rising level of education, factors which are associated with the growth of a more trusting society. Moreover, the government's social policies and a focus on community building have also helped increase social trust (Jones 1999: 47). The ICAC's contribution thus cannot easily be separated from other positive changes taking place in government and the economy.

We argue nonetheless that the ICAC's focus on corruption prevention had a particular impact on exchange relationships. Since the Commission was focused on reducing bribery, the impact of successful corruption prevention was felt especially in interactions between the public and the civil service, in business dealings and in relationships within social networks. At the societal level, the ICAC's successful campaigns to persuade the public to avoid corrupt behaviour inevitably had implications for the ways in which people viewed and treated each other. The Commission became a moral arbiter, laying down the rules on a range of matters such as appropriate behaviour in relationships between civil servants and government contractors, the acceptance of "kickbacks" in the private sector and "sweeteners" in the public sector, gift-giving and tipping public servants. In the process of implementing its zero-tolerance approach to corruption, common social practices were modified or eliminated. Public education likewise meant that from a very early age, children in the school system were exposed to ICAC publicity, which stressed the importance of honesty and fairness. The consequential changes resulting from these efforts were supportive of a new morality which helped both to reduce corruption and increase social trust.

There is some difficulty in assessing whether recent developments have affected the kind of social trust that the ICAC was instrumental in helping to build in the 1970s and 1980s. We consider, first, the initial efforts to change values and social attitudes that affected the development of social trust and, second, the potential consequences of inequality, political conflict and a divided polity on social relationships.

As an example of the ways in which common social practices were changed in ways which were conducive to developing social trust, the attitudes of the public and the ICAC toward tipping public servants are instructive. Although about 86 per cent of the respondents to the early ICAC surveys believed that paying bribes to civil servants was wrong and respondents were clearly aware of the distinction between tipping and corruption, their views on tipping lower-paid civil servants were equivocal (ICAC 1979b: 11). A majority thought that refuse collectors deserved a tip and significant percentages also believed that hospital ward assistants and postmen should be tipped (ICAC 1979b: Tables 2.3, 2.4). However, they did not believe that slightly better paid public servants, such as health inspectors, deserved a tip. The survey asked respondents why they tipped lower-paid civil servants. Most gave multiple reasons for their actions. They appreciated the service (43 per cent), were motivated by custom (39 per cent), sought better service (21 per cent) or wanted to avoid losing face (16 per cent) (ICAC 1979b: 16). Tipping seems to have served as a form of social glue, smoothing relationships and establishing the citizen as a legitimate recipient of a service.

For the ICAC and many of the better educated respondents to its surveys, tipping civil servants amounted to a bribe. The Commission was concerned that tipping would develop into an obligation and eventually turn into situations in which a service would be refused if "tea money" was not forthcoming. Tips were regarded as potential "sweeteners" for future favours from the civil servant. The ICAC's intent to eliminate the tipping of civil servants was clearly shown in a 1978 case in which a postman was prosecuted for soliciting for *lai see* during Chinese New Year (*Attorney General v Chung Fat Ming* 1978; McWalters 2015: 247–249). The postman had said nothing but had made a gesture wishing a resident "happy new year" in the probable expectation of receiving a tip. Although the postman was acquitted, the Attorney-General asked for a statement of the case because it involved the issues of *mens rea* and "sweeteners". The court's findings enabled the ICAC to continue to prosecute without recourse to proving that the accused had corrupt motives when soliciting for a tip. Within a few years, a survey showed that tipping civil servants was less of a problem (ICAC 1981: Table 2.6).

The ICAC's success in changing social attitudes, coupled with greater prosperity and higher levels of education, helped create relationships that were based on clean exchanges (McDonald 1994). It differed from the previous social order in that there were no expectations that bribes would be solicited or received and, more positively, that the importance of values such as honesty and fairness were more assiduously promoted. Portes (1998) has argued that social trust of this kind, if realised through internalised norms, can be appropriable by others in the community and can lead to a more trusting society. Clean exchanges might therefore be expected to promote a more trusting society although there are few studies comparing trust in Hong Kong society before and after corruption was controlled. A 1986 survey did conclude that "the Hong Kong Chinese have progressed quite a bit in their decent level of abstract social trust", although mistrust of others was still a dominant theme (Lau and Kuan 1988: 68). What we can conclude is that since its creation, the ICAC has sought to lay values before the public which, it has argued, would help improve governance and help the development of a cleaner and more prosperous society. Even though political division over the last decade has not been conducive to the maintenance of a trusting society, the ICAC's values still underlie much of its efforts and, in that sense, provide a standard of morality which has had a strong influence on community norms.

We began this chapter by asking whether an ACA that can successfully prevent corruption contributes to good governance and, if so, in what areas. In Hong Kong, the ICAC's virtual elimination of bureaucratic corruption has certainly been a major contribution. It has had widespread positive benefits for improved relationships between the government and the public, and cleaner and more transparent dealings between the government and the private sector. A cleaner civil service also helped reduce the colonial regime's legitimacy deficit and, in the post-1997 period, served as a pillar of good governance and stability when other institutions, such as the Chief Executive and the Legislative Council, were strongly criticised for their behaviour and consequently lost public confidence. The civil service became an example for other organisations of best ethical practices and of how to create an ethical culture. The ICAC also played an important role in improving the atmosphere in which business transactions took place. Bribes, illegal commissions and rebates did not disappear but business people became more aware of the costs of corruption to their businesses, the damage which it could do to the reputations of their companies and the benefits that could be reaped from clean exchanges. In the society, the ICAC helped develop a new morality which was not only antithetical to corruption but was also supportive of building greater social trust and a more trusting society.

These are important good governance achievements. They support the World Bank's belief that corruption is a major obstacle to good governance, even if the methods used to control it in Hong Kong, through an effective ACA, do not entirely follow the Bank's prescriptions. Yet, despite the ICAC's achievements, there have also been some areas in which it has not had much success in improving dubious ethical practices, poor regulations and fears of undercover corrupt behaviour. In the following chapter, we analyse the reasons why an ACA's successful efforts to control corruption do not necessarily always lead to better governance throughout the polity.

References

Aidt, Toke S. (2009) "Corruption, institutions and economic development", *Oxford Review of Economic Policy*, 25(2): 271–291.
Attorney General v Chung Fat Ming CACC00533/1978.
Beetham, David (1991) *The legitimation of power*. Basingstoke: Macmillan.
Chang, Eric C. (2013) "A comparative analysis of how corruption erodes institutional trust", *Taiwan Journal of Democracy*, 9(1): 73–92.
Cheung, Anthony Bing-leung (1996a) "Public sector reform and the re-legitimation of public bureaucratic power", *International Journal of Public Sector Management*, 9(5-6): 37–50.
Cheung, Anthony Bing-leung (1996b) "Performance pledges – power to the consumer or a quagmire in public sector legitimation", *International Journal of Public Administration*, 19(2): 233–259.
Civil Service Bureau (2017) "Civil service code", www.csb.gov.hk/english/admin/conduct/1751.html.
Customs and Excise Department (2015) *Code on conduct and discipline*. 7th edition, www.customs.gov.hk/filemanager/common/pdf/pdf_publications/code_conduct_discipline_e.pdf.
Dzhumashev, Ratbek (2014) "Corruption and growth: The role of governance, public spending and economic development", *Economic Modelling*, 37: 202–2015.

Efficiency Unit (1996) *The service imperative*. Hong Kong: Government Printer.

Finance Branch (1989) *Public sector reform*. Hong Kong: Finance Branch.

Hardin, Russell (2003) "Trust in government" in Margaret Levi and Valerie Brathwaite (eds.) *Trust and governance*. New York: Russell Sage Foundation: 9–27.

Heilbrunn, John R. (2004) *Anti-corruption commissions: Panacea or real medicine to fight corruption?* Washington: World Bank.

Hong Kong Business Ethics Development Centre (2018) "Publications resources", www.hkbedc.icac.hk/english/publications/publications.html

Hong Kong Government (1993) *Hong Kong: Today's successes, tomorrow's challenges*. Hong Kong: Government Printer.

Hong Kong Government (1995) *Serving the community*. Hong Kong: Government Printer.

Hong Kong Government (2018) "CE visits ICAC", 9 January, www.info.gov.hk/gia/general/201801/09/P2018010900856.htm.

Huang, Chiung-Ju (2016) "Is corruption bad for economic growth? Evidence from Asia-Pacific countries", *North American Journal of Economics and Finance*, 35: 247–256.

ICAC (1974–2017) "Annual reports", www.icac.org.hk/en/about/report/annual/index.html.

ICAC (1979a) *Mass survey 1977 final report*. Hong Kong: Community Research Unit, February.

ICAC (1979b) *Mass survey 1978 final report*. Hong Kong: Community Research Unit, November,

ICAC (1981) *Final report of the 1980 mass survey*. Hong Kong: Community Research Unit, September.

ICAC (1984) *ICAC mass survey 1984*. Hong Kong: Community Research Unit.

ICAC (1986) "Annual report 1985", www.icac.org.hk/filemanager/en/Content_27/1985.pdf.

ICAC (1990) "Annual report 1989", www.icac.org.hk/filemanager/en/Content_27/1989.pdf.

ICAC (2017) "Annual report 2016", www.icac.org.hk/filemanager/en/content_27/2016.pdf.

ICAC (2018a) "Annual report 2017", www.icac.org.hk/filemanager/en/content_27/2017.pdf.

ICAC (2018b) "Annual survey 2017", www.icac.org.hk/filemanager/en/content_176/survey2017.pdf.

ICAC (2018c) "Business sector – corporate ethics programme", www.icac.org.hk/en/service/edcuate/business-sector/index.html.

ICAC (2018d) "Business sector – good governance means good business", www.icac.org.hk/en/bs/index.html.

ICAC Corruption Prevention Advisory Service (2016) "Anti-corruption programme: A guide for listed companies", http://cpas.icac.hk/UPloadImages/InfoFile/cate_43/2017/2011e868-01e0-4a6c-bc6e-967e84e6a7eb.pdf.

IMF (1997) "Good governance: The IMF's role: Transparency, accountability, efficiency, fairness", www.imf.org/external/pubs/ft/exrp/govern/govindex.htm.

IMF (2016) "IMF survey: Fighting corruption critical for economic growth and macro-economic stability", *IMF News*, 6 May, www.imf.org/en/News/Articles/2015/09/28/04/53/sores051116a.

Independent Commission Against Corruption Ordinance (ICACO) (Cap 204).

Jones, Carol (1999) "Law as a substitute for politics in Hong Kong and China" in Kanishka Jayasuriya (ed.) *Law, capitalism and power in Asia*. London; New York: 38–57.

Kaufmann, Daniel (2000) "World Bank Institute foreword" in Robert Klitgard, Ronald MacLean-Aboroa and H. Lindsey Parris (eds.) *Corrupt cities: A practical guide to cure and prevention*. Washington, DC: The World Bank.

Klitgaard, Robert, Ronald MacLean-Aboroa and H. Lindsey Parris (2000) *Corrupt cities: A practical guide to cure and prevention*. Washington, DC: The World Bank.

Kochanova, Anna (2015) "How does corruption affect economic growth?" *World Economic Forum*, 6 May, www.weforum.org/agenda/2015/05/how-does-corruption-affect-economic-growth/

Kwok, Man-wai Tony (2005) "Measures to combat economic crime, including money-laundering", Eleventh United Nations Congress on Crime Prevention and Criminal Justice, Bangkok, 18–25 April 2005, www.unafei.or.jp/publications/pdf/11th_Congress/27Talking_Points_4.pdf.

Lateef, K. Sarwar (2016) "Evolution of the World Bank's thinking on governance", Background paper for the 2017 World Development Report, http://pubdocs.worldbank.org/en/433301485539630301/WDR17-BP-Evolution-of-WB-Thinking-on-Governance.pdf.

Lau, Siu-Kai and Kuan Hsin-Chi (1988) *The ethos of the Hong Kong Chinese*. Hong Kong: The Chinese University Press.

Leftwich, Adrian (1994) "Governance, the state and the politics of development", *Development and Change*, 25(2): 363–386.

Li, Raymond (n.d.) "Banking problems: Hong Kong experience in the 1980s", www.bis.org/publ/plcy06d.pdf.

Ma Man, Su-lan Paula (1988) *A study of the ICAC's role in handling non-corruption complaints*. Unpublished M. Soc. Sc. dissertation, Department of Political Science, University of Hong Kong.

Makowski, Grzegor (2016) "Anti-corruption agencies – silver bullet against corruption or fifth wheel to a coach? Analysis from the perspective of the constructivist theory of social problems", *Studia z polityki publicznej*, 2(10): 55–77.

Manion, Melanie (2004) *Corruption by design: Building clean government in Mainland China and Hong Kong*. Cambridge, MA: Harvard University Press.

Marquette, Heather (2003) *Corruption, politics and development: The role of the World Bank*. New York: Palgrave Macmillan.

McDonald, Gael M. (1994) "Value modification strategies on a national scale" in W.Michael Hoffman, Judith Brown. Kamm, Robert E. Frederick and Edward S. Petry (eds.) *Emerging global business ethics*. London: Quorum: 14–35.

McWalters, Ian, David Fitzpatrick and Andrew Bruce (2015) *Bribery and corruption law in Hong Kong*. 3rd edition. Singapore: LexisNexis.

Méon, Pierre Guillaume and Laurent Weill (2010) "Is corruption an efficient grease?" *World Development*, 38(3): 244–259.

Mills, Laurence (2012) *Protecting free trade: The Hong Kong paradox 1947–1997*. Hong Kong: Hong Kong University Press.

Morris, Stephen D. and Joseph L. Klesner (2010) "Corruption and trust: Theoretical considerations and evidence from Mexico", *Comparative Political Studies*, 43(10): 1258–1285.

Newton, Kenneth, Dietlind Stoll and Sonja Zmerli (2018) "Social and political trust" in Eric M. Uslaner (ed.) *The Oxford handbook of social and political trust*. Oxford: Oxford University Press: 37–56.

Ng, Kang-chung (2017) "Illegal funds frozen in Hong Kong up 60 per cent, ICAC says as it prepares to host global conference on money-laundering", *South China Morning Post*, 8 May, www.scmp.com/news/hong-kong/law-crime/article/2093318/illegal-funds-frozen-hong-kong-60-cent-icac-says-it.

Nguyen, Thang V., Thang N. Bach, Thanh Q. Le and Canh Q. Le (2017) "Local governance, corruption and public service quality: Evidence from a national survey in Vietnam", *International Journal of Public Sector Management*, 30(2): 137–153.

Park, Chong-Min (2017) "Political trust in the Asia-Pacific region" in Sonja Zmerli and Tom van der Meer (eds.) *Handbook of political trust*. Cheltenham: Edward Elgar.

Peters, B. Guy (2010) "Institutional design and good governance" in Gjalt de Graaf, Patrick von Maravić and Pieter Wagner (eds.) *The good cause: Theoretical perspectives on corruption*. Opladen and Farmington Hills, MI: Barbara Budrich Publishers: 83–97.

Portes, Alejandro (1998) "Social capital its origins and applications in modern sociology", *Annual Review of Sociology*, 24(1): 1–24.

Quah, Jon S.T. (2015) "Evaluating the effectiveness of anti-corruption agencies in five Asian countries: A comparative analysis", *Asian Education and Development Studies*, 4(1): 143–159.

Rose-Ackerman, Susan (2017) "Corruption in Asia: Trust and economic development" in Ting Gong and Ian Scott (eds.) *Routledge handbook of corruption in Asia*. London: Routledge: 85–96.

Rothstein, Bo (2011) *The quality of government: Corruption, social trust and inequality in international perspective*. Chicago: University of Chicago Press.

Rothstein, Bo and Daniel Eek (2009) "Political corruption and social trust: An experimental approach", *Rationality and Society*, 21(1): 81–112.

Scott, Ian (1993) "Legitimacy and its discontents: Hong Kong and the reversion to Chinese sovereignty", *Asian Journal of Political Science*, 1(1): 55–75.

Scott, Ian and Joan Y.H. Leung (2012) "Integrity management in post-1997 Hong Kong: challenges for a rule-based system", *Crime, Law and Social Change*, 58(1): 39–52.

Seligson, Mitchell A. (2002) "The impact of corruption on regime legitimacy: A comparative study of four Latin American countries", *The Journal of Politics*, 64(2): 408–433.

Snell, Robin Stanley and Neil C. Herndon Jr. (2000) "An evaluation of Hong Kong's corporate code of ethics initiative", *Asia Pacific Journal of Management*, 17(3): 493–518.

TRACE International (2017) "Hong Kong", www.traceinternational.org/Uploads/MatrixFiles/2017/Reports/Hong%20Kong-TRACE%20Matrix%20Individual%20Countries.pdf.

Transparency International (2017) "People and corruption: Asia Pacific – Global corruption barometer", www.transparency.org/whatwedo/publication/people_and_corruption_asia_pacific_global_corruption_barometer.

Transparency International (2018) "Corruption perceptions index", www.transparency.org/news/feature/corruption_perceptions_index_2017.

Tse, Man-shing (2015) "Enhancing corporate governance in the public and private sectors", 6th ICAC symposium, 12 May, www.icac.org.hk/symposium/2015/pdf/TSE%20Man-shing_speech.pdf.

UNDP (United Nations Development Programme) (2005) "Institutional arrangements to combat corruption: A comparative study", www.un.org/ruleoflaw/files/10%20Institutional%20arrangements%20to%20combat%20corruption_2005.pdf

Uslaner, Eric M. (2008) *Corruption, inequality and the rule of law: The bulging pocket makes the easy life*. Cambridge: Cambridge University Press.

Uslaner, Eric M. (2017) "Political trust, corruption and inequality" in Sonja Zmerli and Tom van der Meer (eds.) *Handbook of political trust*. Cheltenham: Edward Elgar.

Ward, Paul R., Loreen Mamerow and Samantha B. Meyer (2014) "Interpersonal trust across six Asia-Pacific countries: Testing and extending the 'high trust' society and 'low trust' society theory", *PLoS One*, 9(4).

Warren, Mark E. (2018) "Trust in democracy" in Eric M. Uslaner (ed.) *The Oxford handbook of social and political trust*. Oxford: Oxford University Press: 75–94.

Wedeman, Andrew (2012) "Growth and corruption in China", *China Currents*, 11(2), www.chinacenter.net/2012/china_currents/11-2/growth-and-corruption-in-china/.

World Bank (1994) "Governance: The World Bank's experience", http://documents.worldbank.org/curated/en/711471468765285964/pdf/multi0page.pdf.

World Bank (1997) *Helping countries combat corruption: The role of the World Bank*. Washington: The World Bank.

World Bank (2005) "Voices for the world's poor: Selected speeches and writings of World Bank President James D. Wolfensohn 1995–2005", www.gfdrr.org/sites/default/files/publication/Voices%20for%20the%20World%27s%20Poor.pdf.

World Bank (2017) "Combating corruption", *Brief*, 26 September, www.worldbank.org/en/topic/governance/brief/anti-corruption.

World Economic Forum (2017) *The Global Competitiveness Report 2017–2018*, https://www.weforum.org/reports/the-global-competitiveness-report-2017-2018.

You, Jong-sung (2017) "Corruption and inequality in Asia" in Ting Gong and Ian Scott (eds.) *Routledge handbook of corruption in Asia*. London: Routledge: 97–112.

10 Bad governance

Bad governance covers a multitude of sins and affects the ability to control corruption in many different ways (Rose and Peiffer 2018: 10). In this chapter, we focus principally on situations in which governments fail to take action against corruption or the environments which are conducive to its development. Based on a belief that they do not have the power to bring about change, governments may feel severely constrained by, for example, intractable constitutional or political obstacles or, in Hong Kong's case, by cross-border geopolitical and socio-economic considerations. Under such circumstances, they may also recoil from introducing remedies within their competence because they fear the consequences of challenging the *status quo*. These circumstances differ from those involving a lack of political will where a government is usually presumed to have the capacity to act, particularly in relation to the powers of an ACA, but chooses not to do so (see Ch. 4). Nevertheless, outcomes resulting from perceptions of a lack of capacity to act against corruption and those stemming from a lack of political will are largely similar. Corruption opportunities and practices emerge by default, perceptions of malpractice grow and trust in government declines.

Bad governance situations arising from a lack of government action are usually well beyond the jurisdiction of the ACA. Forms of corruption develop in areas that are in effect off-limits to the ACA and over which it becomes difficult to exert control. Depending on the extent of the government's inaction, failure to address corruption reduces legitimacy, affects perceptions of the effectiveness of the government in other areas and has a negative impact on the credibility of the ACA (Seligson 2002; Morris and Klesner 2010). Such perceptions are detrimental to positive support for good governance that results from the belief that transparent and effective action is being taken to control corruption. Instead, government inaction breeds conspiracy theories, belief in collusion and suspicions of opaque and illicit dealings. Whether or not the perceptions themselves are based on reliable evidence – and often they may not be – is less important than the damage that they inflict on the standing of the government, on the social fabric and on support for good governance practices.

The ICAC's reputation has suffered less than most ACAs from such circumstances, principally because past performance and high public regard have insulated it from government inaction in some important areas where corruption opportunities are present. Public recognition of the ICAC's role as separate and independent from government has led to an awareness that the government's failure to act in some areas should not be confused with the continuing importance of the work of the Commission in others. Nonetheless, over the past decade, evidence of electoral fraud and corruption, perceptions that corruption is being imported from Mainland China, the conviction of Hui and Tsang on misconduct in public office charges and ICAC investigations of other political office-holders have also fuelled suspicions that a murky sub-culture lurks beneath the surface of an otherwise clean Hong Kong.

In this chapter, we examine the consequences for governance in Hong Kong of ineffective corruption prevention in three major areas: constitutional and organisational arrangements that enable opportunities for electoral fraud and corruption, corruption problems stemming from a porous border and increased economic and social interaction between Mainland China and Hong Kong, and perceptions of government–business collusion.

Elections and corruption

In Hong Kong, elections for the Chief Executive, the Legislative Council and the District Councils are part of a constitutional system which is ultimately under the control of the PRC government. The Standing Committee of the National People's Congress interprets the Basic Law, which provides for the method of election and composition of the major political institutions. The Standing Committee has made specific interventions into the electoral system determining, for example, that candidates should affirm that Hong Kong is an inalienable part of China and declaring that elected members who fail to take the oath of office properly should not be permitted to sit in the legislature (Cheung *et al* 2016; Lau and Chung 2017). Within Hong Kong, the Legislative Council is responsible for making laws regarding the conduct of elections which may affect the ability of the ICAC and other bodies concerned with electoral administration to control corruption. The ICAC has no jurisdiction over the rules governing the election of the Chief Executive, the Legislative Council or the District Councils, even though some electoral arrangements create conditions under which corruption might flourish.

The ICAC does, however, have a mandate under the *Elections (Corrupt and Illegal Conduct) Ordinance (ECICO)* to investigate complaints about corruption in voter registration, in the financial administration of a candidate's election expenses, and in attempts to bribe electors. The ordinance provides that the ICAC should ensure that elections are conducted fairly and honestly, that electoral advertising should be regulated and that candidates should "properly account for the expenditure of money at elections and the soliciting and receipt of election donations and that they do not exceed the prescribed levels of expenditure" (*ECICO*: Section 3). The *ECICO* draws a distinction between corrupt and illegal conduct. Corrupt conduct involves a wide range of offences, including bribery either of candidates or voters, force or duress, deception in standing or not standing for an election, defacing or destroying nomination or ballot papers, providing "food, drinks or entertainment" with a view to inducing voters to vote for a particular candidate and improper use of election donations (*ECICO*: Sections 7–15). Illegal conduct relates principally to expenses in support of a campaign that are paid for by someone other than the candidate or his or her election expenses agent and to making false statements (*ECICO*: Sections 22–29). There are substantial penalties for violations of these rules. On conviction, corrupt conduct can result in fines of up to HK$500,000 and seven years' imprisonment. Conviction for illegal conduct can lead to fines of up to HK$200,000 and three years' imprisonment.

The ICAC is not the only organisation involved in supervising electoral conduct. The *Electoral Affairs Commission Ordinance* (*EACO*) provides for an Electoral Affairs Commission, whose chair must be a judge and which has overall responsibility for the administration of elections and for reviewing constituency boundaries (*EACO*: Section 4). The ordinance gives the Commission powers to make the rules governing the conduct of any election and prescribes penalties for non-compliance (*EACO*: Sections 6, 7). In addition, the Constitutional and Mainland Affairs Bureau has overall responsibility for devising electoral provisions, the Registration and Electoral Office aids the Electoral Affairs Commission in discharging its responsibilities, and the police are involved if there are criminal activities or complaints about noise or other disturbances associated with an election. Yet, despite this considerable legal and organisational commitment to fair elections, compliance with the rules falls short of acceptable standards. There are many examples of attempted vote-rigging in the registration process, dubious and illegal practices in both geographical constituency (GC) and functional constituency (FC) elections, campaign spending that exceeds the permissible limit and issues concerning the sources of campaign finance, illegal conduct and intimidation of candidates (But 2012; Cheung 2013; *South China Morning Post* 2015; Bauhinia Foundation 2016; Siu 2016a; Legislative Council 2018). This contributes, as a think tank report observes, to "low levels of public confidence in the political process" (Bauhinia Foundation 2016: 17).

We argue that these problems stem from the fact that the electoral system has been set up in a way that allows contraventions of the rules to occur, makes detection difficult and comprises multiple regulatory actors who sometimes have insufficient or overlapping powers. We consider, first, the constitutional provisions governing the electoral system and the conditions which permit corruption to develop and, second, the problems posed for the ICAC and other regulatory organisations in trying to ensure free and clean elections under such circumstances.

The electoral system

The Hong Kong election system is a comparatively recent creation and was largely a response to the perceived needs of the British and PRC governments after the signing of the Joint Declaration in 1984. Prior to 1985, the only elections in

Hong Kong were for the Urban Council and the District Boards. In the transition to Chinese sovereignty, the British government was primarily concerned with maintaining political and economic stability which it sought to achieve by formalising the existing power arrangements by means of a corporatist electoral system in the Legislative Council. The first elections to the Council took place in 1985 as functional constituency (FC) elections in which business and professional elites elected one of their members to represent their interests. The growing pressure for direct elections was finally acknowledged in 1991 but attempts to further expand the numbers of directly elected members and to reduce the number of FCs have been a major source of contention between the pan-democrats and the PRC government ever since. The PRC government appears to see the FCs in the same way as the British government – that is, as a means of maintaining stability and entrenching business and professional elites in power. As a consequence, the Legislative Council electoral system is bifurcated. In 2018, there were thirty-five directly elected members from geographical constituencies (GCs) and thirty-five FC members.

There have also been continuing major controversies over the election of the Chief Executive – notably the Occupy Central civil disobedience movement in 2014, which saw demonstrators take possession of parts of three public areas in central Hong Kong for 79 days (Lam 2015). The protesters argued for election of the Chief Executive under universal suffrage with open nomination, but the PRC government insisted that a nominating committee should decide on who was eligible to run. The present system of electing the Chief Executive is an electoral college of 1200 members which draws largely from electors in the FCs. We begin with a discussion of potential and actual corruption offences that have occurred in elections to the Legislative Council. Since many offences are common to the District Council elections, we include examples from those elections to illustrate further the kinds of corruption problems that have arisen.

The directly elected members of the Legislative Council run for office in multi-member constituencies on a list proportional system. Candidates who exceed the quota (the number of votes divided by the number of candidates) are elected, and a Hare quota system is used to calculate who should fill the remaining seats. The system replaced the single seat, "first-past-the-post" arrangements that were used in the last colonial Legislative Council election in 1995, which saw the democrats take 60 per cent of the seats. The list proportional system, which was introduced in 1998, was favoured by pro-establishment politicians in Hong Kong and by the PRC government, neither of whom wanted to see the GCs swept by the democrats.

There is some evidence that list proportional multi-member constituencies lead to greater corruption than other electoral systems. After the 1988 Japanese Recruit scandal, the party list system was thought to be a major cause of fraud and corruption and was replaced with single member constituencies which reduced corruption significantly (Reed and Thiess 2001; Krauss and Pekkanen 2005). In the 2016 Legislative Council elections in Hong Kong, a Liberal Party candidate alleged that he had been warned by "three men from Beijing" that he would be in danger if he did not withdraw from the race (Ng 2016). The apparent reason for the alleged intimidation was that his presence on the list would take votes away from other pro-Beijing candidates. The candidate withdrew and reported the incident to the ICAC, which conducted an investigation but could find no evidence to support the allegation (Cheng 2017a). The list proportional system with multi-member constituencies does, however, seem to create opportunities for illicit pressure on declared candidates on the party list to better the chances of another candidate. Studies have shown that corruption tends to be higher in systems where representatives are elected from party lists (Persson *et al* 2003; Kunicova and Rose-Ackerman 2005).

There have been many other complaints about electoral conduct in Hong Kong that might have occurred whatever electoral system was in place. In the District Council elections, which employs the first-past-the-post system, there has been a long history of attempts to undermine the electoral rules by means of vote-rigging and bribery (Lau 2012; Cheung 2013; Siu 2016a). Legislative Council elections have been similarly affected. In the 2012 Legislative Council election, there were 11,799 complaints to the Electoral Affairs Commission, which dropped to 7,375 in the 2016 election (Electoral Affairs Commission 2012: 89, 2016: 105). Most complaints related to the GCs and were relatively minor – election advertising and disturbances to electors caused by canvassing activities, for example – but some were more serious attempts to subvert the system. The ICAC investigated 327 complaints concerning the 2011 District Council elections and the 2012 Legislative and District Council elections, prosecuting forty-seven persons in 2012 and five persons in 2013 (ICAC 2013: 35, Appendix 10; ICAC 2014: 34, Appendix 10). After the 2016 Legislative and District Council elections, the ICAC conducted 400 investigations into complaints, prosecuting two people in 2016 and four people in 2017 (ICAC 2017a: 14, Appendix 9; ICAC 2018a: 17, Appendix 9). The ICAC itself directly received 162 complaints in both the 2012 and 2016 Legislative Council elections, most concerning bribery in relation to voting, impersonation of other electors and false statements about candidates (Electoral Affairs Commission 2012: Appendix XI[E]; Electoral Affairs Commission 2017a: Appendix XI[E]).

Although complaints are often not pursued because they are without foundation or because of lack of evidence, they illustrate the fractious nature of elections where activists often seem to violate the rules. It is difficult to pursue many complaints of illegality because they are often disguised under an activity that may be legitimate. For example, it is not illegal for a political party to organise trips for elderly people and to provide them with other welfare benefits; the pro-Beijing Democratic Alliance for Betterment of Hong Kong (DAB) and the Hong Kong Federation of Trade Unions (HKFTU), which run candidates in elections, do so frequently. However, it would be an offence if the trip or the offer of free food, drinks or entertainment or bussing to the polls was accompanied by an inducement or instruction to vote for a particular candidate. Newspaper reports have repeatedly drawn attention to cases in both Legislative Council and District Council elections in which elderly residents of care homes have been taken to the polls with instructions on how to vote (Lam 2015a; Lam 2015b; *South China Morning Post* 2015; Lau 2016). But gathering evidence, finding witnesses and persuading those prosecuted to reveal the name of the person behind the corrupt scheme is difficult. Nonetheless, more could probably be done at the polling stations to monitor whether voters are taking instructions from others.

Another issue where malpractice is particularly difficult to detect is campaign finance. The *ECICO* requires a candidate to make an election return, providing receipt to donors for any amount over HK$1000 and limits expenditure to a specific amount in each constituency (*ECICO*: Sections 37–39). The expenditure cap is relatively low compared with some other countries but it is intended to ensure that there is a level playing field in electoral contests. The issues are that the DAB and candidates who support the PRC and Hong Kong governments' position have much better financial support and resources than other parties and candidates, and that political donations are not adequately monitored (*South China Morning Post* 2016). Even by 2011, the DAB's income was greater than the combined income of its three main rivals: the Civic Party, the Democratic Party and the Liberal Party (*Webb-site Reports* 2011). It has been able to staff a network of party branches in all Hong Kong districts and has received consistent support from the HKFTU and the PRC's Hong Kong Liaison Office. The Liaison Office has aided the DAB's fund-raising activities and mobilised its united front network in support of the party (Lam and Lam 2013; Lau 2016; Ng 2016). The DAB's extensive resources and presence across Hong Kong enable its candidates, unlike those of other parties, to spend their time on campaigning rather than raising funds. The admirable intent of the legislation to establish a level playing field has consequently remained symbolic rather than real.

Despite these actual and potential corruption problems, the GC elections are relatively clean compared with some of their FC counterparts. FCs have traditionally been based on occupation, although five new FCs with large electorates based on districts were introduced in the 2012 election. Traditional FCs, which comprise thirty seats, are often based on small electorates. In 2016, fifteen FCs had electorates of less than 1500, composed solely of corporate (company) voters (10), a mixture of individual and corporate voters (3), or solely of individual voters (2) (Electoral Affairs Commission 2016: Appendix IV). A few FCs, such as education, health services and accountancy, and the five "super FCs" based on the districts, have much larger electorates. In the 2016 Legislative Council election, the twelve uncontested seats corresponded almost exactly with FCs with small electorates. In some cases, the constituencies have never been contested since their creation in 1985. This raises the question of how the candidates are actually chosen, since it is obviously not by means of contested elections. At worst, it raises suspicions of influence-peddling, an opaque selection process and deals done to secure nomination.

Even more serious is the composition of the electorate. There are insufficient restrictions on listing companies which are simply there for the purpose of obtaining a vote. In the Sports and Arts FC, for example, Yeung *et al* (2017) found that many legitimate companies were not represented and that over 10 per cent of voters did not have a close relationship with sports or recreation. Registered voluntary organisations in the constituency which proclaimed support for the government were much more likely to receive grants than those which did not. Umbrella organisations, which have a legitimate connection to the sector, often register subsidiary member companies to vote which have little connection with the occupations which they are supposed to represent (Young and Law 2006). In 2016, for example, it was discovered that two pro-Beijing youth groups were listed as electors in the Wholesale and Retail FC, that a property management company was listed as an elector in the Information Technology FC and that a number of corporate voters were companies with a majority of shareholders on the Mainland or in foreign countries (Lam and Ng 2016). Worse was to follow. In 2017, the ICAC arrested seventy-two people, of whom sixty-eight were new electors, in connection with vote-rigging in the Information Technology FC, a constituency with only 5747 electors (ICAC 2017c). They had registered as electors under the auspices of an umbrella organisation but did not themselves have any experience or qualifications in information technology. Some had allegedly accepted money to participate in the illegal registration process (ICAC 2017c).

FC electors play a pivotal role in the election of the Chief Executive. The electoral college is made up of four sectors, each comprising 300 seats. Three sectors are composed largely of FC electors, with the fourth comprising representatives of various kinds including the FC members of the Legislative Council. The subsectors within each sector nominate members to serve in the electoral college, and the Electoral Affairs Commission then supervises an election if the nominees exceed the number of seats allocated to the subsector. In the 2017 election, 300 seats in twelve subsectors and one sub-subsector were returned uncontested (Electoral Affairs Commission 2017b). The PRC government's Hong Kong Liaison Office played a central role in the election, making clear from the outset that its preferred candidate was Carrie Lam Yuet-ngor. Many of the subsectors voted *en bloc* for Lam, and there was never any doubt that she would win the election (Lo 2017).

There were ninety-four complaints about the Chief Executive election, of which three were received directly by the ICAC and fifteen were referred to it by other government departments (Electoral Affairs Commission 2017b: Appendix XI[D]). A serious allegation was that the Beijing-based Asia Infrastructure Bank had offered a senior position to Lam's most serious contender, John Tsang Chun-wah, the former Secretary of Finance, if he would step down (Cheng 2017b). Most other complaints concerned expenses incurred without authorisation. The Chief Executive election was an improvement on the scandal-ridden 2012 election, although it still left unanswered questions about such values as transparency, accountability and popular participation and about whether there was much point in having an election at all if the outcome was decided in advance. As Young and Cullen (2010: 50) remark, the system lacks political legitimacy, and little has been done "to remedy its clear shortcomings".

Constraints on corruption control in elections

Difficulties in controlling electoral corruption occur not only because the constitutional framework within which elections take place is beyond the ICAC's jurisdiction but also because insufficient electoral administrative measures have been taken to prevent corruption. The Electoral Affairs Commission and its administrative arm, the Registration and Electoral Office (REO), do make strenuous efforts to ensure that elections are conducted honestly, fairly and openly. They have had some successes in the GCs. The counting of votes has not attracted many complaints and returning officers are well-schooled in their responsibilities. After the vote-rigging scandals, the government did produce a report on the voter registration system which improved *inter alia* means of verifying the residential addresses of voters (Constitutional and Mainland Affairs Bureau 2016). Illegal registration of voters at false addresses had been a perennial feature of District Council elections.

The improvements in the voter registration system relate mainly to the GCs and the District Councils. The registration system for the FCs remains replete with corruption opportunities, as the ICAC's arrests of electors in the Information Technology FC show. The Electoral Affairs Commission notes that under the law, there is "no direct relationship between the business address and the eligibility of corporate FC electors" (Electoral Affairs Commission 2017a: 25). This means that creating bogus companies with corporate voting rights is that much easier. Equally problematic is ensuring that legitimate electors in the FCs maintain their eligibility to vote. The registrar of electors is only valid for one year and the REO attempts to detect electors who may not meet the criterion. If the elector is not in the same field as the FC, the right to vote is lost. In the 2016 election, 1420 electors did not have sufficient connection with the FC to warrant eligibility to vote (Electoral Affairs Commission 2017a: 26). However, those electors were still on the register. All that the REO could do was to warn them that they would be committing an offence if they did cast a vote.

It is surprising in the light of the considerable evidence of these corruption opportunities that the government and, in particular, the Constitutional and Mainland Affairs Bureau, has not conducted a comprehensive review of voter registration in the FCs. Administering the system, as the Electoral Affairs Commission (2017a) report shows, has become much more difficult and every fresh incident reduces public confidence in the system. The Bureau has only used the services of the ICAC's CPD on one occasion for an assignment study, even though the elections in all of Hong Kong's political institutions suggest that there is a strong case for tightening the regulations. For the ICAC, the present regulations, coupled with the many regulatory actors in the field, tend to mean that it is reactive to electoral corruption. The OD pursues corruption cases whenever there is sufficient evidence to do so, and the CRD provides extensive publicity on the need for clean elections. But the ICAC's ability to control corruption by improving administrative control systems through the CPD, as it has done in the civil service, is much more limited.

Many factors that are detrimental to effective corruption control in Hong Kong elections revolve around the ability of the government to take action. On the FCs, it is constrained in expanding the size of the electorate in some constituencies because constitutional change rests with the PRC government which has shown little inclination to reform the system. The Hong Kong government still has the power, however, to tighten regulations and to ensure that they are enforced and fully accepted by all the parties contesting the elections. Fair and clean elections are a critical means of ensuring the legitimacy of office-holders; effective corruption control may assist in achieving that aim. At present, the prevailing rules and their enforcement are not sufficiently regulated to deter those who wish to subvert the system. The task for the ICAC and other regulatory bodies consequently becomes more difficult. More government action is necessary to ensure cleaner contests.

Geopolitical and socio-economic issues

Hong Kong's location, an increasingly porous border, ever-closer economic integration with Mainland China, rapidly rising migration and the movement of people between the two places present a major corruption prevention challenge for the government and the ICAC. There are two main issues:

- the difficulty for both the PRC and Hong Kong governments to control environments which provide many corruption opportunities; and
- problems of extradition and rendition of suspects relating to the very different legal regimes in Mainland China and Hong Kong.

The corruption environment

The Mainland is Hong Kong's second largest source of direct investment, accounting for nearly 26 per cent of direct investment in 2017 (Trade and Industry Department 2018). Mainland Chinese companies are now dominant forces in the banking sector, in telecoms and the media, and in underwriting new share issues. They are also increasingly influential in real estate and property development (Ho 2017). Some 154 Mainland Chinese companies have established regional headquarters in Hong Kong, and a further 196 have set up regional offices (Trade and Industry 2018). There has been a long-standing perception in Hong Kong that business people from across the border act in ways that may be acceptable on the Mainland but are in violation of local anti-corruption laws and regulations.

Cross-border corruption is a two-way street, however. Tens of thousands of Hong Kong SMEs have set up manufacturing businesses in the Pearl River Delta. In 2017, Guangdong province derived almost 63 per cent of its direct investment from Hong Kong (Trade and Industry Department 2018). The ICAC has no jurisdiction in the Delta where Hong Kong business people could act in ways that would be illegal in the HKSAR. There is moreover a temptation for business people to use bribes in efforts to overcome the numerous bureaucratic hurdles that must be cleared in Mainland China before businesses can operate or products can be exported (Johnson *et al* 2017).

These cross-border capital inflows and outflows have been accompanied by increased emigration from the Mainland to Hong Kong and improved infrastructural links. Over 1.5 million immigrants (about 20 per cent of the population) have arrived in Hong Kong from the Mainland since 1997. Most are on family re-union one-way permits, but a significant number are business and professional people (O'Neill 2017). There is some suspicion, possibly fuelled by social tensions between Mainlanders and Hong Kongers, that new migrants might try to bend the rules, particularly in relationships with government officials (Ma 2015; Hong Kong Institute of Asia-Pacific Affairs 2016; Li and Lo 2017).

Between about 1992 and 2005, there was a widespread belief that an increase in corruption was an inevitable consequence of the resumption of Chinese sovereignty. In a debate on the accountability of the ICAC in the Legislative Council in 1994, for example, some members spoke of public fears that corruption was being imported from Mainland China (Hong Kong Hansard 1994: 2121–2152). Yet, although corruption complaints were rising, the evidence that it was related to closer interaction with the Mainland was slim. The rise in corruption complaints may have been caused by beliefs that the resumption of sovereignty would bring about a new political order and that it was best to try to take advantage while the going was good. But it does not seem to have been caused by greater interaction between Hong Kong and China (see pp. 61–62). Shortly before and just after 1997, the Hong Kong government and the ICAC took strong measures to deal with corruption, which seemed to help dispel perceptions of imported corruption.

With increased migration and economic integration, however, perceptions of imported corruption returned. In 2013, for example, in a survey of District Councillors, Li and Lo (2017) found that "Mainlandisation" – a somewhat blurred concept in the minds of the respondents that seemed to cover many aspects of Mainland China's influence over Hong Kong – was often perceived to be the cause of increased corruption. Yet again, evidence to support the perception is difficult to find. There have been some corruption cases involving Chinese banks, a Mainland businessman who tried to bribe a bank employee with a bottle of Chanel No. 5 perfume, and the reported attempt to persuade John Tsang to drop out of the Chief Executive race for a position at the Asia Infrastructure Bank (Rovnick 2010; Siu 2016b; Cheng 2017b). But there is little concrete evidence of collusion between top government officials and Mainland Chinese business people, which seems to be a major source of the public perception of collusion. The perception nonetheless remains that the rules are being bent in favour of Mainland business people and to the advantage of senior Hong Kong government officials.

Research on the behaviour of Hong Kong business people in the Pearl River Delta suggests that corruption is an accepted part of doing business. It appears difficult to avoid officials who are soliciting for bribes; for example, only 12 per cent of Hong Kong business respondents to a survey said that they had never been asked for a bribe (Johnson *et al* 2017). Hong Kong business people may not simply be passive victims in a corrupt environment. In the same study, a manager in a Guangdong non-government agency was quoted as saying that Hong Kong business people often offered bribes or supplied fake documents (Johnson *et al* 2017). The ICAC has an agreement with the Guangdong Provincial People's Procuratorate (GPPP), subsequently extended to the rest of the Mainland, which enables the agencies to interview witnesses (but not suspects) in their respective regions. The ICAC and the GPPP have also organised conferences for owners of Hong Kong SMEs in the Delta and, with the Commission Against Corruption in Macao, have produced guidelines on good practice for those companies (ICAC, GPPP and Commission Against Corruption, Macao 2012; Legislative Council Panel on Security 2014). Given the perceived extent of the problem, this alone does not seem to be sufficient.

Legal systems, extradition and rendition

There has been long-standing concern about the legal relationship between Hong Kong and Mainland China over the detection and prosecution of crimes which are committed in one place but where the offender escapes to the other. Under the Basic Law, a person accused of a crime committed in Hong Kong should be tried in the Hong Kong courts under Hong Kong laws. Similarly, a person accused of an offence elsewhere may be extradited from Hong Kong under agreements between the HKSAR and other states. But there is no such agreement with the PRC government. In 1998, the "Big Spender", Cheung Tze-keung, who had been involved in abductions, murder, robbery and arms-smuggling in Hong Kong, was apprehended on the Mainland and subsequently executed. Hong Kong legal experts believed that he should have been returned to the HKSAR to face trial. PRC officials thought that as the crimes had been planned in China and there was no agreement on extradition, it was appropriate that Cheung should be tried in Mainland China. Shortly after the case was concluded, the Hong Kong government sought to negotiate a rendition agreement, but, to date, little progress has been made.

What this state of affairs meant initially was that those committing corruption offences in Hong Kong could attempt to flee to the PRC. In 2000, for example, the two most senior officials in the China Travel Service were ordered back to the Mainland by their parent body before the ICAC could question them; in the following year, a similar situation resulted in a leading Chinese banker taking the same course of action (Choy and Fu 2009: 228). Officials in PRC government-funded bodies tended to return quickly to the Mainland if the ICAC had any questions about the integrity of their actions. After Xi Jinping's anti-corruption drive began in 2012, Mainland China became less of a sanctuary for the corrupt. Instead, those in Hong Kong who could assist in enquiries or who were suspected of corruption were liable to face pressure from PRC government security forces. In 2017, for example, the security forces wanted a tycoon, Xiao Jianhua, to help in their investigations, and he was spirited back to the Mainland. It was initially thought that he had been abducted, but it was later claimed that he went back voluntarily. In 2018, he was reported to be under house arrest awaiting trial (Zhou and Xie 2018). In April 2018, employees of a PRC state-owned enterprise in Hong Kong were asked to surrender their travel documents when the head of the enterprise was investigated for corruption offences in Beijing (Wienland and Lockett 2018). Both the intervention by the security forces and the request to surrender travel documents were illegal under Hong Kong law.

This situation is clearly unsatisfactory. It would be in the interests of all the governments, PRC, Hong Kong and Macao, to work in collaboration to improve anti-corruption efforts in the Delta and to establish due process for the rendition of suspects. Yet there are major obstacles in the way. Despite calls for the signing of a rendition agreement (*South China Morning Post* 2017), the PRC government seems to have little enthusiasm for more formalised legal arrangements which would probably slow down the completion of cases. On the Hong Kong side, there are also difficulties in conceiving how such an agreement would work since, presumably, the HKSAR government would want assurances that someone extradited to the Mainland would not be executed. As it stands, the ICAC has to deal with situations which do not help effective corruption prevention but about which the government has been able to do very little.

Government–business collusion

Collusion is regarded as one of the most difficult forms of corruption to detect but it is also one of the most dangerous. Individual acts of corruption, if discovered and successfully prosecuted, might be seen as confirmation that an anti-corruption system is working well. Collusion involves at least two parties, often occupying positions of authority within their organisations and is usually based on reciprocal advantages. If discovered, it may lead to the suspicion that the problem is systemic and that many more cases have not been detected. In worst-case scenarios, unchecked collusion may come to be seen as normal practice with damaging effects for the polity and public confidence (Gong 2002).

It is instructive to consider the various forms that collusion have taken in Hong Kong and the form of the public perceptions that have arisen from them. Corruption has gone through phases, some of which relate to collusion and some of which do not. Syndicated corruption within the police force and other government departments could be regarded as a form of collusion, but it was usually based within a single department and there was no reciprocal advantage for the victims of extortion and rent-seeking. Once the ICAC broke the syndicates, corruption in the public sector was largely restricted to individual cases, which could be dealt with under the *POBO*. Private sector corruption cases did not normally involve collusion with government officials because the public sector was clean. Toward the end of the 1990s, a different form of corruption began to emerge in which there was a collusive government–business nexus but not one that necessarily gave an immediate or obvious direct pecuniary advantage to the public servant committing the offence.

The landmark case concerned the government's former chief property manager, Shum Kwok-sher (*Shum Kwok-sher v HKSAR* 2002). Shum was charged under the common law offence of misconduct in public office for awarding major contracts worth over HK$150 million to a company controlled by brothers of his sister-in-law. He was originally sentenced to nine months' imprisonment but appealed and the sentence was increased to 30 months. The essence of the charges was that they involved a conflict of interest. He had failed to declare his family relationships when making decisions on contracts and had therefore subverted the integrity of the tendering process. The Shum decision paved the way for the use of misconduct in public office to bring charges in similar cases by extending the scope of the definition of corruption beyond simple bribery, giving the ICAC a new weapon to combat collusion (see p. 98).

Many subsequent cases of misconduct in public office mirrored the Shum case. They involved government contracts in which civil servants were able to subvert a fair tendering process in favour of friends or relatives who owned companies (*HKSAR v Chung Sim-ying, Tracy* 2001; *HKSAR v Wong Hon-ching, San Stephen* 2003; *HKSAR v Chan Chung-ching and Others* 2004; *HKSAR v Wong Kong-shun, Paul* 2007). In none of these cases did the amount of the contract match the sums in the Shum case, but they contained the common elements of failing to disclose close personal or family relationships (a conflict of interest) and providing an unfair advantage to a company owned by the relatives or friends. Over the period from 1998 to 2012, the ICAC effectively controlled government–business collusion, using the misconduct in public office offence to secure a number of convictions.

Until 2002, the Hong Kong government was entirely composed of civil servants with the Governor or, after 1997, the Chief Executive in overall command. After 2002, the heads of government bureaus were political appointees on contract and could be drawn from any occupation. The change did not necessarily foreshadow an increase in corruption but, especially after 2012 when Leung Chun-ying became Chief Executive, appointees were more likely to have connections with business. In 2012, the Hui and Tsang cases provided evidence that the relationships between government and business were too close and could lead to corruption. In March 2012, Hui, who had previously been the Chief Secretary for Administration, was arrested and charged with misconduct in office (Lau 2017). He had received loans from Sun Hung Kai Properties, a major Hong Kong company, from whom he was also alleged to have accepted HK$8.5 million in bribes and the use of a rent-free apartment. Hui's lawyers argued that no offence had actually been committed but the appeal judges accepted the prosecution's contention that the payments were bribes made to persuade him to act favourably toward the company and its interests. In 2014, Hui was convicted and sentenced to seven and a half years in prison. The former joint chairman and managing director of Sun Hung Kai Properties, Thomas Kwok Ping-kwong, received a five-year sentence (*HKSAR v Rafael Hui Si-yan and Others* 2014).

In 2017, after a scandal that was first revealed in 2012, the former Chief Executive, Donald Tsang Yam-kuen, was charged with two counts of misconduct in public office. The first charge concerned awarding an honour to his interior decorator on which he was acquitted. The second involved approving three applications for a digital broadcasting licence for a company which was 20 per cent owned by a tycoon, Bill Wong Cho-bau, with whom Tsang was negotiating to rent a residence at below market rates (Scott 2014). He was convicted and sentenced to twenty months in prison on the second charge. At the time of his arraignment, the Court of First Instance added a further charge of bribery under Section 4 of the *POBO* of accepting, as inducement or reward to perform an act as Chief Executive, the refurbishment and redecoration of his residence. In November 2017, jurors, for the second time, were unable to reach a verdict and the prosecutors decided not to pursue a third trial (Lau and Siu 2017).

For the two leading public figures of their time to be charged with such serious offences shook public confidence in the probity of the government and reinforced the perception that there was a growing collusive relationship between government and business. As the judge in the Hui case remarked,

> There has been a perception for many years of . . . government and business leaders cosying up to one another . . . regrettably this case will have done nothing to dispel that perception.
>
> (*HKSAR v Rafael Hui Si-yan and Others* 2014)

The impact of the cases was compounded by political scandals during the Leung administration. Some of the allegations against senior members of the administration, including against Leung himself, remained unproven; others had nothing to do with government–business collusion, but both helped create an atmosphere of suspicion and mistrust (see Scott 2017: Table II). There was no immediate resolution to the Hui or Tsang cases for both appealed the original decision and the process dragged on through the courts between 2012 and 2017, probably resulting in increasingly negative public perceptions of collusion at the apex of the Hong Kong government. In our 2015 survey, we found that government–business collusion was the principal reason why some respondents thought that the ICAC was not effective. The ICAC's own survey shows that the main reason why respondents considered that the Commission was ineffective was that it had been unsuccessful in cracking cases or had a low detection rate. Those who regarded the ICAC as ineffective for this reason rose to 60 per cent in 2015 but had dropped back to 42 per cent by 2017 (ICAC 2017b: Table 5d; ICAC 2018b). The Hong Kong government, mired in its own political problems, seemed to have no answers to reducing perceptions of government–business collusion, although they were affecting both its own credibility and perceptions of the effectiveness of the ICAC. The result was to reduce trust and increase cynicism.

We have argued that, despite this and because of the institutionalisation of the ICAC, there has been little significant negative impact on its broad, long-term support or the belief that it is still highly effective in dealing with traditional forms of corruption such as bribery. Smart (2018) notes that the effectiveness of corruption prevention has meant that opportunities for corruption at the lower levels of the civil service no longer exist and that corrupt behaviour "had better be worth it". He argues that this is not simply a matter of pushing corruption further up the bureaucratic or political hierarchy, but rather that changes in formal and informal rules which have resulted from the ICAC's efforts and Hong Kong's greater dependence on Beijing have created a new environment in which a different kind of corruption may flourish. For the ICAC, to be effective in such circumstances may require adapting its strategies to capture the new dimensions of government–business collusion and the increased impact and behaviour of Mainland Chinese businesses in Hong Kong. For the government, it requires much more attention to the ways in which its most senior political officials interact with business and how this affects its reputation for probity.

We have examined three areas in which potential or actual corruption problems have occurred, largely because the government believed it could do nothing about them. These bad governance situations have helped create more corruption opportunities and have affected the credibility of the government itself and perceptions of the effectiveness of the ICAC. Analysis suggests that government inaction based on a belief in its lack of efficacy can hinder corruption prevention in different ways.

In the case of elections, the constitutional arrangements have created situations, particularly in the FCs, which encourage corruption. Although the ICAC has made arrests and prosecuted in some instances, small electorates and corporate voting, coupled with transactions which are victimless, make it difficult to detect offences. If the PRC government is not willing to take action to reform the FCs, there is still a need for the Hong Kong government to conduct a thorough review of electoral administration, party financing and better policing of campaign activities.

In the case of cross-border corruption, the government has taken the view that what happens in the Delta is beyond its jurisdiction. The ICAC has cooperation agreements with the GPPP and other Mainland agencies, but they need to be extended, and that requires action at an inter-governmental level. On the thorny issue of rendition, the government needs to finish what it originally started in 1998 and seek a rendition agreement with the PRC government. The alternative seems to be more instances of PRC security interventions which violate Hong Kong laws.

In the case of government–business collusion, the absence of government action on probity at the highest level, together with some high-profile corruption cases, seem to have contributed to a public perception that government–business collusion is widespread. The government should acknowledge that the integrity of political appointees is an issue and take measures to deal with it. It could, for example, appoint an Ethics Commissioner to administer and strengthen the code governing political appointees. The ICAC also requires stronger powers to investigate misconduct in public office offences.

If these problems are to be resolved, the Hong Kong government will need to take more decisive action. It must provide the necessary policy and administrative measures to assure the public that it remains committed to clean elections, the preservation of a corruption-free environment on its borders and the legal processes required for an acceptable form of rendition, and the integrity of top-level political appointees. Failure to do so will result in a continuing downward spiral in areas which are beyond the ICAC's ability to control.

References

Bauhinia Foundation (2016) "Rethinking campaign finance laws in Hong Kong: Reform for a new generation", www.bauhinia.org/assets/document/doc216.pdf.

But, Joshua (2012) "Candidates' campaign expenses shed little light on source of funds", *South China Morning Post*, www.scmp.com/news/hong-kong/article/1088582/candidates-campaign-expenses-shed-little-light-source-funds.

Cheng, Kris (2017a) "Corruption watchdog drops investigation into pro-Beijing candidate's sudden election withdrawal", *Hong Kong Free Press*, 21 June, www.hongkongfp.com/2017/06/21/corruption-watchdog-drops-investigation-pro-beijing-candidates-sudden-election-withdrawal/.

Cheng, Raymond (2017b) "Graft-buster issues guides on election rules amid suspicions of foul play in Chief Executive race", *South China Morning Post*, 3 February, www.scmp.com/news/hong-kong/politics/article/2067733/graft-buster-issues-guides-election-rules-amid-suspicions.

Cheung, Gary, Tony Cheung and Joyce Ng (2016) "China's top body lays down the law on oath-taking", *South China Morning Post*, 30 November, www.scmp.com/news/hong-kong/politics/article/2043768/chinas-top-body-lays-down-law-hong-kong-oath-taking.

Cheung, Simpson (2013) "Mastermind in ICAC's biggest vote-rigging case slips through the net", *South China Morning Post*, 3 April, www.scmp.com/news/hong-kong/article/1205693/mastermind-icacs-biggest-vote-rigging-case-slips-through-net.

Choy, Dick Wan and Fu Hualing (2009) "Cross-border relations in criminal matters" in Mark S. Gaylord, Danny Gittings and Harold Traver (eds.) *Introduction to crime, law and justice in Hong Kong*. Hong Kong: Hong Kong University Press: 223–242.

Constitutional and Mainland Affairs Bureau (2016) "Consultation report on the enhancement of the voter registration system", www.cmab.gov.hk/doc/issues/electoral_matters/VR_con_report_en.pdf.

Elections (Corrupt and Illegal Conduct) Ordinance (Cap 554).

Electoral Affairs Commission (2012) "Report on the 2012 Legislative Council election held on 9 September 2012", www.legco.gov.hk/yr12-13/english/panels/ca/papers/ca1217cb2-306-e.pdf.

Electoral Affairs Commission (2017a) "Report on the 2016 Legislative Council election", www.eac.gov.hk/en/legco/2016lce_report.htm.

Electoral Affairs Commission (2017b) "Report of the 2017 Chief Executive election", www.legco.gov.hk/yr16-17/english/panels/ca/papers/cacb2-1777-e.pdf.

Electoral Affairs Commission Ordinance (EACO) (Cap 541).

Gong, Ting (2002) "Dangerous collusion: Corruption as a collective venture in China", *Communist and Post-Communist Studies*, 35(1): 85–103.

HKSAR v Chan Chung-ching and Others (2004) DCCC 337/2004.

HKSAR v Chung Sim-ying, Tracy (2001) HCMA 267A/2001.

HKSAR v Rafael Hui Si-yan and Others (2014) HCCC 98/2013.

HKSAR v Wong Hon-ching, San Stephen (2003) DCCC 503/2003.

HKSAR v Wong Kong-shun, Paul (2007) CACC 390/2007.

Ho, Prudence (2017) "Chinese giants are taking over Hong Kong: Banks, real estate, telecoms show biggest Chinese influence", *Bloomberg*, 7 June, www.bloomberg.com/news/features/2017-06-06/chinese-giants-are-taking-over-hong-kong.

Hong Kong Hansard 26 January 1994.

Hong Kong Institute of Asia-Pacific Affairs (2016) "Survey findings on views of new immigrants from China", 11 November, www.cpr.cuhk.edu.hk/resources/press/pdf/582568e8b35c5.pdf.

ICAC (2013) "Annual report 2012", www.icac.org.hk/filemanager/en/content_27/2012.pdf.

ICAC (2014) "Annual report 2013", www.icac.org.hk/filemanager/en/content_27/2014.pdf.

ICAC (2017a) "Annual report 2016", www.icac.org.hk/filemanager/en/content_27/2016.pdf.

ICAC (2017b) *Annual survey 2016*. Hong Kong: mimeo.

ICAC (2017c) "ICAC arrests 72 for alleged corrupt conduct at 2016 Legco election", www.icac.org.hk/en/press/index_id_391.html.

ICAC (2018a) "Annual report 2017", www.icac.org.hk/filemanager/en/content_27/2017.pdf.

ICAC (2018b) "Annual survey 2017", www.icac.org.hk/filemanager/en/content_176/survey2017.pdf.

ICAC, GPPP and Commission Against Corruption, Macao (2012) "Business success: Integrity and legal compliance: Corruption prevention guide for SMEs in Guangdong, Hong Kong and Macao", www.hkbedc.icac.hk/english/files/publications/1._Eng.pdf.

Johnson, Thomas, Ting Gong and Wen Wang (2017) "Regulatory capture, as a two-way street: Hong Kong small and medium enterprises in the Pearl River Delta" in Ting Gong and Ian Scott (eds.) *Routledge handbook of corruption in Asia*. London: Routledge: 144–161.

Krauss, Elliot S. and Robert Pekkanen (2005) "Explaining party adaptation to electoral reform: The discreet charm of the LDP", *Journal of Japanese Studies*, 30(1): 1–34.

Kunicova, Jana and Susan Rose-Ackerman (2005) "Electoral rules and constitutional structures as constraints on corruption", *British Journal of Political Science*, 35(4): 573–606.

Lam, Jeffie (2015a) "Exposed: Pro-establishment supporters bussed elderly people to polling stations and directed them to vote in Hong Kong elections", *South China Morning Post*, 22 November, www.scmp.com/news/hong-kong/politics/article/1881785/hong-kong-district-council-elections-elderly-people-bussed.

Lam, Jeffie (2015b) "Hong Kong poll candidate accused of bussing elderly residents for votes 'handed gifts' to them", 28 November, www.scmp.com/news/hong-kong/politics/article/1884329/hong-kong-poll-candidate-accused-bussing-elderly-residents.

Lam, Jeffie and Joyce Ng (2016) "Dubious voters for Hong Kong's functional constituency revealed", *South China Morning Post*, 4 July, www.scmp.com/news/hong-kong/politics/article/1984913/dubious-voters-hong-kongs-legislative-council-functional.

Lam, Jermain T.M. (2015) "Political decay in Hong Kong after the Occupy Central Movement", *Asian Affairs: An American Review*, 42(2): 99–121.

Lam, Wai-man and Kay Lam Chi-yan (2013) "China's united front work in civil society: The case of Hong Kong", *International Journal of Chinese Studies*, 4(3): 301–325.

Lau, Chris (2017) "How a small team of graft-busters tightened the net in Hong Kong's most explosive corruption case", *South China Morning Post*, 7 August, www.scmp.com/news/hong-kong/law-crime/article/2105628/how-small-team-graft-busters-tightened-net-hong-kongs-most.

Lau, Chris and Jasmine Siu (2017) "Former Hong Kong leader Donald Tsang avoids conviction on bribery – for now – as jury unable to reach verdict", *South China Morning Post*, 3 November, www.scmp.com/news/hong-kong/law-crime/article/2118106/former-hong-kong-leader-donald-tsang-avoids-conviction-now.

Lau, Chris and Kimmy Chung (2017) "Court ruling disqualifying Hong Kong lawmakers is a 'declaration of war'", *South China Morning Post*, 15 July, www.scmp.com/news/hong-kong/politics/article/2102609/four-more-hong-kong-lawmakers-disqualified-over-oath-taking.

Lau, Stuart (2012) "Five more jailed for vote-rigging in Hong Kong District Council election", *South China Morning Post*, 29 August, www.scmp.com/news/hong-kong/article/1024758/five-more-jailed-vote-rigging-hong-kong-district-council-election.

Lau, Stuart (2016) "Reports of irregularities and influencing tarnish Hong Kong Legco vote", *South China Morning Post*, 4 September, www.scmp.com/news/hong-kong/politics/article/2014642/reports-irregularities-and-influencing-tarnish-hong-kong.

Legislative Council (2018) "Database on particular policy issues: Electoral matters", www.legco.gov.hk/database/english/data_ca/ca-electoral-and-registration-system.htm.

Legislative Council Panel on Security (2014) "Anti-corruption work against cross-boundary corruption", LC Paper No. CB (2)1453/13–14(04), www.legco.gov.hk/yr13-14/english/panels/se/papers/se0513cb2-1453-4-e.pdf.

Li, Li and T. Wing Lo (2017) "Mainlandization, the ICAC and the seriousness attached by local politicians to corruption in post-1997 Hong Kong", *Journal of Offender Therapy and Comparative Criminology*, 62(6): 1742–1760.

Lo, Shiu-hing (2017) "Faction and Chinese-style democracy: The 2017 Chief Executive election", *Asia Pacific Journal of Public Administration*, 39(2): 101–119.

Ma, Ngok (2015) "The rise of 'Anti-China' sentiment in Hong Kong and the 2012 Legislative Council elections", *China Review*, 15(1): 39–66.

Morris, Stephen D. and Joseph L. Klesner (2010) "Corruption and trust: Theoretical considerations and evidence from Mexico", *Comparative Political Studies*, 43(10): 1258–1285.

Ng, Ellie (2016) "Pro-Beijing DAB party raised tens of millions of dollars at dinner attended by top officials", *Hong Kong Free Press*, 22 November, www.hongkongfp.com/2016/11/22/pro-beijing-dab-party-raises-tens-millions-dollars-dinner-attended-top-officials/.

Ng, Kang-chung (2016) "Ken Chow alleges Beijing warned him to quit Hong Kong's Legco elections", *South China Morning Post*, 8 September, www.scmp.com/news/hong-kong/politics/article/2017295/ken-chow-alleges-beijing-trio-warned-him-quit-hong-kongs.

O'Neill, Mark (2017) "1.5 million mainland immigrants change Hong Kong", *ejinsight*, 19 June, www.ejinsight.com/20170619-1-5-million-mainland-migrants-change-hong-kong/.

Persson, Torsten, Guido Tabellini and Francesco Trebbi (2003) "Electoral rules and corruption", *Journal of the European Economic Association*, 1(4): 958–989.

Reed, Steven R. and Michael F. Thiess (2001) "The causes of Japanese electoral reform" in Mathew S. Shugart and Martin P. Wattenberg (eds.) *Mixed member electoral systems.* Oxford: Oxford University Press.

Rose, Richard and Caryn Peiffer (2018) *Bad governance and corruption.* Basingstoke: Palgrave Macmillan.

Rovnick, Naomi (2010) "ICBC chief on corruption charges", *South China Morning Post*, 8 October, www.scmp.com/article/726833/icbc-chief-corruption-charges.

Scott, Ian (2014) "Political scandals and the accountability of the Chief Executive in Hong Kong", *Asian Survey*, 54(5): 966–986.

Scott, Ian (2017) "The challenge of preserving a successful anti-corruption agency", *Asian Education and Development Studies*, 6(3): 227–237.

Seligson, Mitchell A. (2002) "The impact of corruption on regime legitimacy: A comparative study of four Latin American countries", *The Journal of Politics*, 64(2): 408–433.

Shum Kwok-sher v HKSAR (2002) 5 HKCFAR 381.

Siu, Jasmine (2016a) "Hong Kong radio host convicted over plan to pay localists to win votes in district council elections", *South China Morning Post*, 24 October, www.scmp.com/news/hong-kong/law-crime/article/2039644/hong-kong-waiter-convicted-over-plan-pay-localists-win.

Siu, Jasmine (2016b) "Mainland businessman jailed for six months after trying to bribe HSBC staffer with Chanel No. 5", *South China Morning Post*, 27 September, www.scmp.com/news/hong-kong/law-crime/article/2023017/fragrant-offence-jail-businessman-who-tried-bribe-hong-kong.

Smart, Alan (2018) "The unbearable discretion of street-level bureaucrats: Corruption and collusion in Hong Kong", *Current Anthropology*, 59(supplement 18) (April): S37-S47.

South China Morning Post (2015) "Elderly people bussed to polling stations during Hong Kong's District Council elections", www.facebook.com/scmp/videos/10153695173314820/.

South China Morning Post (2016) "Hong Kong must find a way for public to monitor donations to political parties", 4 January, www.scmp.com/comment/insight-opinion/article/1897843/hong-kong-must-find-way-public-monitor-donations-political.

South China Morning Post (2017) "Hong Kong must sign rendition treaty with mainland China", 13 February, www.scmp.com/comment/insight-opinion/article/2070279/hong-kong-must-sign-rendition-treaty-mainland-china.

Trade and Industry Department (2018) "Hong Kong and Mainland of China: Some important facts", 9 April, www.tid.gov.hk/english/aboutus/publications/factsheet/china.html.

Webb-site Reports (2011) "Party finance in HK", https://webb-site.com/articles/partyfinance.asp.

Wienland, Don and Hudson Lockett (2018) "China anti-corruption drive stretches to Hong Kong", *Financial Times*, 26 April, www.ft.com/content/aa5daa92-4856-11e8-8ee8-cae73aab7ccb.

Yeung, Rikkie L.K., Francesca T.C. Chiu and James Y.C. Kwok (2017) "Corporatist governance in Hong Kong: The case of the sports and arts functional constituency", *Asia- Pacific Journal of Public Administration*, 39(3): 163–176.

Young, Simon N.M. and Anthony Law (2006) "Privileged to vote: Inequalities and anomalies of the FC system" in Christine Loh and Civic Exchange (eds.) *Functional constituencies: A unique feature of the Hong Kong Legislative Council*. Hong Kong: Hong Kong University Press: 59–109.

Young, Simon N.M. and Richard Cullen (2010) *Electing Hong Kong's Chief Executive*. Hong Kong: Hong Kong University Press.

Zhou, Xin and Xie Yu (2018) "Chinese tycoon, Xiao Jianhua, missing for 15 months since vanishing in Hong Kong, could face trial in June", *South China Morning Post*, 13 April, www.scmp.com/news/china/economy/article/2141462/chinese-tycoon-xiao-jianhua-missing-15-months-vanishing-hong-kong.

11 Institutionalising ACAs
Constraints and possibilities

In this chapter, we summarise our conclusions on corruption prevention in Hong Kong and assess what this experience might contribute to the institutionalisation of ACAs elsewhere. We consider, first, the obstacles that ACAs are likely to confront on the road to institutionalisation, the conditions that are necessary for building public trust, and the value that such agencies may add to the polity and the society. We then analyse the problems associated with transfer of anti-corruption practices from one jurisdiction to another with specific reference to Mainland China. Finally, we identify the conditions under which ACAs can help achieve more effective corruption control and assess the benefits for better governance.

Obstacles to institutionalising ACAs

We have argued that success for ACAs depends on whether they are institutionalised and perceived to have value for the probity of the governance system and for the quality of life of citizens. Achieving this status is difficult. Many obstacles lie in the way of those ACAs which are genuinely committed to reducing corruption and improving governance. At their inception, they often face challenges to their very existence or to the scope of their investigations; once in action, there are often design flaws in their structures and processes which affect their capacity and impede effective action; and, most important, they may have difficulties in gaining the trust of their societies. Each of these problems has to be overcome on the road to institutionalisation.

Subverting the ACA

The challenges to an ACA's authority often occur soon after its creation in disputes over its jurisdiction and powers. Subsequent issues may also arise from regime change and declining political will or government inaction or from organised groups that are detrimentally affected by successful corruption measures. Differing political, economic and cultural settings mean that crises will take divergent forms in different places. Generally, however, they involve political interference from either or both the executive and the legislature and those with authority or influence such as the police or business. The ICAC was perhaps fortunate that its opponents were the police, who had been shown to be corrupt, business associations who admitted that some of their members were engaged in illegal activities, and the Legislative Council's Finance Committee, who could be persuaded to loosen the purse strings under more favourable economic circumstances. As serious as these crises were, the ICAC was backed by firm support from the political executive and an independent and largely corruption-free judicial system. The challenges were resolved in its favour and the Commission was then able to extend its investigations without interference into all parts of the public and private sectors.

Other ACAs have faced challenges which have been less easy to resolve. If the executive is lukewarm or hostile toward an ACA, if the legislature is not willing to enact effective anti-corruption laws, if legislators are themselves corrupt and seek to reduce the powers of the ACA and if courts do not convict offenders unless the bribes are large enough, then the chances of success are sharply reduced. In East Timor, Scambary (2017: 273) found that executive interference with the legal system was the major obstacle to the effective operation of the ACA, especially when it tried to investigate a former Finance Minister, Emilia Pires. In Indonesia, the parliament has repeatedly sought to dissolve the Komisi Pemberantasan Korupsi (KPK) or to weaken its powers, and the police have conducted sustained investigations and public attacks on its Commissioners (Schütte 2017; Widoyoko 2017). In Mongolia, Quah (2013: 397–399) discovered that the salaries and living conditions of judges made them highly vulnerable to corruption. Multiple examples from around the world confirm that these are not isolated incidents (Tangri and Mwenda 2006; Doig *et al* 2007; Batory 2012). There are many groups who are well aware of an ACA's potential to prosecute offenders, reduce corruption, and change the rules of the game. Driven by self-interest, they will act to prevent it from becoming effective.

It is tempting in the light of these experiences to suggest that there is little point in pursuing the ACA model. It might be argued that there are too many fundamental governance problems for the model to be successful and that if it has a role, it might be better to come on the scene after these problems have been resolved (De Maria 2010). This assumes that governance will improve, not deteriorate, and that it will result in a reduction in corruption to the point where it is no longer an impediment to clean government. The widespread perception that world-wide corruption is increasing does not give much reason for confidence in this prognosis (Transparency International 2018). While many ACAs fall significantly short of best practice and others, for anti-corruption purposes, are effectively useless, there are few viable short-term alternatives for improving corruption prevention. Some ACAs do show signs of greater effectiveness over time and even an ability to manoeuvre in sometimes hostile political environments. The KPK successfully prosecuted many leading figures for corruption, including eighty-two parliamentarians (Widoyoko 2017: 253). Despite political interference, East Timor's Anti-Corruption Commission did eventually succeed in bringing Emilia Pires to court although she had left the country before sentencing (Barker 2017). Incremental changes and small successes may help

ACAs to weather the difficulties caused by political attacks on their independence; increased public trust may dissuade their opponents from mounting attacks to dissolve or emasculate them.

Challenges to ACAs may occur even after they have been in operation for many years. In the case of the ICAC, there was a rise in the level of corruption which was reflected in an increase in corruption reports just before and after 1997. Although most of the public still believed that the ICAC was able to control corruption, the perception was growing that it would be less effective under a new regime. For the corrupt, this may have meant that opportunities should be taken when they could, a situation which was compounded by the difficult economic circumstances prevailing immediately after 1997 (Lai 2001). When it became clear that the ICAC would continue to be effective and the economy improved, the number of corruption reports dropped back to their previous level.

Under the Leung administration, the rise in conflicts of interests and perceptions of government–business collusion and cross-border corruption posed a different kind of challenge. The question was whether the ICAC could deal effectively with these issues. Because it was well institutionalised, there was acceptance on both sides of the political divide that the ICAC should continue to perform its traditional functions. Had there been serious moves to do otherwise, politically instability would have increased substantially. The ICAC experience indicates that insulation from political interference aids autonomy and provides the best protection for ACAs seeking to avoid attempts to subvert them. But it can only be achieved if the ACA develops the capacity to deal with corruption effectively and shows that it has value for the society.

Design flaws

Even assuming that an ACA is fully committed to reducing corruption, there are many different ways in which political support and institutional design can detrimentally affect its performance. Funding is a first and fundamental issue. Political will has to be matched with the resources to allow the ACA to do its work. Most ACAs will not receive funding at the ICAC's level; for that reason alone, the universal model is not feasible in most cases. Nevertheless, it is still possible to design effective ACAs if political will remains constant and if objectives are clearly stated and supported by appropriate organisational design and processes.

Research has found that dividing anti-corruption responsibilities between agencies is not desirable (Quah 2013: 121, 196; Ko *et al* 2015; Quah 2017). The concentration on establishing and defending often-competing jurisdictions detracts from the objective of fighting corruption and spreads resources too thinly. A single independent agency is the organisational form by far the most likely to succeed. Even then, the agency must be given sufficient powers to investigate corruption. In South Korea, for example, continuing concerns over perceived high levels of corruption have been linked to the existence of multiple agencies with inadequate powers (Quah 2017). If an ACA has insufficient investigative powers, it is scarcely surprising that corruption tends to flourish.

Adequate investigative powers are only the first step. The anti-corruption laws must be sufficiently related to the offence to ensure convictions and lead to punishments that may serve as a deterrent. For more than 100 years, Hong Kong law met neither criterion and corruption permeated the government and the society. Until the passage of the *POBO* in 1970, the law was too imprecise to permit many convictions. Corruption was considered to be morally reprehensible but not something that warranted severe penalties. It is not only the deterrent effect of penalties that makes a difference. Laws must be matched to the kind of corruption that is most prevalent and should reflect the social norms of a society. If they do so, then the impact of upholding the law will strengthen those norms and aid anti-corruption efforts. Of course, the government and the ACA may feel, as in Hong Kong, that society itself should condemn improprieties and uphold anti-corruption values. But the ACA must also be careful that what it is engaged in condemning as immoral is appropriately sanctioned under the law. If there is a disjunction between the law and the norms which the society holds or between the law and the publicity which the ACA is propagating, then anti-corruption initiatives will probably fall on deaf ears.

The problem stretches beyond a single, simple solution. Forms of corruption change in response to effective laws. As the ICAC discovered, if simple bribery can no longer be sustained, then other offences such as serious conflicts of interest are likely to become more prevalent. The law may need to be amended to counter these developments, but there are often major impediments. Many ACAs lack access to the legal expertise to develop appropriate responses and, even if guidance is available, a reluctant legislature or entrenched groups may not support change. There is a tendency for ACAs to lag behind the pace of change, which may be exacerbated by such organisational problems as out-of-date technology and inadequately trained staff. At worst, the law becomes set in stone and is used as a means of defending an agenda that has lost its relevance for many citizens.

If conviction rates are high in the first few years of its operation, the public usually perceive the ACA to be successful. The conviction of offenders who are seen to be the main perpetrators of corruption, such as the police in Hong Kong and politicians in Indonesia, gives it credibility and coincides with what the public often considers to be the primary function of the agency. Almost all respondents to the early ICAC surveys associated the role of the Commission with the investigative work of the OD and the complaint-handling function of the regional offices and were not as familiar with the liaison efforts of the CRD or the corruption prevention activities of the CPD (ICAC 1979a: III; ICAC n.d.: 49). About 30 per cent of respondents to an ICAC mass survey thought that the Commission's most important work should be catching "big tigers" rather than "small flies" (ICAC 1979a: 22); a later survey found clear links between positive assessments of the ICAC's performance and its ability in "cracking big corruption cases" (ICAC 1984: para 86). The ICAC's Community Research Unit thought, probably correctly, that this was too narrow a base on which to construct support for the Commission (ICAC 1979a: III). It wanted wider recognition and knowledge of public education and corruption prevention activities which were later achieved by effective publicity and extensive liaison work. An ACA may base its support largely on the success of its investigations and prosecutions, as Singapore's CPIB does, but deepening and widening engagement with the community embeds an agency more firmly in the society.

ACAs come in a variety of organisational forms, but if they are to be successful, basic organisational principles need to be observed. There should be leadership, independent and sufficient powers, appropriate objectives which are achievable within budgets, strategic alliances within the jurisdiction and with international networks, adequate technology for efficient complaint-handling, and constant attention to the ACA's level of support within society (Doig and Norris 2012). Whatever form the organisation takes, it needs time to consolidate because, as the ICAC's experience shows, the public is unlikely to be fully aware of all ACA functions within a short period. Major changes in structure are likely to detract from attempts to publicise its work and may even create suspicions. Many ACAs fall well short of realising even basic organisational requirements. As de Sousa (2010) remarks, there are "no silver bullets but a mixture of successes and failures and no quick fixes but a long and hard learning process". An ACA that overcomes its challenges and failures with its basic strategy and structure intact is more likely to become institutionalised than those which change tack and see organisational reforms as the answer to every setback.

Gaining trust

Overcoming immediate challenges to its anti-corruption investigations, building capacity and demonstrating effectiveness are essential first steps for an ACA. Gaining trust is a less tangible, more elusive objective which may depend on the consistency with which the ACA performs over time and the expectation that it will continue to seek to reduce corruption and prevent its re-emergence. We distinguish three domains where trust relationships between the agency and the public are important but have different consequences for citizen perceptions of the ACA.

The first domain concerns the probity of the ACA and its officials, which is a necessary pre-condition for positive perceptions of effectiveness. A second domain relates to procedures and processes, particularly in the investigation of complaints, which must be sufficiently consistent, transparent and fair to be able to generate trust. A third domain is trust derived from public perceptions of the effectiveness of an ACA. These perceptions may vary depending on the form of corruption involved, whether it affects citizens directly and whether the issue is seen to be within the competence of the ACA. We consider each of these forms of trust in turn.

Trust might be considered as a quality that extends outward from the ACA to its operations in the community. ACAs are usually set up because there is evidence that corruption is widespread. If corruption is perceived to be endemic, citizens might logically assume that there would also be corrupt personnel within the ACA. Consequently, an organisational priority for any ACA is to ensure that its employees meet the highest ethical standards. In the beginning, there often seems to be doubt in the public mind about the probity of anti-corruption officers. The reasons for this may vary considerably from specific suspicions that the officials are political appointees on a mission to line their own pockets to beliefs that human nature means that there is corruption everywhere and in all organisations. Whatever the source of the belief, it is potentially destructive of any attempt to control corruption. If the public does not believe in the probity of the ACA itself, they are scarcely likely to trust its commitment to reducing corruption in the wider system.

The early ICAC surveys found that there were major public concerns about corruption within the agency. In the first major survey conducted in 1977, 39 per cent of respondents believed that there was corruption within the ICAC, 42 per cent said that they did not know whether or not there was corruption, and only 19 per cent thought that there was no corruption at all (ICAC 1979b: 33). Although 77 per cent of respondents believed that the ICAC would act if corruption was found within the Commission, the high percentage of those who thought that the ICAC had some corrupt personnel serves as an indication of the fragility of trust in anti-corruption efforts (ICAC 1979b: 33). However, a survey taken three years later showed that confidence in the probity of the Commission had increased: 42 per cent now thought that there was no corruption in the ICAC, while the number who thought there was corruption had declined to 28 per cent (ICAC 1981: 39). Concerns about ethical standards within the agency are a continuing problem for ACAs. For the ICAC, they have resulted in investigations into the work of the Commission in 1994, several enquiries and a select committee into the over-spending of the ICAC Commissioner in 2013 and 2014 and calls for a select committee into the decision to revert the Acting Head of Operations to her substantive position in 2016 (see Ch. 5).

A second domain which is helpful for gaining trust is to ensure that procedures and processes are consistent, transparent and fair. Trust stems from the reliability of anti-corruption measures, but it also rests on the expectation that rules will be applied fairly and not used to favour or penalise particular groups. Transparency is also important. If citizens are fully aware of how their complaints are being processed and of the safeguards in place to ensure that the information remains confidential, they are more likely to be willing to report corruption. In its early years, the ICAC wanted to encourage more people to report corruption and promised that all complaints would be treated confidentially. Survey evidence showed that respondents did not always believe that this was so. In the 1982 survey, the percentage who believed that corruption reports were always kept confidential declined from 79 per cent in the 1980 survey to 53 per cent two years later (ICAC 1984: para 100). As time went on, there was a gradual increase in the numbers who believed that the ICAC would respect confidentiality (ICAC n.d.: Table 4.15). More people were willing to give their names and addresses when lodging corruption reports, a development that was taken to be a sign of greater confidence and trust that the ICAC would treat all complaints appropriately.

Based on the ICAC's experience, we conclude that it is necessary for any ACA to monitor closely what the public thinks about its procedures and processes.

Social attitudes can change quite rapidly and may not always coincide with what the ACA believes are citizens' views on corruption and its prevention. The sudden decline in the belief that information provided to the Commission would not be treated confidentially took the ICAC by surprise. Similarly, in the 1990s, there was pressure from some legislators and groups to make the ICAC more accountable and transparent in view of the resumption of Chinese sovereignty over Hong Kong, the passage of a Bill of Rights ordinance and possible abuse of the Commission's extensive powers (Independent Review Committee 1994: 16, 21–23). The ICAC did not appear to have anticipated the pressure for change and thought that its existing powers were necessary, but it accepted the Committee's recommendations on increasing transparency and accountability (Independent Review Committee 1994: 36). Trust also derives from the effective implementation of procedures and processes based on the anti-corruption laws. Although the law may be fit for purpose, implementation may be weak (Transparency International and CHR Michelsen Institute 2016: 1). There must be constant repetition of fair and transparent procedures which the community supports and believes to have value if institutionalisation is to be achieved. The process takes time and, without losing the fundamental attributes of consistency, transparency and fairness, may need sensitive modification when public opinion changes.

The third domain is trust derived from perceptions of effectiveness. We have argued that there are differing public perceptions of the effectiveness of the ICAC based on its overall record over time and perceptions of its ability to deal with corruption problems in the political environment. In 1984, more than 90 per cent of survey respondents believed that the ICAC had made a great contribution to restoring justice and fair play and that it had become less prevalent to use corruption to get things done (ICAC n.d.: Table 4.15). The positive response may be explained partly by the immediacy of the citizens' experience. What the ICAC had done was to clean up corruption on the streets and in the civil service where there was most likely to be direct contact between the public and corrupt officials. Its effectiveness in bringing about this change was greatly appreciated and was a factor that contributed to increased trust and the institutionalisation of the Commission. Suspected political corruption in more recent times is a perception which is less easily resolved. Occasional scandals and prosecutions suggest that it may be present, but the ICAC cannot demonstrate as easily as in the past that it is in control of newer forms of corruption which are opaque and more difficult to detect. In addition, stamping out some types of electoral corruption requires action that is beyond the jurisdiction of the ICAC. Perceptions reflect these difficulties, and the Commission is consequently seen to be less effective in dealing with them. Nonetheless, in the 2017 ICAC annual survey, more than 96 per cent of respondents still said that the Commission "deserved their support" – mostly, it seemed, because it had maintained a corruption-free society (ICAC 2018: Table C).

Many ACAs face situations in which the political leadership is perceived to be corrupt. There is often scepticism about whether the ACA can take on entrenched political elites and about whether there is genuine intent to combat corruption. In the rare cases when there is an attempt to clean up government at higher levels, as with the KPK, there is strong public support for its actions. More often, ACAs are content to deal with petty corruption; in some worst-case scenarios, such as Bangladesh and Cambodia, they seem to have been used primarily to investigate alleged corruption in opposition parties (Jamil *et al* 2016; Transparency International and CHR Michelsen Institute 2016; Baniamin and Jamil 2017). Even if the ACAs are effective in dealing with petty corruption, perceptions of their inability to deal with corruption on a grand scale are likely to hamper the development of trust. The prospects for improvement look bleak unless there are fundamental changes in political attitudes and ACA practices and procedures. Does the ICAC experience offer any useful lessons which are transferable across jurisdictions?

Transferring the ICAC model

Meagher (2005) observes that the ICAC model has "proven enormously influential" and estimates that thirty to forty national level ACAs around the world have drawn on the idea of a single, powerful, centralised anti-corruption agency. Not all these ACAs have taken on Hong Kong's full panoply of anti-corruption laws, the ICAC's three-pronged approach or its organisational structure. Even among the small number of ACAs that might be regarded as successes, the extent of borrowing from the model has differed considerably. Botswana, where the Directorate on Corruption and Economic Crime is regarded as Africa's most successful ACA, borrowed quite extensively from the model and several senior officials, including the first Director, had previously served with the ICAC (Theobald and Williams 1999). In Indonesia, the KPK adopted the ICAC's three-pronged approach but chose a different organisational format (Schütte 2012). The Malaysian Anti-Corruption Commission is also formally modelled on the ICAC although its ability to control corruption effectively has been seriously compromised by the 1MDB scandal involving the former Prime Minister, Najib Razak (Dahlan and Hasani 2018). Aside from political interference, budgetary constraints are also a major reason for failure to adopt the model successfully. Makowski (2016) notes, for example, that the Philippines, Thailand and Uganda all found that ICAC practice was too expensive to implement on their limited budgets.

Successful policy transfer is premised on two conditions: whether specific policies and institutions can be turned into knowledge and practice beyond their original locations and whether contextual factors in the target location support the intended effects of the policy transfer (Williams *et al* 2014). Both conditions have been considered carefully in academic discussions on whether the ICAC model, or parts of it, can be transferred to Mainland China (Li 2004; Manion 2004; Cheung 2007; Michael 2014; Holmes 2015). At first sight, the prospects do not look promising. The ICAC model was developed in response to particular conditions and drew upon a long history of failed efforts to control corruption. Those conditions and that history cannot be replicated elsewhere. It is evident that the political institutions, the legal system and anti-corruption policies in Hong Kong are very different from those in Mainland China and that a simple block transfer of ICAC institutions, laws and policies would not work. If there were any doubts about that, then the many failures of attempts to transfer the ICAC model to other places would surely give pause for thought.

There are nonetheless some similarities in the pervasive extent of corruption in Hong Kong before the creation of the ICAC and in Mainland China today. Despite many nationwide anti-corruption campaigns and strong disciplinary and legal sanctions against corrupt officials, corruption in Mainland China has resulted in serious damage to state coffers and leadership legitimacy and has even led to social instability in some locations (Wedeman 2017). In response, the PRC government has substantially intensified its anti-corruption drive in recent years. An unprecedented number of corrupt officials, including many senior ones, have been brought to trial; strict rules have been imposed on bureaucratic behaviour; excessive position-related consumption in government institutions has been regulated; and an extensive campaign has been launched to raise public awareness of corruption (Quah 2015; Manion 2016; Gong and Xiao 2017).

What lessons might be learned from the ICAC model to increase the effectiveness of ACAs elsewhere? At the institutional level, bearing in mind the caveats we have already considered, the ICAC's organisation is more a reference to best practice than a model to be transferred without modification. Much more important and potentially less expensive, in our view, is changing social attitudes toward corruption. The ICAC has vast experience of the central issues involved: the means to discover what the public is really thinking about corruption and its prevention, building trust and developing positive perceptions of effectiveness, and using publicity, the media and other social and economic organisations to disseminate the anti-corruption message. In the following paragraphs, we consider, first, the institutional lessons that might be drawn from the model and, second, practical means, derived from the ICAC's experience, which an ACA can use to change social attitudes toward corruption.

In Chapter 8, we examined the virtuous circle in which improved capacity leads to more effective control over corruption which in turn creates greater trust, a critical element in promoting institutionalisation. Capacity is composed of the ACA's ability to act, to respond, to engage, to adapt and to change. While there are many ways that these abilities can be developed and achieved, some factors, such as strong political support, appropriate funding, independence, effective anti-corruption laws and a well-defined jurisdiction, personnel who meet the highest standards of integrity and dedication, and coordinated strategies within the ACA, are clearly necessary. The most appropriate organisational format, however, is probably not going to be found by the wholesale importation of an external model.

Some institutional principles and policies may nonetheless serve as guidance for ACAs which are seeking to improve their capacity and effectiveness. An initial concentration on public sector corruption, if successful, has important spin-off benefits and generally receives strong community approval (see pp. 155–160). Cheung (2007) also notes the value of the single agency approach which was pioneered by Singapore's CPIB and the ICAC. The approach gave the ICAC a monopoly over corruption control which enabled it to penetrate deeply into government and society. In Mainland China, corruption control was divided among several agencies, which focused on different targets and tasks (Holmes 2015). In 2018, the PRC government decided to create a single agency, an important institutional reform which is a more effective way of dealing with corruption (Gueorguiev and Stromseth 2018). Similar institutional changes may also assist the more effective transfer of policies.

The other important condition of successful policy transfer is whether the transferred policies and practices are compatible with the political, social and cultural context in which they are to be lodged. It is at this interface between ACAs and the public where the ICAC's experience has most relevance. We envisage three possible types of relationships between ACAs and the public that might arise. The first type might occur if an ACA is set up in a place which already has strong anti-corruption values and attitudes. There might be questions about why an ACA is needed under such circumstances, since there is presumably not much corruption and little need to change values, but it could conceivably play a watchdog role. The second type, which is characteristic of many developing societies, is a situation in which people engage in corrupt transactions because it is seen to be the normal way of life. If the ACA or the government does nothing to change values, and even if there are severe penalties for corrupt activities and some offenders are caught, it is likely that corruption will continue.

The third type is the ACA which has actively engaged with civil society, changed social attitudes toward corruption and presented and received positive public support for a moral agenda which clearly points out the adverse consequences of corruption. It is the transformation from the second type of relationship to the third type where the ICAC's experience is particularly relevant.

In their comparative analysis of public attitudes toward corruption in Mainland China and Hong Kong, Gong *et al* (2015) found that the Mainland respondents tended to believe that corruption was part of human nature, that it was everywhere and that it could not be controlled. Hong Kong respondents, on the contrary, thought – probably as a result of their experience of a largely corruption-free environment – that corruption could be controlled. There were also significant differences in definitions of corruption. Hong Kong respondents defined it as bribery. For their Mainland counterparts, corruption had a much wider connotation, describing many different criminal and social evils. Manion (2004: 1, 4) has argued that the problem of corruption is not simply a matter of reducing the level of corruption but also of changing shared expectations that there will be corrupt payoffs and avoiding the danger that informal corrupt rules may subvert formal clean ones. Hong Kong's experience in this respect is highly relevant. Social attitudes towards corruption in the 1970s changed quite quickly once the ICAC began to engage with the community and to tell people what would be permitted and what would not (Scott and Gong 2015). In Mainland China, by contrast, anti-corruption campaigns to date have been top-down and there have been little attempts to base reform on efforts which are "unambiguously bottom-up"(Holmes 2015).Provided there is sufficient political will to support effective corruption prevention, three ICAC initiatives may be particularly relevant for Mainland China and for some ACAs in developing countries:

- discovering what social attitudes toward corruption are;
- developing policies and practices which are aimed at building trust between the ACA and the community; and
- designing specific strategic alliances with the community and business to change values.

We consider each of these in turn.

Discovering what social attitudes are

Many ACAs think they know about social attitudes toward corruption and its prevention and thus do not make efforts to understand public opinion. Yet, unless they make rigorous efforts to identify precisely what the public thinks about corruption through surveys and liaison work, there is some danger that resources may be misallocated and that the public mood on critical issues could be inadvertently ignored. The ICAC in its early years, for example, had good reason to believe that the public thought that corruption was a serious problem because there had been demonstrations calling on the government to take strong measures. But the first survey undertaken showed conclusively that most respondents did not regard corruption as a serious problem compared to other social problems. In order to persuade people otherwise, the ICAC had to change its publicity to link corruption to what the public regarded as more serious social problems such as crime, housing and employment. If an ACA is not fully aware of prevailing social attitudes, it may continue to act on incorrect or inaccurate assumptions.

What kinds of information on social attitudes does an ACA need to collect? A first issue is whether the public is willing to report corruption. If it is not, then the ACA's operation will be hampered because corruption complaints are the leads upon which a large portion of an ACA's work depends. Citizens' willingness to report corruption also reflects their trust in, and support for, the ACA. Besides knowing whether people are willing to report corruption, it is also important to know why some are not willing to do so in order to allay their concerns.

Second, knowledge of the anti-corruption laws and regulations give some indication of people's willingness to comply with them. Clearly, those who are not aware of the law are more likely to tolerate or even engage in corruption. The threat of enforceable penalties will act as a deterrent and persuade some people not to act corruptly while others will accept the ACA's argument that specific legal provisions are a necessary means of achieving a corruption-free society. While there will still be others who are not convinced that the law can be enforced or that the offence can be detected, providing the public with information about the law and its consequences is a valuable means of generating support for the ACA's agenda.

Third, the issue of whether an ACA is trusted can be assessed indirectly in many different ways. For example, it may be measured by asking people what they know about an ACA's commitment to corruption prevention and whether they believe that government officials act with integrity. Trust is also related to perceptions of the ACA's effectiveness. If the public feels that the ACA is not effective, then it is unlikely that corruption will be reported or that the agency will be trusted. Understanding perceptions of effectiveness is valuable because it reveals the areas on which the public would like the ACA to focus and may draw attention to any doubts about the ACA's ability to deal with particular issues. It may also provide specific information and leads on types of corruption. A positive relationship between perceptions of effectiveness and trust is vital for the success of an ACA. If survey evidence or other information reveals that an agency is not perceived to be effective, then the ACA must address the problem as a matter of priority.

In each of these areas, establishing what the public thinks about corruption is important and provides guidance on how the ACA might translate the information into evidence-based policy.

Developing policies and practices aimed at building trust

It is important for building trust and supporting institutionalisation that ACA procedures should be seen to be transparent, consistent, fair and effective. Perhaps the most critical interface between an ACA and the public is the way in which it handles complaints. Even if a citizen is not lodging a corruption report, knowledge of how to do so and what will happen once a report has been made is a necessary first step if an ACA is to be successful. The ICAC has also always stressed the ease of making a complaint. If lodging a complaint is inconvenient, some citizens will not report corruption, as some of the ICAC surveys discovered. A 1978 survey reported that nearly half of all respondents who said that they would not report corruption cited that doing so would be inconvenient (ICAC 1979a: 27). The researchers accepted that this was a legitimate reason in some cases, although probably an excuse in others, and advised that the ICAC should publicise the ease of making a complaint.

Once a complaint is in the system, a second step is to ensure that procedures are speedy and linear and that the complainant is informed of the outcome of the investigation. The ICAC prides itself on the speed with which complaints are processed, information received from the complainant, classification made of the type of complaint and investigations pursued. The process is designed to ensure as rapid a completion of the case as possible. This would seem a commonsensical objective but, in many ACAs, complaints seem to get lost in the system and the complainant is not informed of the outcome. A target set for speed of completion of cases and a monitoring committee to ensure that it is met is beneficial for the efficiency of the agency and also serves the purpose of assuring the complainant – and the public – that the ACA is treating corruption reports seriously.

A final step is to ensure that procedures are properly and consistently carried out and that information is treated confidentially. The behaviour of ACA officials during the course of the investigation is also important. If officials break the law and this is revealed – in a court case, say – it can have a damaging impact on public confidence in the agency. If the ACA violates legal and social norms in its investigations, it can hardly expect that its integrity will not be impugned. Transparency is equally important for public confidence in the ACA. If there is no transparency in an ACA's procedures or if there is suspicion that the procedures might be abused, it is unlikely that the agency will be able to win trust (Fijnaut and Huberts 2002; Buckley 2017). Institutionalisation depends on the repeated performance of accepted procedures that correspond with expected social norms. Violation of those norms undermines the acceptability of all its procedures.

Building strategic alliances

The difficulty for ACAs, particularly those with small budgets operating over large areas, is that resources do not usually permit extensive engagement with the community. ACAs, in consequence, need to galvanise support from peak organisations, such as chambers of commerce, and from local governments, NGOs, the media and various sectoral organisations, especially in education and labour. The ICAC has received substantial support from these organisations which has significantly reduced its cost of engaging with the public. Its regional offices have liaised with district councils to produce annual programmes and there have also been campaigns across Hong Kong, such as the "All for Integrity" programme, which have aimed at including the whole community in anti-corruption activities. The media have also been very supportive and assisted in the production of television drama series and anti-corruption publicity. Even though it is well-funded, the ICAC has still needed this kind of support. New ACAs, with more limited budgets, are even more dependent on this kind of alliance if they want to change social attitudes. The alliances reduce their costs, because the participants may use their own resources to produce anti-corruption publicity, and may also help increase the visibility of the ACA through the networks of partner organisations.

The transfer of any anti-corruption model, or part of it, requires careful planning. Pre-conditions for successful transfer are that there should be sufficient political will, adequate funding and a supportive culture. If there is not, the danger is that half-baked models will be transferred that do not work in the new environment. For these reasons, we do not believe that the transfer of the full institutional framework of a universal model is practicable or desirable. At best, it may serve as a reference point for possible ACA structures which will almost invariably have to be modified to suit local circumstances. We are more in favour of policy transfers which strengthen the relationships between the ACA and the public. In situations where an ACA is confronted with an indifferent public or one which is supportive of corrupt practices, the ACA needs to acquire a better understanding of the attitudes and values of citizens and to keep them informed of what the ACA is attempting to accomplish. Such interactions can be achieved through means which have been employed to great effect by the ICAC: surveys, publicity, liaison work with the community and the building of strategic alliances. There is also, critically, the need to ensure that the ACA's procedures are transparent, fair and do not violate social norms. The procedures must be repeated consistently and show results so that the agency becomes respected in the community and is eventually institutionalised as a necessary element of good governance.

The debate about the future of ACAs is set to continue. There is little doubt that many ACAs do not justify their expenditure. Yet trying to control corruption by means of top-down good governance reforms does not seem to be a feasible alternative. In many cases, the problem of corruption at the centre and its insidious effects on institutions and people throughout the political and social system represents an entrenched obstacle to change. So long as it persists, neither the good governance approach nor an ACA-centred effort, nor an attempt to combine both approaches, is likely to make much difference.

The debate becomes more interesting in conditions where efforts to bring about change are supported by the political leadership or the public or both and there is a commitment to ensuring that corruption will no longer be tolerated. Under these circumstances, an ACA-centred approach can have a significant impact, as the ICAC experience has shown. Political commitment helps create effective top-down agencies emphasising the penalties that will be applied to offenders enhancing a rule-based anti-corruption approach. Equally important is mobilising public support and making efforts to change social attitudes toward corruption. If the two can be combined, corruption opportunities will be reduced, and it will be difficult for new street-level forms of corruption to emerge. At the centre, successful efforts in combating corruption in government enhance perceptions of a corruption-free government and society and have positive outcomes in developing a more trusting society and in institutionalising the ACA itself.

The ICAC provides the most compelling example of how an ACA can bring about such change which also serves as a reminder that new forms of corruption can shift the focus of an ACA. The change in the form of corruption from the prevention of simple bribery to more complex conflicts of interest and from a focus on public sector corruption to private sector corruption required successful new legal measures and initiatives. But the political environment is not always conducive to making appropriate changes. The long-running saga of the attempted amendment of Sections 3 and 8 of the *POBO* to cover the Chief Executive, the failure to reach a rendition agreement with the PRC government and the lack of new measures to strengthen the ICAC's powers to investigate conflicts of interest are all testimony to the problems that may arise through political inaction. If an ACA is not able to adapt to changes in the corruption environment, however, then its efficacy and value may begin to be questioned.

Political will in support of anti-corruption measures may decline over time, but institutionalisation can serve as a counterweight to political inconstancy. Because institutionalisation depends on public perceptions that the ACA has value and that the community would be worse off without it, the agency is insulated from the adverse effects of declining political will and its autonomy and independence may be protected by community support. Political attacks on the ACA are likely to be seen as a violation of anti-corruption norms held in common by the agency and the public. Yet, for many ACAs, the path to achieving institutionalisation is littered with formidable obstacles many of which may be fatal to its survival as an effective agency. The battle is nevertheless worth fighting. An effective and institutionalised ACA, as the ICAC's efforts show, leads to a cleaner government and society, greater economic certainty and more investment, and enhances the values of transparency, fairness, accountability and integrity.

References

Banaimin, Hassan Muhammad and Ishtiaq Jamil (2018) "Dynamics of corruption and citizens' trust in anti-corruption agencies in three South Asian countries", *Public Organization Review*, 18(3): 381–398.

Barker, Anne (2017) "Australian citizen, former East Timorese minister fights 'unfair' seven year jail sentence for corruption", *ABC News*, 10 February, www.abc.net.au/news/2017-02-10/australian-fights-against-east-timors-unfair-jail-sentence/8256952.

Batory, Agnes (2012) "Political cycles and organizational life cycles: Delegation to anti-corruption agencies in Central Europe", *Governance*, 25(4): 639–660.

Buckley, Chris (2017) "In China, fears that new anticorruption agency will be above the law", *New York Times*, 29 November, www.nytimes.com/2017/11/29/world/asia/china-xi-jinping-anticorruption.html.

Cheung, Anthony B.L. (2007) "Combating corruption as a political strategy to rebuild trust and legitimacy: Can China learn from Hong Kong?" *International Public Management Review*, 8(2): 45–72.

Dahlan, Rosli and Muhammed Faizal Faiz Mohd Hasani (2018) "Malaysia", *The Anti-Bribery and Anti-Corruption Review*, 6th edition, https://thelawreviews.co.uk/edition/the-anti-bribery-and-anti-corruption-review-edition-6/1151858/malaysia.

De Maria, William (2010) "The failure of the African anti-corruption effort: Lessons for managers", *International Journal of Management*, 27(1): 117–122.

de Sousa, Luis (2010) "Anti-corruption agencies: Between empowerment and irrelevance", *Crime, Law and Social Change*, 53(1): 5–22.

Doig, Alan and David Norris (2012) "Improving anti-corruption agencies as organizations", *Journal of Financial Crime*, 19(3): 255–273.

Doig, Alan, David Watt and Robert Williams (2007) "Why do developing country anti-corruption commissions fail to deal with corruption? Understanding the three dilemmas of organisational development, performance expectation and government cycles", *Public Administration and Development*, 27(3): 251–259.

Fijnaut, Cyrille and Leo Huberts (2002) "Corruption, integrity and law enforcement" in Cyrille Fijnaut and Leo Huberts (eds.) *Corruption, integrity and law enforcement*. Den Haag: Kluwer Law International: 3–34.

Gong, Ting and Hanyu Xiao (2017) "The formation and impact of isomorphic pressures: Extravagant position-related consumption in China", *Governance*, 30(3): 387–405.

Gong, Ting, Shiru Wang and Jianming Ren (2015) "Corruption in the eye of the beholder: Survey evidence from Mainland China and Hong Kong", *International Public Management Journal*, 18(1): 458–482.

Gueorguiev, Dimitar and Jonathan Stromseth (2018) "New Chinese agency could undercut other anti-corruption efforts", www.brookings.edu/blog/order-from-chaos/2018/03/06/new-chinese-agency-could-undercut-other-anti-corruption-efforts/.

Holmes, Leslie (2015) "Combating corruption in China: The role of the state and other agencies in comparative perspective", *Economic and Political Studies*, 3(1): 42–70.

ICAC (1979a) *Mass survey 1978 final report*. Hong Kong: ICAC Community Research Unit.

ICAC (1979b) *Mass survey 1977 final report*. Hong Kong: ICAC Community Research Unit.

ICAC (1981) *Final report of the 1980 mass survey*. Hong Kong: ICAC Community Research Unit.

ICAC (1984) *Final report of the 1982 mass survey*. Hong Kong: ICAC Community Research Unit.

ICAC (2018) "Annual survey 2017", www.icac.org.hk/filemanager/en/content_176/survey2017.pdf.

ICAC (n.d.) *ICAC mass survey 1984*. Hong Kong: ICAC Community Research Unit.

Independent Review Committee (1994) *Report of the ICAC review committee*. Hong Kong: Government Printer.

Jamil, Ishtiaq, Steinar Asvik and Hasan Muhammed Baniamin (2016) "Citizens' trust in anti-corruption agencies: A comparison between Bangladesh and Nepal", *International Journal of Public Administration*, 39(9): 676–685.

Ko, Ernie, Yu-chang Su and Chilik Yu (2015) "Sibling rivalry among anti-corruption agencies in Taiwan: is redundancy doomed to failure?", *Asian Education and Development Studies*, 4(1): 101–124.

Lai, Alan N. (2001) "Keeping Hong Kong clean: Experiences of fighting corruption post-1997", *Harvard Asia Pacific Review*, 5(2): 51–54.

Li, Shaomin (2004) "Can China learn from Hong Kong's experience in fighting corruption?", *Global Economic Review*, 33(1): 1–9.

Makowski, Grzegor (2016) "Anti-corruption agencies – silver bullet against corruption or fifth wheel to a coach? Analysis from the perspective of the constructivist theory of social problems", *Studia z polityki publicznej*, 2(10): 55–77.

Manion, Melanie (2004) *Corruption by design: Building clean government in Mainland China and Hong Kong*. Cambridge, MA: Harvard University Press.

Manion, Melanie (2016) "Taking China's anticorruption campaign seriously", *Economic and Political Studies*, 4(1): 3–18.

Meagher, Patrick (2005) "Anti-corruption agencies: Rhetoric versus reality", *Journal of Economic Policy Reform*, 8(1): 69–103.

Michael, Bryane (2014) "Can the Hong Kong ICAC help reduce corruption on the Mainland?", *The Chinese Journal of Comparative Law*, 2(1): 78–119.

Quah, Jon S.T. (2013) *Curbing corruption in Asian countries: An impossible dream?* Singapore: ISEAS Publishing.

Quah, Jon S.T. (2015) *Hunting the corrupt 'tigers' and 'flies' in China: An evaluation of Xi Jinping's anti-corruption campaign (November 2012 to March 2015)*. Baltimore, MD: Carey School of Law, University of Maryland.

Quah, Jon S.T. (2017) "Learning from Singapore's effective anti-corruption strategy: Policy recommendations for South Korea", *Asian Education and Development Studies*, 6(1): 17–29.

Scambary, James (2017) "The road to nowhere: The rise of the neo-patrimonialist state" in *East Asia Pacific: Current perspectives and future challenges*. Amsterdam: Elsevier: 267–280.

Schütte, Sofie Arjon (2012) "Against the odds: Anti-corruption reform in Indonesia", *Public Administration and Development*, 32(1): 38–48.

Schütte, Sofie Arjon (2017) "Two steps forward, one step backwards: Indonesia's winding (anti-) corruption journey" in Ting Gong and Ian Scott (eds.) *Routledge handbook of corruption in Asia*. London: Routledge: 42–55.

Scott, Ian and Ting Gong (2015) "Evidence-based policy-making for corruption prevention in Hong Kong: A bottom-up approach", *Asia Pacific Journal of Public Administration*, 37(2): 87–101.

Tangri, Roger and Andrew M. Mwenda (2006) "Politics, donors and the ineffectiveness of anti-corruption institutions in Uganda", *Journal of Modern African Studies*, 44(1): 101–124.

Theobald, Robin and Robert Williams (1999) "Combating corruption in Botswana: Regional role model or deviant case", *Journal of Commonwealth and Comparative Politics*, 37(3): 117–134.

Transparency International (2018) *Corruption perceptions index 2017*, www.transparency.org/news/feature/corruption_perceptions_index_2017.

Transparency International and CHR Michelsen Institute (2016) "Cambodia: Overview of corruption and anti-corruption", www.transparency.org/files/content/corruptionqas/Country-profile-Cambodia-2016.pdf.

Wedeman, Andrew (2017) "Corruption and collective protest in China" in Ting Gong and Ian Scott (eds.) *Routledge handbook of corruption in Asia*. London: Routledge: 179–195.

Widoyoko, Johannes Danang (2017) "Indonesia's anti-corruption campaigns: Civil society versus the political cartel" in Marie dela Rama and Chris Rowley (eds.) *The changing face of corruption in the Asia Pacific: Current perspectives and future challenges*. Amsterdam: Elsevier: 253–266.

Williams, Colin C., Rositsa Dzhekova, Marijana Baric, Josip Franic and Lyubo Mishkov (2014) "Assessing the cross-national transferability of policy measures for tackling undeclared work", http://dx.doi.org/10.2139/ssrn.2501688.

Selected bibliography

Official sources

Advisory Committee on Corruption (1960) *First report*. Hong Kong: mimeo.
Advisory Committee on Corruption (1961) *Sixth report*. Hong Kong: mimeo.
Attorney-General v Hui Kin-hong (1995) HKCLR 227.
Attorney-General v Chung Fat-ming CACC000533/1978.
Basic Law of the Hong Kong Special Administrative Region of the People's Republic of China (1990), www.basiclaw.gov.hk/en/basiclawtext/images/basiclaw_full_text_en.pdf.
Blair-Kerr, Sir Alastair (1973a) *First report of the Commission of Inquiry under Sir Alastair Blair-Kerr*. Hong Kong: Government Printer.
Blair-Kerr, Sir Alastair (1973b) *Second report of the Commission of Inquiry under Sir Alastair Blair-Kerr*. Hong Kong: Government Printer.
British Parliamentary Papers (1971) *China 25 Hong Kong 1862–1881*. Shannon: Irish University Press.
Civil Service Bureau (2005) *Civil servants' guide to good practices*. 2nd edition. Hong Kong: mimeo.
Civil Service Bureau (2009) *Civil service code*, www.csb.gov.hk/english/admin/conduct/1751.html.
Competition Commission (2016) *Fighting bid-rigging*, www.compcomm.hk/en/media/press/files/Press_release_Fighting_bid_rigging_kick_off_ceremony_e.pdf.
Constitutional and Mainland Affairs Bureau (2016) *Consultation report on the enhancement of the voter registration system*, www.cmab.gov.hk/doc/issues/electoral_matters/VR_con_report_en.pdf.
Customs and Excise Department (2015) *Code on conduct and discipline*, 7th edition, www.customs.gov.hk/filemanager/common/pdf/pdf_publications/code_conduct_discipline_e.pdf.
Director of Audit (2013) "Report No. 60 – Chapter 7", www.legco.gov.hk/yr12-13/english/pac/reports/60a/app_11.pdf.
Efficiency Unit (1996) *The service imperative*. Hong Kong: Government Printer.
Elections (Corrupt and Illegal Conduct) Ordinance (ECICO) (Cap 554).
Electoral Affairs Commission Ordinance (EACO) (Cap 541).
HKSAR v Chan Chung-ching and Others (2004) DCCC 337/2004.
HKSAR v Cheung Chi-ying, Teresa (2008) DCCC 203/2008.
HKSAR v Chung Sim-ying, Tracy (2001) HCMA 267A/2001.
HKSAR v Ho Mi-mi and Cheng Sai-man (2002) ESCC410/2002.

HKSAR v Lew Mon-hung (2013) DCCC819/2013.
HKSAR v Rafael Hui Si-yan and Others (2014) HCCC 98/2013.
HKSAR v So Yau-hang and Two Others (2009) KTCC 5923/2009.
HKSAR v Tsang Yip-fat (2002) HCMA1125/2002.
HKSAR v Wong Hon-ching, San Stephen (2003) DCCC 503/2003.
HKSAR v Wong Kong-shun, Paul (2007) CACC 390/2007.
HKSAR v Wong Lin Kay (2012) 2 HKLRD 898.
Hong Kong Bill of Rights Ordinance (Cap 383).
Hong Kong Government (1902) "Report of the Commission to enquire into the Public Works Department", http://sunzi.lib.hku.hk/hkgro/view/s1907/1993.pdf.
Hong Kong Government (1907a) "Report of the Public Health and Buildings Ordinance Commission", http://sunzi.lib.hku.hk/hkgro/view/s1907/1993.pdf.
Hong Kong Government (1907b) "Minute of the Principal Civil Medical Officer on the report of the Public Health and Buildings Ordinance Commission", http://sunzi.lib.hku.hk/hkgro/view/s1907/1993.pdf.
Hong Kong Government (1907c) "Minute by the Colonial Secretary on the report of the Commission to enquire into the working of the Public Health and Building Ordinance in the Sanitary Department", http://sunzi.lib.hku.hk/hkgro/view/s1907/1993.pdf.
Hong Kong Government (1908) "Report on the blue book for 1907", http://sunzi.lib.hku.hk/hkgro/view/s1907/1993.pdf.
Hong Kong Government (1924) "Report of the Superintendent of Imports and Exports for the year 1923", http://sunzi.lib.hku.hk/hkgro/view/s1907/1993.pdf.
Hong Kong Government (1940) "Report of the Commissioner of Police, 1939", http://sunzi.lib.hku.hk/hkgro/view/s1907/1993.pdf.
Hong Kong Government (1941) *The Hong Kong Government Gazette*, 31 October, http://sunzi.lib.hku.hk/hkgro/view/s1907/1993.pdf.
Hong Kong Government (1963) *Hong Kong 1962*. Hong Kong: Government Press.
Hong Kong Government (1967) *Kowloon disturbances 1966: Report of the Commission of Enquiry*. Hong Kong: Government Printer.
Hong Kong Government (2016) "Code of practice (issued pursuant to Section 63 of the Interception of Communications and Surveillance Ordinance)", www.sb.gov.hk/eng/special/sciocs/2016/ICSO%20CoP%20-%20June%202016%20(E).pdf.
Hong Kong Government (2017) "Annual report to the Chief Executive by the Commissioner on Interceptions of Communications and Surveillance, 2016", www.info.gov.hk/info/sciocs/en/pdf/Annual_Report_2016.pdf.
Hong Kong Hansard 16 May 1907; 21 June 1919; 19 March 1936; 16 November 1938; 11 July 1948; 21 October 1970; 17 October 1973; 13 February 1974; 11 February 1976; 4 October 1984; 7 October 1992; 26 November 1994; 11 October 1995; 10 July 1996; 8 October 1997; 7 October 1998; 11 July 2007; 25 June 2008; 29 February 2012; 17 October 2012; 16 January 2013; 29 October 2014; 5 November 2014; 6 November 2014; 11 November 2015; 9 November 2016; 10 November 2016; 18 January 2017; 11 October 2017.
ICAC (1975–2018) "Annual reports", www.icac.org.hk/en/about/report/annual/index.html
ICAC (1979–1990) *Mass surveys*. Hong Kong: ICAC Community Research Unit.
ICAC (1992–2018) *Annual surveys*. Hong Kong: mimeo.

ICAC (2008) "Defining and developing an effective code of conduct for organizations", www.hkbedc.icac.hk/english/publications/practical_guides.php.

ICAC (2014) *40 years in the Operations Department.* Hong Kong: ICAC.

ICAC (2014) "Sample code of conduct for employees of public bodies", www.icac.org.hk/en/resource/publications-and-videos/ps/index.html.

ICAC (2015) "Integrity and corruption prevention guide on managing relationships with public servants", www.icac.org.hk/filemanager/en/Content_216/ps.pdf.

ICAC (2017) "Sample code of conduct", www.hkbedc.icac.hk/english/files/publications/Sample_English.pdf.

ICAC (2018) "Hong Kong business ethics development centre", www.hkbedc.icac.hk.

ICAC (n.d.) "Integrity and corruption prevention guide on managing relationships with public servants", www.icac.org.hk/filemanager/en/Content_216/ps.pdf.

ICAC (n.d.) "Reference package on conflict of interest for managers in the civil service", www.icac.org.hk/en/resource/publications-and-videos/ps/index.html.

ICAC and Civil Service Bureau (n.d.) *Ethical leadership in action: Handbook for senior managers in the civil service.* Hong Kong: ICAC and Civil Service Bureau.

ICAC, GPPP and Commission Against Corruption, Macao (2012) "Business success: Integrity and legal compliance: Corruption prevention guide for SME's in Guangdong, Hong Kong and Macao", www.hkbedc.icac.hk/english/files/publications/1._Eng.pdf.

ICAC, Hong Kong Monetary Authority, the DTC Association and the Hong Kong Institute of Bankers (n.d.) "Bank on integrity: A practical guide for bank managers", http://cpas.icac.hk/UPloadImages/InfoFile/cate_43/2016/194ad8e4-d904-4a24-b992-aa0f6812a2e9.pdf.

ICAC Operations Review Committee (2017) "Annual report 2016", www.icac.org.hk/filemanager/en/content_27/2016.pdf.

ICAC Review Committee (1994) *Report of the ICAC review committee.* Hong Kong: Government Printer.

Independent Commission Against Corruption Ordinance (Cap 204).

Independent Review Committee (2012) "Report of the Independent Review Committee for the prevention and handling of conflicts of interest", www.legco.gov.hk/yr11-12/english/panels/ca/papers/ca0604-rpt20120531-e.pdf.

Independent Review Committee (2013) "Report of the Independent Review Committee on ICAC's regulatory systems and procedures for handling official entertainment, gifts and duty visits", www.gov.hk/en/theme/irc-icac/pdf/irc-icac-report.pdf.

Interception of Communications and Surveillance Ordinance (Cap 589).

Legislative Council (1997) "Report of the select committee into the circumstances surrounding the departure of Mr. Leung Ming-yin from the government and related issues", http://ebook.lib.hku.hk/HKG/B36226270V1.pdf.

Legislative Council (2008) "Report of the Bills Committee on the Prevention of Bribery (Amendment Bill) 2007", LC Paper No. CB (2)2365/07–08, 19 June.

Legislative Council (2014) "Report on matters relating to Mr. Timothy Tong's duty visits, entertainment, and bestowing and receipt of gifts during his tenure as Commissioner of the Independent Commission Against Corruption, Hong Kong", www.legco.gov.hk/yr13-14/english/counmtg/papers/cm0709-ttong-members-rpt-e.pdf.

Legislative Council (2018) "Database on particular policy issues: Electoral matters", www.legco.gov.hk/database/english/data_ca/ca-electoral-and-registration-system.htm.

Legislative Council, Panel on Administration of Justice and Legal Services (2011) "Response to the background brief provided by the Legco Secretariat entitled 'An independent Director of Public Prosecutions'", LC Paper No. CB (20 2154/10–11(01), www.legco.gov.hk/yr10-11/english/panels/ajls/papers/aj0627cb2-2154-1-e.pdf.

Legislative Council, Panel on Public Service (2008) "Integrity enhancement initiatives for public servants", LC Paper No. CB (1)764/07–08(05), 18 February, www.legco.gov.hk/yr07-08/english/panels/ps/papers/ps0218cb1-764-5-e.pdf.

Legislative Council, Panel on Security (1994) *Enquiry into the circumstances surrounding the termination of the employment of Mr. Alex Tsui Ka-kit, former Senior Assistant Director of the Independent Commission Against Corruption.* Hong Kong: mimeo.

Legislative Council, Panel on Security (2013) "Background brief prepared by the Legislative Council Secretariat", LC Paper No. CB (2)696/12–13, 25 February, www.legco.gov.hk/yr12-13/english/panels/se/papers/se0301cb2-696-4-e.pdf.

Legislative Council, Panel on Security (2014) "Anti-corruption work against cross-boundary corruption", LC Paper No. CB (2)1453/13–14(04), www.legco.gov.hk/yr13-14/english/panels/se/papers/se0513cb2-1453-4-e.pdf.

Legislative Council, Panel on Security (2016) "Briefing by the Commissioner, Independent Commission Against Corruption", LC Paper No. CB (2) 654/14–15(06), 2 February.

Legislative Council, Panel on Security (2017) "Report of the Panel on Security", www.legco.gov.hk/yr16-17/english/panel/se/reports/se20170705cb2-1752-e.pdf.

Legislative Council, Public Accounts Committee (2013) "Report 60A-part 4: Preventive education and enlisting public support against corruption", www.legco.gov.hk/yr14-15/english/pac/reports/63/m_4.pdf.

Legislative Council Secretariat (2017) "Information note: The UGL incident", 23 February, www.legco.gov.hk/research-publications/english/1617in03-the-ugl-incident-20170223-e.pdf.

Legislative Council, Select Committee (2010) "Report of the select committee to inquire into matters relating to the post-service work of Mr. Leung Chin-man", www.legco.gov.hk/yr08-09/english/sc/sc_lcm/report/lcm_rpt-e.pdf.

Legislative Council, Select Committee (2016) "Select committee to inquire into matters about the agreement between Mr. Leung Chun-ying and the Australian firm UGL Limited", www.legco.gov.hk/yr16-17/english/sc/sc_lcyugl/general/sc_lcyugl.htm.

Prevention of Bribery Ordinance (POBO) (Cap 201).

Shum Kwok-sher v HKSAR (2002) 5 HKCFAR 381.

Sin Kam-wah and Another v HKSAR (2005) 8HKCFAR 192.

Yeung, Chun Kuen and Lee Jark Pui (2007) "Report of the Commission of Inquiry on allegations relating to the Hong Kong Institute of Education", www.commissionofinquiry.gov.hk/pdf/Commission%20Report_e.pdf.

Academic publications

Aidt, Toke S. (2009) "Corruption, institutions and economic development", *Oxford Review of Economic Policy*, 25(2): 271–291.

Andrews, Matt (2008) "The good governance agenda: Beyond indicators without theory", *Oxford Development Studies*, 36(4): 379–407.

Ankamah, Samuel Siebie and S.M. Manzoor E. Khoda (2018) "Political will and government anti-corruption efforts: What does the evidence say?" *Public Administration and Development*, 38(1): 3–14.

Baniamin, Hassan Muhammad and Ishtiaq Jamil (2018) "Dynamics of corruption and citizens' trust in anti-corruption agencies in three South Asian countries", *Public Organization Review*, 18(3): 381–398.

Beetham, David (1991) *The legitimation of power*. Basingstoke: Macmillan.

Brewer, Brian, Joan Y.H. Leung and Ian Scott (2015) "Value-based integrity management and bureaucratic organizations: Changing the mix", *International Public Management Journal*, 18(3): 390–410.

Brinkerhoff, Derick W. (2000) "Assessing political will for anti-corruption efforts: An analytical framework", *Public Administration and Development*, 18(2): 239–252.

Burns, John P. (2004) *Government capacity and the Hong Kong civil service*. Hong Kong: Oxford University Press.

Carpenter, Daniel (2001) *The forging of bureaucratic autonomy*. Princeton: Princeton University Press.

Chan, Kin-man (1997) "Combating corruption and the ICAC" in Joseph Y.S. Cheng (ed.) *The other Hong Kong report, 1997*. Hong Kong: The Chinese University Press: 101–121.

Chan, Thomas (2001) "Corruption prevention-the Hong Kong experience" in *UNAFEI, Resource material series No.56*, www.unafei.or.jp/publications/Resource_Material_56.htm, 365–377.

Chang, Eric C. (2013) "A comparative analysis of how corruption erodes institutional trust", *Taiwan Journal of Democracy*, 9(1): 73–92.

Cheung, Anthony B.L. (1996) "Public sector reform and the re-legitimation of public bureaucratic power", *International Journal of Public Sector Management*, 9(5/6): 37–50.

Cheung, Anthony B.L. (2008) "Combating corruption as a political strategy to rebuild trust and legitimacy" in Bidya Bowornwathana and Clay Westcott (eds.) *Corruption governance reform in Asia: Democracy, corruption and government trust*. Bingley: Emerald: 55–84.

Cheung, Arthur K.C. (1997) "Bill of Rights – hotbed of challenge" in Joseph Y.S. Cheng (ed.) *The other Hong Kong report, 1997*. Hong Kong: The Chinese University Press: 123–135.

Cheung, Tak-sing and Chong-chor Lau (1981) "A profile of syndicate corruption in the police force" in Rance P.L. Lee (ed.) *Corruption and its control in Hong Kong*. Hong Kong: The Chinese University Press: 199–221.

Choi, Jin-wook (2009) "Institutional structures and the effectiveness of anti-corruption agencies: A comparative analysis of South Korea and Hong Kong", *Asian Journal of Political Science*, 17(2): 195–214.

Choi, Jin-wook (2017) "Corruption prevention: Successful cases" in Ting Gong and Ian Scott (eds.) *Routledge handbook of corruption in Asia*. London: Routledge: 262–276.

Dahlan, Rosli and Muhammed Faizal Faiz Mohd Hasani (2018) "Malaysia", *The Anti-Bribery and Anti-Corruption Review*, 6th edition, https://thelawreviews.co.uk/edition/the-anti-bribery-and-anti-corruption-review-edition-6/1151858/malaysia.

David, Roman (2010) "Transitions to clean government: Amnesty as an anticorruption measure", *Australian Journal of Political Science*, 43(3): 391–406.

de Sousa, Luis (2010) "Anti-corruption agencies: Between empowerment and irrelevance", *Crime, Law and Social Change*, 53(1): 5–22.

de Speville, Bertrand (2010) "Anticorruption models: The 'Hong Kong model' revisited", *Asia Pacific Review*, 17(1): 47–71.

Doig, Alan and David Norris (2012) "Improving anti-corruption agencies as organizations", *Journal of Financial Crime*, 19(3): 255–273.

Doig, Alan, David Watt and Robert Williams (2006) "Hands-on or hands-off? Anti-corruption agencies in action, donor expectations, and a good enough reality", *Public Administration and Development*, 26(2): 163–172.

Donald, David C. (2013) "Countering corrupting conflicts of interest: The example of Hong Kong" in Jeremy Horder and Peter Allridge (eds.) *Modern bribery law*. Cambridge: Cambridge University Press: 66–94.

Dzhumashev, Ratbek (2014) "Corruption and growth: The role of governance, public spending and economic development", *Economic Modelling*, 37: 202–2015.

Elliot, Elsie (1971) *The avarice, bureaucracy and corruption of Hong Kong*. Hong Kong: Friends Commercial Printing Factory.

Fijnaut, Cyrille and Leo Huberts (2002) "Corruption, integrity and law enforcement" in Cyrille Fijnaut and Leo Huberts (eds.) *Corruption, integrity and law enforcement*. Den Haag: Kluwer Law International: 3–34.

Fritzen, Scott A. and Sherya Basu (2011) "The strategic use of public information in anti-corruption agencies: Evidence from the Asia-Pacific region", *International Journal of Public Administration*, 31(14): 893–904.

Galtung, Frederik (2006) "Measuring the immeasurable: Boundaries and functions of (macro) corruption indices" in Charles Sampford, Arthur Shacklock, Carmel Connors and Frederik Galtung (eds.) *Measuring corruption*. Aldershot: Ashgate: 101–130.

Ganahl, Joseph Patrick (2012) *Corruption, good governance and the African state: A critical analysis of the political-economic foundations of corruption in sub-Saharan Africa*. Potsdam: Potsdam University Press.

Gittings, Danny (2013) *Introduction to the Basic Law*. Hong Kong: Hong Kong University Press.

Gomomo, Nceba (2001) "Community participation: A 'sine qua non' for an effective anti-corruption strategy" in Joseph Rotblat (ed.) *Confronting the challenges of the 21st century*. Singapore: World Scientific: 456–468.

Gong, Ting (2002) "Dangerous collusion: Corruption as a collective venture in China", *Communist and Post-Communist Studies*, 35(1): 85–103.

Gong, Ting and Hanyu Xiao (2017a) "The formation and impact of isomorphic pressures: Extravagant position-related consumption in China", *Governance*, 30(3): 387–405.

Gong, Ting and Hanyu Xiao (2017b) "Socially embedded anti-corruption governance: Evidence from Hong Kong", *Public Administration and Development*, 17(3): 176–190.

Gong, Ting and Ian Scott (2015) "Conflicts of interest and ethical decision-making: Mainland China and Hong Kong comparisons" in Alan Lawton, Leo Huberts and Zeger van der Wal (eds.) *Ethics in public policy and management: A global research companion*. London: Routledge: 257–276.

Gong, Ting and Ian Scott (2017) "Introduction" in Ting Gong and Ian Scott (eds.) *Routledge handbook of corruption in Asia*. London: Routledge: 1–10.

Gong, Ting and Shiru Wang (2013) "Indicators and implications of zero tolerance of corruption", *Social Indicators*, 112(3): 569–586.

Gong, Ting, Shiru Wang and Jianming Ren (2015) "Corruption in the eye of the beholder: Survey evidence from Mainland China and Hong Kong", *International Public Management Journal*, 18(1): 458–482.

Goodstadt, Leo F. (2005) *Uneasy partners: The conflict between public interest and private profit in Hong Kong*. Hong Kong: Hong Kong University Press.

Gregory, Robert (2014) "Assessing 'good governance': 'Scientific' measurement and political discourse", *Policy Quarterly*, 10(1): 15–25.

Grindle, Merilee (2012) "Good governance: The inflation of an idea" in Bishwapira Sanyai, Lawrence J. Vale and Christina D. Rosen (eds.) *Planning ideas that matter*. Cambridge, MA: Massachusetts Institute of Technology Press: 259–282.

Heilbrunn, John R. (2004) *Anti-corruption commissions: Panacea or real medicine to fight corruption?* Washington: World Bank.

Heywood, Paul (1997) "Political corruption: Problems and perspectives", *Political Studies*, 45(3): 417–435.

Heywood, Paul and Jonathan Rose (2014) "Close but no cigar: The measurement of corruption", *Journal of Public Policy*, 34(3): 507–529.

Holmes, Leslie (2015) "Combating corruption in China: The role of the state and other agencies in comparative perspective", *Economic and Political Studies*, 3(1): 42–70.

Hong Kong Institute of Asia-Pacific Affairs (2016) "Survey findings on views of new immigrants from China", 11 November, www.cpr.cuhk.edu.hk/resources/press/pdf/582568e8b35c5.pdf.

Huang, Chiung-Ju (2016) "Is corruption bad for economic growth? Evidence from Asia-Pacific countries", *North American Journal of Economics and Finance*, 35: 247–256.

Hui, Cora Y.T. and T. Wing Lo (2016) "Anti-corruption" in Wing Chong Chui and T. Wing Lo (eds.) *Understanding criminal justice in Hong Kong*. 2nd edition. London: Routledge: 175–193.

Jamil, Ishtiaq, Steinar Asvik and Hasan Muhammed Baniamin (2016) "Citizens' trust in anti-corruption agencies: A comparison between Bangladesh and Nepal", *International Journal of Public Administration*, 39(9): 676–685.

Johnson, Thomas, Ting Gong and Wen Wang (2017) "Regulatory capture, as a two-way street: Hong Kong small and medium enterprises in the Pearl River Delta" in Ting Gong and Ian Scott (eds.) *Routledge Handbook of Corruption in Asia*. London: Routledge: 144–161.

Johnston, Michael (1999) "A brief history of anticorruption agencies" in Andreas Schedler, Larry Diamond and Marc F. Plattner (eds.) *The self-restraining state: Power and accountability in new democracies*. Boulder, CO: Lynne Reiner: 217–226.

Johnston, Michael (2017) "Thinking about corruption as though people mattered" in Ting Gong and Ian Scott (eds.) *Routledge handbook of corruption in Asia*. London: Routledge: 165–178.

Joutsen, Matti (2011) "The United Nations Convention Against Corruption" in Adam Graycar and Russell G. Smith (eds.) *Handbook of global research and practice in corruption*. Cheltenham: Edward Elgar: 303–318.

Kaufman, Daniel (2005) "Myths and realities of governance and corruption", http://siteresources.worldbank.org/INTWBIGOVANTCOR/Resources/2-1_Governance_and_Corruption_Kaufmann.pdf.

Kaufmann, Daniel, Aart Kraay and Massimo Mastruzzi (2004) "Governance matters III: Governance indicators 1996,1998, 2000 and 2004", *The World Bank Economic Review*,18(2): 253–287.

Khan, Mustaq (2006) "Governance and anti-corruption reform in developing countries: Policies, evidence and ways forward", *G-24 Discussion Paper Series*, http:// unctad.org/en/docs/gdsmdpbg2420064_en.pdf.

Klitgaard, Robert, Ronald MacLean-Aboroa and H. Lindsey Parris (2000) *Corrupt cities: A practical guide to cure and prevention*. Washington, DC: The World Bank.

Ko, Ernie, Yu-chang Su and Chilik Yu (2015) "Sibling rivalry among anti-corruption agencies in Taiwan: Is redundancy doomed to failure?" *Asian Education and Development Studies*, 4(1): 101–124.

Kpundeh, Sahr J. (1998) "Political will in fighting corruption" in Sahr J. Kpundeh and Irene Hors (1998) *Corruption and integrity development initiatives*. New York: UNDP: 91–110.

Kuan, Hsin-chi (1981) "Anti-corruption legislation in Hong Kong – a history" in Rance P.L. Lee (ed.) *Corruption and its control in Hong Kong*. Hong Kong: The Chinese University Press.

Kurer, Oskar (2015) "Definitions of corruption" in Paul M. Heywood (ed.) *Routledge handbook of political corruption*. London: Routledge, 30–41.

Kwok, Man-wai Tony (2005) "Measures to combat economic crime, including money-laundering", Eleventh United Nations Congress on Crime Prevention and Criminal Justice, Bangkok, 18–25 April 2005, www.unafei.or.jp/publications/ pdf/11th_Congress/27Talking_Points_4.pdf.

Lai, Alan N. (2001) "Keeping Hong Kong clean: Experiences of fighting corruption post- 1997", *Harvard Asia Pacific Review*, 5(2): 51–54.

Lam, Wai-man and Kay Lam Chi-yan (2013) "China's united front work in civil society: the case of Hong Kong", *International Journal of Chinese Studies*, 4(3): 301–325.

Lateef, K. Sarwar (2016) "Evolution of the World Bank's thinking on governance", Background paper for the 2017 World Development Report, http:// pubdocs.worldbank.org/en/433301485539630301/WDR17-BP-Evolution-of-WB-Thinking-on-Governance.pdf.

Lee, Ambrose (2006) "The public as our partner in the fight against corruption" in Charles Sampford, Arthur Shacklock, Carmel Connors and Frederik Galtung (eds.) *Measuring corruption*. Aldershot: Ashgate: 221–232.

Lee, Francis L.F. (2015) "How citizens react to political scandals surrounding government leaders: A survey study in Hong Kong", *Asian Journal of Political Science*, 23(1): 44–62.

Lee, Rance P.L. (1981a) "The folklore of corruption in Hong Kong", *Asian Survey*, 21(3): 355–368.

Lee, Rance P.L (ed.) (1981b) *Corruption and its control in Hong Kong*. Hong Kong: The Chinese University Press.

Lethbridge, Henry James (1978) "The emergence of bureaucratic corruption as a social problem in Hong Kong" in H.J. Lethbridge, *Hong Kong: Prosperity and stability: A collection of essays*. Hong Kong: Oxford University Press: 214–237.

Lethbridge, Henry James (1985) *Hard graft in Hong Kong: Scandal, corruption and the ICAC*. Hong Kong: Oxford University Press.

Li, Li and T. Wing Lo (2018) "Mainlandization, the ICAC and the seriousness attached by local politicians to corruption in post-1997 Hong Kong", *Journal of Offender Therapy and Comparative Criminology*, 62(6): 1742–1760.

Lo, Sonny S.H. (2017) "Comparative grand corruption and protection pacts among elites: The cases of Ao Man Long in Macao and Hui Si-yan in Hong Kong", *Asian Journal of Political Science*, 25(2): 234–251.

Lo, T. Wing (1991) "Law and order" in Sung Yung-wing and Lee Ming-kwan (eds.) *The other Hong Kong report 1991*. Hong Kong: The Chinese University Press.

Lo, T. Wing (1993) *Corruption and politics in Hong Kong and China*. Milton Keynes: Open University Press.

Lo, T. Wing (2003) "Minimizing crime and corruption in Hong Kong" in Roy Godson (ed.) *Menace to society: Political-criminal collaboration around the world*. New Brunswick: Transaction: 231–256.

Lo, T. Wing and Ricky C.C. Yu (2000) "Curbing draconian powers: The effects on Hong Kong's graft-fighter", *The International Journal of Human Rights*, 4(1): 54–73.

Lusty, David (2014) "Revival of the common law offence of misconduct in public office", *Criminal Law Journal*, 38: 337–363.

Ma, Ngok (2015) "The rise of 'Anti-China' sentiment in Hong Kong and the 2012 Legislative Council elections", *China Review*, 15(1): 39–66.

Makowski, Grzegor (2016) "Anti-corruption agencies – silver bullet against corruption or fifth wheel to a coach? Analysis from the perspective of the constructivist theory of social problems", *Studia z polityki publicznej*, 2(10): 55–77.

Manion, Melanie (2004) *Corruption by design: Building clean government in Mainland China and Hong Kong*. Cambridge, MA: Harvard University Press.

Manion, Melanie (2016) "Taking China's anticorruption campaign seriously", *Economic and Political Studies*, 4(1): 3–18.

Marquette, Heather (2003) *Corruption, politics and development: The role of the World Bank*. New York: Palgrave Macmillan.

Marquette, Heather (2007) "The World Bank's fight against corruption", *The Brown Journal of World Affairs*, XIII(2): 27–39.

McDonald, Gael M. (1994) "Value modification strategies on a national scale" in W.Michael. Hoffman, Judith. Brown Kamm, Robert E. Frederick and Edward S. Petry (eds.) *Emerging global business ethics*. London: Quorum: 14–35.

McWalters, Ian, David Fitzpatrick and Andrew Bruce (2015) *Bribery and corruption law in Hong Kong*. 3rd edition. Singapore: LexisNexis.

Meagher, Patrick (2005) "Anti-corruption agencies: Rhetoric versus reality", *Journal of Economic Policy Reform*, 8(1): 69–103.

Miners, Norman (1987) *Hong Kong under imperial rule*. Hong Kong: Oxford University Press.

Mishler, William and Richard Rose (1997) "Trust, distrust and skepticism: Popular evaluations of civil and political institutions in post-communist societies", *The Journal of Politics*, 59(2): 418–451.

Mok, W.H. (n.d.) "Corruption prevention in public organizations – the Hong Kong experience", http://unpan1.un.org/intradoc/groups/public/documents/undpadm/unpan049657.pdf.

Moran, Jonathan (1999) "The changing context of corruption control: The Hong Kong Special Administrative Region, 1977–1999", *Journal of Commonwealth and Comparative Politics*, 37(3): 98–116.

Morris, Stephen D. and Joseph L. Klesner (2010) "Corruption and trust: Theoretical considerations and evidence from Mexico", *Comparative Political Studies*, 43(10): 1258–1285.

Munn, Christopher (1997) "'Giving justice a second chance': The criminal trial in early British Hong Kong, 1841–1866", *China Information*, 12(1/2): 36–65.

Munn, Christopher (2001) *Anglo-China: Chinese people and British rule in Hong Kong, 1841–1880*. Richmond: Curzon Press.

Neoh, Anthony (2010) "An impartial and uncorrupted civil service: Hong Kong's fight against corruption in the past 34 years" in Christopher Forsythe, Mark Elliott, Swati Javeri, Michael Ramsden and Anne Scully Hill (eds.) *Effective judicial review: A cornerstone of good governance*. New York: Oxford University Press: 216–242.

Nguyen, Thang V., Thang N. Bach, Thanh Q. Le and Canh Q. Le (2017) "Local governance, corruption and public service quality: Evidence from a national survey in Vietnam", *International Journal of Public Sector Management*, 30(2): 137–153.

Norton-Kysshe, James (1971) *The history of the laws and courts of Hong Kong from the earliest period until 1898*. Vols. 1 and 2. Hong Kong: Vetch and Lee.

Paine, Lynn S. (1994) "Managing for organizational integrity", *Harvard Business Review*, (March-April): 106–115.

Palmier, Leslie (1985) *The control of bureaucratic corruption in Asia*. New Delhi: Allied Publishers.

Park, Chong-Min (2017) "Political trust in the Asia-Pacific region" in Sonja Zmerli and Tom van der Meer (eds.) *Handbook of political trust*. Cheltenham: Edward Elgar.

Peh, Simon Yun-lu (2015) "Culture building and systemic prevention – a twin pillar anti-corruption strategy of Hong Kong", paper delivered to the 8th Annual Conference and General Meeting of IAACA, 31 October, www.icac.org.hk/filemanager/en/content_77/c-iaaca-2015.pdf.

Persson, Anna and Martin Sjöstedt (2012) "Responsive and responsible leaders: A matter of political will", *Perspectives on Politics*, 10(3): 617–632.

Peters, B. Guy (2010) "Institutional design and good governance" in Gjalt de Graaf, Patrick von Maravić and Pieter Wagner (eds.) *The good cause: Theoretical perspectives on corruption*. Opladen and Farmington Hills, MI: Barbara Budrich Publishers: 83–97.

Philp, Mark (2015) "The definition of political corruption" in Paul M. Heywood (ed.) *Routledge handbook of political corruption*. London: Routledge: 17–29.

Pope, Jeremy and Frank Vogl (2000) "Making anticorruption agencies more effective", *Finance and Development*, 37(2): 6–9.

Quah, Jon S.T. (2013) *Curbing corruption in Asian countries: An impossible dream?* Singapore: ISEAS Publishing.

Quah, Jon S.T. (2015a) "The critical importance of political will in combating corruption in Asian countries", *Public Administration and Policy*, 18(2): 12–23.

Quah, Jon S.T. (2015b) *Hunting the corrupt 'tigers' and 'flies' in China: An evaluation of Xi Jinping's anti-corruption campaign (November 2012 to March 2015)*. Baltimore, MD: Carey School of Law, University of Maryland.

Quah, Jon S.T. (2017a) "Controlling corruption in Asian countries: The elusive search for success" in Ting Gong and Ian Scott (eds.) *Routledge handbook of corruption in Asia*. London: Routledge: 241–261.

Quah, Jon S.T. (2017b) "Minimizing corruption in Hong Kong and Singapore: Lessons for Asian policy makers", *Public Administration and Policy*, 20(2): 7–22.

Quah, Jon S.T. (2017c) *Combating Asian corruption: Enhancing the effectiveness of anti-corruption agencies*. Baltimore MD: Carey School of Law, University of Maryland.

Quah, Jon S.T. (2018) "Combating corruption in Asian countries: Learning from success and failure", *Dædalus*, 147(3): 201–215.

Roberts, Robert (2009) "The rise of compliance-based ethics: Implications for organizational ethics", *Public Integrity*, 11(3): 261–278.

Rose-Ackerman, Susan (2017) "Corruption in Asia: Trust and economic development" in Ting Gong and Ian Scott (eds.) *Routledge handbook of corruption in Asia*. London: Routledge: 85–96.

Rose-Ackerman, Susan and Bonnie J. Palifka (2016) *Corruption and government: Causes, consequences and reform*. 2nd edition. Cambridge: Cambridge University Press.

Rose, Jonathan (2015) "Corruption and the problem of perception" in Paul Heywood (ed.) *Routledge handbook of political corruption*. London: Routledge: 172–182.

Rose, Richard and Caryn Peiffer (2018) *Bad governance and corruption*. Basingstoke: Palgrave Macmillan.

Rotberg, Robert I. (2017) *The corruption cure: How leaders and citizens can combat graft*. Princeton: Princeton University Press.

Rothstein, Bo (2011) *The quality of government: Corruption, social trust and inequality in international perspective*. Chicago: University of Chicago Press.

Rothstein, Bo and Daniel Eek (2009) "Political corruption and social trust: An experimental approach", *Rationality and Society*, 21(1): 81–112.

Salminen, Ari and Rinna Ikola-Norrbacka (2010) "Trust, good governance and unethical actions in Finnish public administration", *International Journal of Public Sector Management*, 23(7): 647–668.

Scott, Ian (1989) *Political change and the crisis of legitimacy in Hong Kong*. London: Hurst.

Scott, Ian (2013a) "Institutional design and corruption prevention in Hong Kong", *Journal of Contemporary China*, 22(79): 77–92.

Scott, Ian (2013b) "Engaging the public: Hong Kong's Independent Commission Against Corruption's community relations strategy" in Jon S.T. Quah (ed.) *Different paths to curbing corruption: Lessons from Denmark, Finland, Hong Kong, New Zealand and Singapore*. Bingley: Emerald: 79–108.

Scott, Ian (2014) "Political scandals and the accountability of the Chief Executive in Hong Kong", *Asian Survey*, 54(5): 966–986.

Scott, Ian (2015) "Governance and corruption prevention in Hong Kong" in Leon van den Dool, Frank Hendriks, Alberto Gianoli and Linze Schaap (eds.) *The quest for good governance: Theoretical reflections and international practices*. Wiesbaden: Springer: 185–204.

Scott, Ian (2017) "The challenge of preserving a successful anti-corruption agency", *Asian Education and Development Studies*, 6(3): 227–237.

Scott, Ian and Joan Y.H. Leung (2008) "Managing integrity: The regulation of post public employment in Britain and Hong Kong", *Public Organization Review*, 8(4) (October): 365–380.

Scott, Ian and Joan Y.H. Leung (2012) "Integrity management in post-1997 Hong Kong: Challenges for a rule-based system", *Crime, Law and Social Change*, 58(1): 39–52.

Scott, Ian and Ting Gong (2015) "Evidence-based policy-making for corruption prevention in Hong Kong: A bottom-up approach", *Asia Pacific Journal of Public Administration*, 37(2): 87–101.

Schütte, Sofie Arjon (2017) "Two steps forward, one step backwards: Indonesia's winding (anti-) corruption journey" in Ting Gong and Ian Scott (eds.) *Routledge handbook of corruption in Asia*. London: Routledge: 42–55.

Seligson, Mitchell A. (2002) "The impact of corruption on regime legitimacy: A comparative study of four Latin American countries", *The Journal of Politics*, 64(2): 408–433.

Smart, Alan (2018) "The unbearable discretion of street-level bureaucrats: Corruption and collusion in Hong Kong", *Current Anthropology*, 59(supplement 18) (April): S37-S47.

Snell, Robin Stanley and Neil C. Herndon Jr. (2000) "An evaluation of Hong Kong's corporate code of ethics initiative", *Asia Pacific Journal of Management*, 17(3): 493–518.

Tangri, Roger and Andrew M. Mwenda (2006) "Politics, donors and the ineffectiveness of anti-corruption institutions in Uganda", *Journal of Modern African Studies*, 44(1): 101–124.

Theobald, Robin and Robert Williams (1999) "Combating corruption in Botswana: Regional role model or deviant case", *Journal of Commonwealth and Comparative Politics*, 37(3): 117–134.

Tsang, Steve (ed.) (1995) *A documentary history of Hong Kong: Government and politics*. Hong Kong: Hong Kong University Press.

Tse, Man-shing (2015) "Enhancing corporate governance in the public and private sectors", 6th ICAC symposium, 12 May, www.icac.org.hk/symposium/2015/pdf/TSE%20Man-shing_speech.pdf.

Tu, Elsie (2003) *Colonial Hong Kong through the eyes of Elsie Tu*. Hong Kong: Hong Kong University Press.

Uslaner, Eric M. (2008) *Corruption, inequality and the rule of law: The bulging pocket makes the easy life*. Cambridge: Cambridge University Press.

Uslaner, Eric M. (2018) "The study of trust" in Eric M. Uslaner (ed.) *The Oxford handbook of social and political trust*. Oxford: Oxford University Press: 3–14.

Wedeman, Andrew (2017) "Corruption and collective protest in China" in Ting Gong and Ian Scott (eds.) *Routledge handbook of corruption in Asia*. London: Routledge: 179–195.

Widoyoko, Johannes Danang (2017) "Indonesia's anti-corruption campaigns: Civil society versus the political cartel" in Marie dela Rama and Chris Rowley (eds.) *The changing face of corruption in the Asia Pacific: Current perspectives and future challenges*. Amsterdam: Elsevier: 253–266.

Wong, Hok-wui Stan, Ngok Ma and Wai-man Lam (2016) "Migrants and democratization: The political economy of Chinese immigrants in Hong Kong", *Contemporary Chinese Political Economy and Strategic Relations: An International Journal*, 2(2): 909–940.

Yep, Ray (2013) "The crusade against corruption in the 1970s: Governor MacLehose as a zealous reformer or a reluctant hero?" *China Information*, 27(2): 197–221.

Yeung, Rikkie L.K., Francesca T.C. Chiu and James Y.C. Kwok (2017) "Corporatist governance in Hong Kong: The case of the sports and arts functional constituency", *Asia-Pacific Journal of Public Administration*, 39(3): 163–176.

You, Jong-sung (2017) "Corruption and inequality in Asia" in Ting Gong and Ian Scott (eds.) *Routledge handbook of corruption in Asia*. London: Routledge: 97–112.

Young, Simon N.M. (2013) "Prosecuting bribery in Hong Kong's human rights environment" in Jeremy Horder and Peter Alldridge (eds.) *Modern bribery law*. Cambridge: Cambridge University Press: 267–293.

Young, Simon N.M. and Anthony Law (2006) "Privileged to vote: Inequalities and anomalies of the FC system" in Christine Loh and Civic Exchange (eds.) *Functional constituencies: a unique feature of the Hong Kong Legislative Council.* Hong Kong: Hong Kong University Press: 59–109.

Young, Simon N.M. and Richard Cullen (2010) *Electing Hong Kong's Chief Executive.* Hong Kong: Hong Kong University Press.

Yu, Chilik (2017) "Measuring public perceptions of corruption in Asia" in Ting Gong and Ian Scott (eds.) *Routledge handbook of corruption in Asia.* London: Routledge: 224–238.

Dissertations

Cook Liu, Sau-fong Bernadette (1992) *Civil liberties and the ICAC: An evaluative study.* Unpublished M. Soc. Sc. dissertation, Department of Political Science, University of Hong Kong.

Ho, Chi-hang (1992) *Corruption and its complainants: Reasons for complaining to the ICAC- a theoretical model.* Unpublished M. Soc. Sc. dissertation, Department of Political Science, University of Hong Kong.

Leung, Sui-ying, Katie (1981) *Public education as a means of combating corruption.* Unpublished M. Soc. Sc. dissertation, Department of Political Science, University of Hong Kong.

Ma Man, Su-lan Paula (1988) *A study of the ICAC's role in handling non-corruption complaints.* Unpublished M. Soc. Sc. dissertation, Department of Political Science, University of Hong Kong.

Corruption reports: international agencies and NGOs

Bauhinia Foundation Research Centre (2016) *Rethinking campaign finance laws in Hong Kong: Reform for a new generation,* www.bauhinia.org/assets/document/doc216.pdf.

Global Witness (2015) *Banks and dirty money,* www.globalwitness.org/en-gb/campaigns/corruption-and-money-laundering/banks-and-dirty-money/.

IMF (1997) *Good governance: The IMF's role: Transparency, accountability, efficiency, fairness,* www.imf.org/external/pubs/ft/exrp/govern/govindex.htm.

Jakarta Statement on Principles for Anti-Corruption Agencies (2012), www.unodc.org/documents/corruption/WG-Prevention/Art_6_Preventive_anti-corruption_bodies/JAKARTA_STATEMENT_en.pdf.

OECD (2013) *Specialised anti-corruption institutions: Review of models.* 2nd edition. OECD: OECD Publishing.

TRACE (2017) *The TRACE matrix – the global business risk index for compliance professionals,* www.traceinternational.org/trace-matrix.

Transparency International (2014) *Fighting corruption: The role of the anti-corruption commission,* www.transparency.org/news/feature/fighting_corruption_the_role_of_the_anti_corruption_commission.

Transparency International (2017) *People and corruption: Asia Pacific.* Berlin: Transparency International.

U4 Anti-Corruption Resource Centre (2010) *Unpacking the concept of political will to confront corruption,* www.u4.no/publications/unpacking-the-concept-of-political-will-to-confront-corruption/.

UNCAC (2003) *United Nations convention against corruption*, www.unodc.org/documents/treaties/UNCAC/Publications/Convention/08-50026_E.pdf.

UNDP (2005) *Institutional arrangements to combat corruption: A comparative study*, www.un.org/ruleoflaw/files/10%20Institutional%20arrangements%20to%20 combat%20corruption_2005.pdf.

World Bank (1994) *Governance: The World Bank's experience*, http://documents. worldbank.org/curated/en/711471468765285964/pdf/multi0page.pdf.

World Bank (1997) *Helping countries combat corruption: The role of the World Bank*. Washington: The World Bank.

Index

1MDB 199

Advisory Committee on Corruption 28
Airport Authority Board 142
Anstey, Thomas 20
anti-corruption agencies (ACAs) 8–13,
80–82, 134–140, 142–144, 160,
166–167; anti-corruption agenda 4,
8; crises 37, 193–194; definition of
8; effectiveness of 13, 44, 143–144,
146, 172, 200–201, 203; failure
of 1–2, 9–10, 74, 132–133, 140,
192–196; funding of 37–38, 50,
66, 74, 194; independence of
10–11, 74, 194, 200, 206 (*see also*
Independent Commission Against
Corruption (ICAC), independence
of); institutionalisation of 13, 58,
70, 92, 148, 192–206; and political
will 57–59, 198–199; success factors
10–13, 55–149, 154, 194, 196;
transferring the model 1, 5, 9, 192,
199–206; trust in 131–132, 146;
use of information 116; *see also*
Independent Commission Against
Corruption (ICAC); World Bank,
and ACAs
Anti-Corruption Branch (later Anti-
Corruption Office) 26, 29–30
anti-corruption laws 3, 8–12, 92–107,
136–137, 140–141, 182–183,
198–200; *see also* corruption
prevention approaches, compliance-
based; misconduct in public office;
Misdemeanors Punishment Ordinance;

Prevention of Bribery Ordinance
(*POBO*), *Prevention of Corruption
Ordinance*
Anti-Corruption Office 20, 31–33, 39
Aw Sian, Sally 105

Bangladesh 199
banks 118–120, 154, 162, 180–181;
Asia Infrastructure Bank 179, 181;
Bank Bumiputra Malaysia Berhad
49, 120; Hong Kong Association of
Banks 120; Hong Kong Institute of
Bankers 120; Ka Wah Bank 49–50;
Overseas Trust Bank 49–50, 161; *see
also* business; Hong Kong Monetary
Authority
Basic Law 63, 80, 82, 173, 182
Beetham, David 155
Blair-Kerr, Sir Alastair 32–33, 38, 47
Botswana 199
bribery 2–4, 22, 93–97, 162–165, 195,
205; offering or accepting a bribe 24,
77–78, 94, 122; *see also Prevention of
Bribery Ordinance* (*POBO*); TRACE
Bribery Index
British government 20–21, 24–25, 29,
175
Buildings Department 119
business 23–24, 139–140, 143–145,
160–165, 175, 180–186, 192–194;
attitudes towards corruption 47–49,
161; chambers of commerce 11, 115,
162–163, 204; illegal commissions
32, 38, 47–50, 115, 123, 138, 145;
Mainland Chinese businesses in